CW00376858

GRIFFITH JOHN
apostle to Central China

Griffith John
apostle to Central China

Noel Gibbard

BRYNTIRION PRESS

© Noel Gibbard, 1998
First published 1998

ISBN 1 85049 150 X

All rights reserved. No part of this publication may be reproduced,
stored in a retrieval system, or transmitted, in any form or by any
means, electronic, mechanical, photo-copying, recording or
otherwise, without the prior permission of Bryntirion Press.

Cover design:
Phil Boorman & burgum boorman ltd

Published by Bryntirion Press
Bryntirion, Bridgend CF31 4DX, Wales, UK
Printed by WBC Book Manufacturers, Bridgend

Acknowledgements

I would like to thank all those who have helped me to write this book. Most of the research was done at the School of Oriental and African Studies, London, but it also involved visits to the University Library, Cambridge, and the National Library of Wales, Aberystwyth. The staff of these institutions gave me most helpful assistance. The Evangelical Fellowship of Congregational Churches, through its secretary, the Rev. Alan Tovey, showed much interest in the biography, and a gracious expression of the interest was the financial contribution towards the publication of the work.

The Cambridge University Press gave permission to reproduce two maps, 'China in the nineteenth century' and 'The Taiping Rebellion'. The photograph of Griffith John and Hudson Taylor is from the Overseas Missionary Fellowship Collection in the School of Oriental and African Studies, with the permission of the School and the Fellowship; and the Griffith John Family Tree and photograph of the printing shop are included with the permission of the NLW. A number of individuals contributed in different ways, by letter, phone or tracing of books, including the Rev. Ioan Wyn Gruffydd, Swansea, and Mr John Creasey, Librarian of Dr Williams's Library, London.

Dr R. Tudur Jones, Bangor, readily agreed to read the work and write the Foreword. I am most grateful to him for doing so. This is just one of his many kindnesses to me over a long period of time, indeed, since I was a student at Bala-Bangor College.

These words concerning Dr Tudur Jones were written at the end of June, but now, because of his death on 23 July, I join with others to pay tribute to this great man. He was a scholar, historian, theologian, lecturer, essayist and a powerful preacher of the gospel. He was one of God's giants.

Lastly, I must record my thanks to the Revs David Kingdon and Edmund Owen, Mrs Jill Richards, and Misses Mair Jones and Brenda Lewis for their thorough work in preparing the biography for the press.

Cardiff   Noel Gibbard
July 1998

To
Helen

Foreword

During the nineteenth century Christianity spread to more countries than ever before. That was a direct consequence of the evangelical and missionary enthusiasm that animated the churches of the Western world during that century. It was an enthusiasm that inspired a host of men and women to dedicate their lives to the dissemination of the Christian Faith. Amongst them was Griffith John, the subject of this book. And amongst the heroic characters that worked in the various mission fields, none was more distinguished than he was. His first ambition was to labour on the island of Madagascar, but when that proved impossible he agreed to go to China, and it was there that he worked for over fifty years.

In this book Dr Noel Gibbard offers us a new account of Griffith John's career. It is, like all Dr Gibbard's work, meticulously researched and based throughout on the original sources. The evidence which they provide has been carefully sifted and analysed. The result is that we have here not only a welcome recital of one man's story but a valuable insight into what the missionary enterprise entailed. We are provided with vivid illustrations of the challenges and difficulties, the risks and dangers, the disappointments and joys which characterised the lives of missionaries.

China was a very distant country when Griffith John went there in 1855. Going there meant embarking on a long and tedious sea voyage. Its distance from Wales meant that frequent home visits were out of the question. On arrival, there was a new language to be learnt with very few of the linguistic aids that are available today. The delicacies of courtesy in a completely unfamiliar culture had to be mastered. In China it was a serious challenge to have to confront scholars who were deeply versed in religious traditions that were very different from those of Christianity. In this context it took time to discover how best to convey the Christian message effectively.

This was true of almost all the mission fields, but there were hindrances in China that added to the difficulties of Griffith John and his colleagues. The intrusion of the Western powers, and their insistence on securing special access to the Chinese market and enjoying special privileges in the seaports of China, did not endear Westerners to the Chinese. And the political instability of China caused trepidation. It was so during the Taiping uprising of 1860 and the Boxer rising of

1899–1900. Such disturbances and the cruelties associated with them created fear amongst missionaries as they saw their neighbours massacred, their chapels demolished and their homes set alight. It was small wonder that such occurrences brought about spiritual depression and, as Dr Gibbard explains, even a man of profound faith like Griffith John was not immune from it.

We are reminded in this book that although Griffith John was a short man, he was a spiritual giant. The picture presented to us here is entirely honest. There is no need to flatter him because the evidence speaks for itself. He was greatly admired in his own day. It has been fashionable in some circles to denigrate the work of the missionaries and to portray them as the religious lackeys of militant imperialism. It will be seen that this accusation does not hold with regard to Griffith John. His conviction was that 'If we would convert China, we must begin with the common people.' And he had deep sympathy with them. His frequent journeys through large areas of China brought him face to face with poverty, social degradation and oppression. Of course, his primary task was to spread the gospel, whether by preaching it publicly or by testifying to it in private conversation. But for him the gospel had social implications too. He made a noble contribution in the field of education. He organised health care and built hospitals. He struggled unceasingly to help those whose lives had been blighted by smoking opium.

In addition to all this, he devoted an enormous amount of time to translating the Bible and to producing tracts and pamphlets. One impression that reading about all this activity leaves is that Griffith John was possessed of enormous energy. It was an energy that was sustained by a simple but powerful Christian faith. True, there were times when he was overwhelmed by grief at the death of loved ones and by disappointments connected with his work, but even when his mind had become clouded by senility in his final months, he did not feel abandoned by his Saviour.

Dr Gibbard's fine study of the life, character and contribution of Griffith John will be warmly welcomed by all those who have drawn inspiration from the example of dedicated Christians of the past, and they will find in it much that is relevant to the propagation of the Christian faith today.

Bangor   R. Tudur Jones
June 1998

Contents

Map—'China in the nineteenth century'   11
Map—'The Taiping Rebellion'   12
Chinese place names   13
Abbreviations   13

1. **From Swansea to Shanghai**, 1831–1855   15
   Early influences   15
   Boy preacher and theological student   22
   Further preparation and long-awaited destination   28

2. **Shanghai: an open door and many adversaries**, 1855–1861   35
   Spying out the land and first attacks   37
   Methods and message   45
   The Taiping rebels   53

3. **Hankow: the heart of the Empire**, 1861–1873   65
   Planting and watering   66
   Some notable national workers   71
   Doubt and assurance   74
   Reaching out from Hankow   77
   A remarkable journey   81

4. **Hankow: city and interior**, 1873–1883   89
   Church work and personal faith   90
   Hupeh and Hunan   98
   Relationships   107

5. **Hankow: increased activity**, 1883–1890   115
   Tensions and compensations   115
   The care of the churches in Hupeh   118
   Workers: need, training and support   126
   Literary activity   130

6. **Hankow: riot and fruit**, 1890–1900   141
   Healing and rioting   141
   Advancing and convalescing   146

    Hunan   150
    Schools and Boxers   157

7. From Hankow to Swansea, 1900–1912   167
    Hunan is open   167
    Education and health   172
    America   178
    Hankow and Swansea   182

8. Griffith John: character, creed and contribution   191

References   208
Sources   239
    Manuscripts   239
    Bibliography   239
    Periodicals and Newspapers   242
Glossary   242
Index   243
The Griffith John Family Tree   250

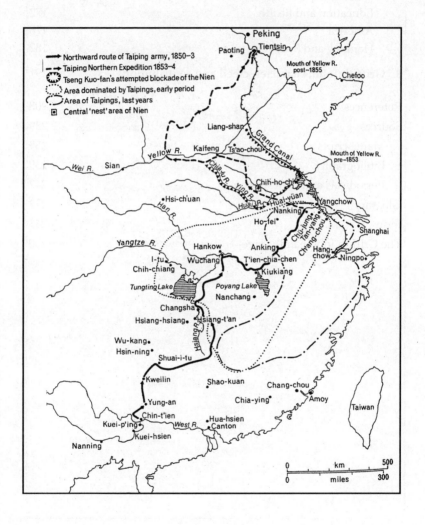

Map legend:
- Northward route of Taiping army, 1850–3
- Taiping Northern Expedition 1853–4
- Tseng Kuo-fan's attempted blockade of the Nien
- Area dominated by Taipings, early period
- Area of Taipings, last years
- Central 'nest' area of Nien

Peking
Paoting
Tientsin
Mouth of Yellow R. post–1855
Chefoo
Liang-shan
Grand Canal
Yellow R.
Kaifeng
Ts'ao-chou
Chih-ho-chi
Mouth of Yellow R. pre–1853
Wei R.
Sian
Chia-lu R.
Ying R.
Huai R.
Huai-yüan
Yangchow
Hsi-ch'uan
Han R.
Ho-fei
Nanking
Shanghai
Yangtze R.
Hankow
Anking
Chü-jung
Tan-yang
Chang-chou
Hang-chow
Ningpo
I-tu
Wuchang
T'ien-chia-chen
Chih-chiang
Tungting Lake
Kiukiang
Poyang Lake
Nanchang
Changsha
Hsiang-hsiang
Hsiang-t'an
Hsiang R.
Wu-kang
Hsin-ning
Shuai-i-tu
Kweilin
Shao-kuan
Chang-chou
Chia-ying
Amoy
Taiwan
Yung-an
Chin-t'ien
Kuei-p'ing
West R.
Hua-hsien
Canton
Kuei-hsien
Nanning

0   km   500
0   miles   300

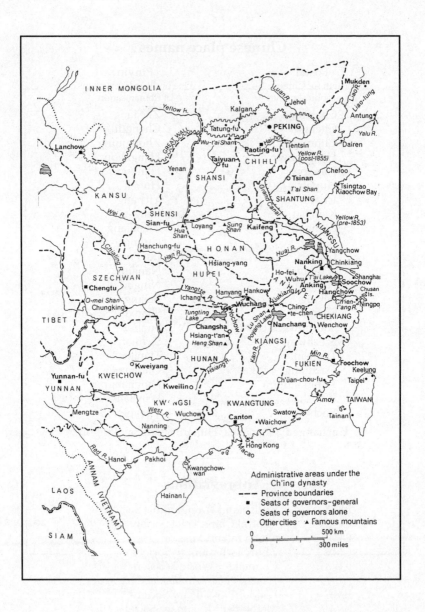

INNER MONGOLIA

Yellow R.

Luan R. Jehol

Mukden

Liao R.

Liao-tung

Antung

Yalu R.

Dairen

Kalgan

GREAT WALL

Tatung-fu

Wu-t'ai Shan ▲

PEKING

Tientsin

Hai R.

Paoting-fu

Yellow R.
(post-1855)

Chefoo

Lanchow

Yenan

Taiyuan-
fu

CHIHLI

Tsinan

Tsingtao
Kiaochow Bay

Wei R.

SHANSI

T'ai Shan ▲

SHANTUNG

KANSU

SHENSI

Grand Canal

Sian-fu

Hua
Shan ▲ Loyang ▲ Sung
Shan

Kaifeng

Yellow R.
(pre-1853)

KIANGSU

Ch'ialing R.

Hanchung-fu

Han R.

HONAN

Huai R.

Yangchow

Hsiang-yang

Nanking ▪ Chinkiang

Hanyang Hankow

Ho-fei
Wuhu ▲ T'ai Lake

Shanghai

Soochow

SZECHWAN

Chengtu

HUPEI

Anking

ANHWEI

Hangchow

Chusan
Is.

Ichang

Yangtze R.

Chien-
t'ang R. Ningpo

Wuchang

O-mei Shan ▲
Chungking

Tungting
Lake

Kukiang

Ching-
te-chen

CHEKIANG

TIBET

Changsha

Lu Shan ▲

Nanchang

Wenchow

Hsiang-t'an

Poyang Lake

Heng Shan ▲

Kan R.

KIANGSI

HUNAN

Hsiang R.

Min R.

Kweiyang

FUKIEN

Foochow

Yunnan-fu

KWEICHOW

Kweilin

Ch'üan-chou-fu

Keelung

Taipei

YUNNAN

KWANGSI

West R.

Wuchow

KWANGTUNG

Amoy

TAIWAN

Mengtze

Nanning

Swatow

Tainan

Canton ▪ Waichow

Red R.

Hanoi

Pakhoi

Macao

Hong Kong

Kwangchow-
wan

ANNAM (VIETNAM)

LAOS

Hainan I.

SIAM

Administrative areas under the
Ch'ing dynasty
--- Province boundaries
▪ Seats of governors-general
○ Seats of governors alone
• Other cities ▲ Famous mountains

0   500 km
0   300 miles

Chinese place names

Postal		Pinyin
System for Chinese geographical names		One of the major systems of Romanisation
Chekiang	....	Zhejiang
Chengtu	....	Chengdu
Chunking	....	Zhongjuing
Hangchow	....	Hangzhou
Hankow	....	Hankou
Hupeh	....	Hubeh
Ichang	....	Yichang
Kiangsu	....	Jiangsu
Kiangyin	....	Zhenjiang
Kuling	....	Guling
Loo	....	Luzhou
Nanking	....	Nanjing
Ningpo	....	Ningbo
Peking	....	Beijing
Shansi	....	Shanxi
Soochow/Suchow	....	Suzhou
Szechwan	....	Sichuan
Tientsin	....	Tianjin
Tsientang	....	Qiantang
Tsingkiangpu	....	Quigjiangpu
Wooshan	....	Wushan
Yochow	....	Yueang

Unchanged: Changsha; Hunan; Shanghai; Pinghu

Abbreviations

BFBS	British and Foreign Bible Society
CCTS	Central China Tract Society
CIM	China Inland Mission
CMS	Church Missionary Society
CWM	Council for World Mission
HEAC	*Hanes Eglwysi Annibynol Cymru*
LMS	London Missionary Society
MMS	Methodist Missionary Society
NLW	National Library of Wales
PRO	Public Record Office
SOAS	School of Oriental and African Studies

'I entered college with two desires in my mind—a higher and a lower. The higher desire was to serve man and to glorify God; the lower desire to become one of the great preachers of Wales. The higher desire was there all the time, and occupied, I hope, the highest place; but the lower was there also, and occupying, I am bound to say, no mean place. When, however, the missionary desire came in and took full possession of my heart, the lower desire was driven out never to return again. That was a great victory, one of the greatest victories ever won on the arena of my soul and one for which I have never ceased to feel truly thankful to God.'

Griffith John
quoted in R. Wardlaw Thompson, *Griffith John*, 18-19

1
From Swansea to Shanghai
1831–1855

Griffith and Ann John, Emma Street, Swansea, were very conscious of the industrial unrest during 1831.[1] As a copperman employed by Vivian & Son he knew very well what effect it could have on the locality. It is true that because of the diversity of work in Swansea the situation was more stable there than in Merthyr Tydfil,[2] where the colliers especially were angry about their bad working conditions and low wages. Neither did Swansea have such colourful leaders as Lewsyn yr Heliwr and Dic Penderyn, but there was an awareness of possible rapid changes in both places, with some hope of political changes as the Reform Bill was being prepared to be presented to Parliament. Fears in the John household were intensified because they were expecting their fourth child. There would be another mouth to feed and less space in the small house. The baby boy arrived on 14 December 1831,[3] and was given the same name as his father.

Early influences
A few months after Griffith's birth, cholera broke out in Swansea, raging from July until October 1832. Approximately 150 people died during this period,[4] including the mother in the John household. It must have been a gruesome experience for the family. Not only had the mother and wife died but she had been taken by the Asiatic plague, 'A specific infectious disease of high mortality, characterised clinically by violent vomiting and purging leading rapidly to collapse, the cholera stools having a typical appearance that is generally described as "rice-water"—a term that well illustrates their colour and consistency.'[5]

Griffith John was left a widower with four children aged between a few months and eight years. He was a resolute and godly character, and his personal faith and the help of relatives sustained him during this trying period. The little boy Griffith was surrounded by the same influences, but as he grew up he became acutely conscious of the fact that he had no mother. This loss he regarded 'as one of the greatest, if not the greatest, privations of my life'.[6] Such a feeling of loss, the invasion of death, and the sensitive kindnesses of those around him, made Griffith John, at a young age, sensitive morally and spiritually.

The religious awareness of Griffith John and the family was nurtured in Ebenezer Independent Chapel, built in 1806 and rebuilt in 1826, situated between the industrial north and the more fashionable Burrows. The roots of the cause had been planted in Commonwealth soil and the young plant watered by such men as Marmaduke Matthews, Daniel Higgs and Stephen Hughes. Fruit became evident at Tirdwncyn, where there was a Welsh cause, and in the town, where there was an English cause which, theologically, turned Unitarian. The Welsh cause was transplanted to Mynyddbach, and as was general during the eighteenth century they held services not only in the chapel but in the homes of members as well. Non-conformity was domestically orientated in a way that would not have been possible within the Established Church. It was from one of these meetings, held in the home of one of the members of Mynyddbach, that the cause in the town commenced. When the lady of the house died in 1776, the worshippers moved to a room in the town and worshipped there until Ebenezer was built. Under the ministry of David Davies (1795-1816) there was a marked increase in membership, as the minister received two thousand persons into the fellowship of the church.[7] A good number of these were from outside Swansea, having come into the area to find work. It was during this period that the workers became prominent in the congregation, creating in Ebenezer a mixed fellowship of farmers, industrial workers, servants and artisans.

Not only was the immediate area looked upon as a mission field, but it was also a period of awakening interest in overseas mission work. A significant meeting for the London Missionary Society (LMS, formed in 1795) was held in

Ebenezer in 1814, and David Davies, David Peter, Morgan Jones and Thomas Phillips championed the cause in South Wales, drawing the attention of their people to Brittany, the South Sea Islands and Madagascar.[8] By the time Griffith John was born, Thomas Bevan, David Jones and David Griffiths of Madagascar were household names in Wales.

Such was the religious activity during the early part of the nineteenth century that there were 31 chapels in Swansea in 1851, which could provide for two-thirds of the population.[9] These churches had a strong influence on their members, religiously and denominationally. The evangelical gospel, common to all the orthodox churches, was proclaimed in a denominational setting. Ebenezer was an Independent church, evangelical, missionary-minded and practising infant baptism. This was the spiritual home of the John family, and here Griffith, the son, was received into membership when he was only eight years old. He was led to apply for membership when he saw his sister being welcomed into fellowship. On that Communion Sunday morning the boy was sitting in the gallery, and when he saw his sister Mary receiving the right hand of fellowship he started questioning himself concerning his spiritual condition and his dedication to the church. He revealed his feelings to the deacons, and they watched him closely to see if there were marks of grace in his life. Even at this tender age they expected to see some spiritual fruit in the lad's life, and eventually they were convinced 'that the change in the little boy was genuine'.[10] One of the deacons did express a strong reservation because the candidate was so young but was persuaded to agree with his fellow officers.[11] The little boy himself thought of the step in three ways: as consecration to God, as a duty to be a member of the church, and as a privilege to partake of the Lord's Supper. There was a personal aspect, a church aspect and a sacramental aspect, which could be strong within Nonconformity.

In the fellowship of the church Griffith John's development was deeply influenced by the intense prayer meetings, which quickened his spirit, and the practice of learning portions of Scripture by heart, which disciplined his mind. He would also take down the heads of sermons, which was a discipline in the Puritan tradition. In the Saturday night prayer meeting the young lad would listen to his uncles, David and Rees, who were like Jacob pleading with God (Genesis 32:32). Griffith was even taken to the mothers' prayer meeting.[12] Soon after becoming a member he offered his first prayer in public. The members were drenched in prayer; as well as the gatherings mentioned, there were meetings on two afternoons, Tuesday and Saturday.[13] William Rees, one of the deacons, and Thomas Davies,[14] the minister, encouraged the boy to learn the Scriptures, and would occasionally ask him to recite a portion during the Sunday service. This he would do from the gallery, regarding it as 'a most stimulating and inspiring exercise'.[15]

The man who mostly encouraged Griffith John to learn the Scriptures and take down the heads of sermons was William Rees; of him the young member said, 'He taught me to *think*, and was the first who ever tried to do so.'[16] William Rees was also Griffith John's Sunday school teacher, and it is proper to emphasise that he was a thinker, not only in terms of his influence on his pupil but also in the light of critical remarks made of Ebenezer Sunday school in 1846. The inspectors reported, 'It appeared to be conducted with little system; chiefly on the old plan of continuously reading the Scripture.'[17] This would not have been true of William Rees's class. On the day of inspection these were some of the relevant figures:

Present Scholars		Teachers		No. att. day school
M	F	M	F	
90	96	32	30	82

There was a strong Sunday school, made up of children and adults, and the number of children attending a day school was quite high. While 82 attended school, 106 could read the Scriptures, having been taught either in the Sunday school or at home, or both. Griffith John himself attended a day school, although he does not give much detail in his autobiography, simply stating that he attended 'one of the common schools of the day' and made the progress that was expected in such a school under such circumstances.[18]

A further contribution to the self-help nature of the education was the Library formed at Ebenezer. This consisted of Welsh and English books, although most of the education was conducted through the medium of Welsh. The Welsh non-conformists were conscious of the need of the non-Welsh population. Earlier in 1814 they had established an English cause in Castle Street, and when Joseph Harries (Baptist) was in Swansea he had held English services. Many from outside would be English-speaking, while others from rural Wales would be Welsh-speaking, thus creating two groups having the same needs spiritually but differing culturally and linguistically. During the same period St John's, the Anglican Church, was making an effort to hold Welsh services; there must have been some awareness of the need to break the Tory-English-Established-Church mould. On the day of the inspection the commissioners commented that most present were well clad, and that very few of the females belonged to the labouring class.

In the fellowship of the church the young lad had many heroes, whom he revered as if they had come from another world. He highly esteemed William Rees, his Sunday school teacher; the elder Dafydd Huw, Tregenydd, who was a strict disciplinarian; and another elder, Daniel Daniel, Waun-wen (later the Strand), known as *'mellt Sinai'* (Sinai lightning). A third elder, Peter Williams, Waun-wen, had told Griffith John about the 'pagans' in other countries, and John Hughes, cobbler, could speak English very well, creating in the young lad a desire to do the same. These were some of the heroes which loomed large on the screen of the young member's life. There were a few notable ladies too, such as Nansi Powell (Nansi'r Berllan), who would tap her right foot to the beat of the music, and when moved would walk down the aisle and then back to her seat. Pegen Tŷ Coch was a poor lady who sold needles and combs for a living, and when she was full of praise she would sway her body to and fro. In sharp contrast was the nosy widow, Sali Howell.[20] At least two features of the church's life emerge from this evidence. First, in terms of church government, Ebenezer had elders and deacons as well as a minister. This was characteristic of nonconformist churches from the beginning of their history, the elders looking after the teaching in the church and the deacons being responsible for the practical aspects. Secondly, in terms of worship, there was a fusion of preaching and lively worship.

It was in Ebenezer that members of the John family were continually reminded that they were citizens of heaven, but that its principles had to be applied to the earthly realm as well; they were citizens of two worlds. Griffith John the father became a foreman employed by Vivian & Son; J. H. Vivian MP (1832–1855) was the driving force behind the Hafod industrial machine. The rapidly increasing process of industrialisation had changed the face of Swansea, 'If in the eighteenth century Swansea could be referred to as the "Brighton" of Wales, "Copperopolis" was a far more appropriate name in the century which followed.'[21] The availability of work brought men and women from other parts of Glamorgan, as well as from other parts of Wales, England and Ireland. Strong groups of Irishmen were to be found in Llangyfelach Street, Charles Street, Emma Street, Angel Street, Greenhill, and some of the courts adjacent to High Street. Many of these courts were regarded as immoral by the more respectable citizens of the town because they were associated with prostitution and drunkenness. Most of them were demolished during the seventies of the last century.

In some of those streets (Llangyfelach Street and Emma Street, for example) many Welshmen would also be found, but the tendency of the Welsh incomers was to settle in Hafod, Cwmbwrla, Plasmarl and Glandŵr. Leading southwards from Ebenezer was High Street, a typical street in a thriving and developing town, having several good houses and the Bush Inn, described as 'most pleasantly situated'. Here too was the office of Evan Griffiths the printer, a deacon at Ebenezer and a true friend to Griffith John.[22] Evan Griffiths, an ordained man, was regarded as a kind of bishop of nonconformity in Swansea and district. Other Ebenezer members pursued occupations typical of townspeople, such as ironmonger, watchmaker, cabinet maker and brandy merchant.

Having a brandy merchant as a member would not then have alarmed the people of Ebenezer. It was accepted practice in the chapels to provide alcohol and tobacco for the preacher, and Ebenezer was no exception. Listed in the 'Cash Paid' were 'Feb 16 Ale 2 Coffee 4 6d March 16 Ale 2 Tobacco 7½ 9½d.'[23] The older ministers—and Daniel Evans, Mynyddbach, would be a good representative—were quite happy with this arrangement. On many occasions chapel members enjoyed drinking together: after a funeral, a wedding, potato setting or a wake; even religious occasions could be an excuse to meet in a public house, as some youngsters did when they gathered together at the Powell's Arms after attending a meeting at Ebenezer.[24] The situation, however, was changing. In about 1830 temperance movements were established, and from 1835 total abstinence movements. Many clashes over the use of alcohol took place, in print, pulpit and pew. *Y Cymedrolwr* (1835) and *Yr Adolygydd* (1838) championed moderation, while *Yr Athraw* (1836) and *Y Dirwestydd* (1836) advocated total abstinence.[25]

In 1837, when a procession for abstainers was held in the town, it attracted 500 people.[26] In Ebenezer Chapel there were two strong groups. One of the leading moderates was David Gibbs, while the champion of teetotalism was Evan Griffiths the printer. Under Griffiths' leadership the abstainers' group grew quickly and had 40 members in 1838. It was not just a clash between two sides, because the position of Thomas Davies, the minister, created real difficulties. He liked his drink and therefore could not support the teetotallers, but he could also drink too much. He was criticised by the moderates, but sympathy was felt for him, especially from within the moderate group. The congregation became divided for and against the minister.

Matters came to a head in 1842 when Thomas Davies was dismissed, followed by his wife: 'Drunkenness Excluded 14 June 1842', and 'Wife Not Regarding Discipline 6 Sept 1842'.[27] Included in the unusually high number dismissed that year were ten members of the family of Edward and Martha Charles of the Plough & Harrow. The reason was 'Regarding Discipline', which could mean that they were staunch supporters of the minister. The Sunday after his dismissal Thomas Davies went as usual to Ebenezer and entered the pulpit to begin the service, but one of the deacons took the Bible from him and prevented him from continuing. Thomas Davies had to leave Ebenezer and took eighty members with him, but he remained in the area, ministering in the town and in Pentre Estyll.[28] He was succeeded by the Rev. Elijah Jacob, who was ordained in 1843. The situation then improved in Ebenezer, although there was not complete harmony until 1844. A few men still opposed the total abstinence emphasis, including David Gibbs, Daniel Daniel and Peter Williams, and a few members queried Jacob's theological orthodoxy. The three men left in 1844, amidst great sorrow as they were highly respected in the church. The work of Evan Griffiths and others was confirmed with the coming of the new minister, who was a staunch teetotaller. Not only did he champion the cause in Swansea, but he also travelled the country lecturing on the Maine Law.[29]

Elijah Jacob took an interest in Griffith John, and the minister was the greatest single influence on the young lad. He himself said later, 'One of the greatest fortunes of my life was to come into close contact with this truly noble man.'[30] He regarded Jacob as a father, brother and friend. However, they spent only a few months together during this period, because in 1843 Griffith John moved to Onllwyn, Seven Sisters, where he had found work.

Boy preacher and theological student

Griffith John's move to Onllwyn was arranged by William Rees, his Sunday school teacher, who was originally from Nant-y-glo, Gwent. He had a friend who had opened iron and coal mines, smelting furnaces and a large store at which the workers were expected to buy their goods.[31] John Williams is a good example of a small industrialist who took to heart the social, educational and religious needs of his workers. He commenced a religious service in a room above the stable, and both he and his wife took a keen interest in the welfare of the newcomer from Swansea. John Williams gave the young lad the responsibility of working in the grocer's shop,[32] and if he had stayed on in Onllwyn he would have become its manager.

It was during this period that Griffith John began to preach. The desire must have been planted in him when he was very young, because it is known that he used to preach to the chairs and walls at Cwm-nant, Crwys, on the Gower, the home of some of his relatives.[33] The consistent teaching and the prayer meetings at Ebenezer must have prepared him, though perhaps unconsciously, during the early years. He himself does not give specific reasons, but only mentions the influences of his background. His first attempt was made when he was 14

years old, at a prayer meeting in a private house. He realised
that he was too young for the work, and postponed the consideration of continuing until a later date. That came very soon,
for within two years, at the age of 16, he preached again from
the text Romans 1:18.[34] The dominant note was the 'gospel',
that is, good news. This marked the beginning of a long period
of over sixty years during which the same message sounded
forth from his lips.

There is no doubt that he had a passion for preaching, a
characteristic that emerged during a visit to Alltwen Independent Chapel. A lay preacher, and a friend of Griffith
John, had persuaded him to preach at the chapel. When the
boy preacher arrived the deacons were taken aback by his
youthfulness, and were greatly relieved when a well-known
preacher arrived on his way home from an engagement in the
area. He was pressed to preach, and Griffith John opened the
service by reading and praying. By the time he had finished
the prayer the deacons were on the steps of the pulpit urging
him to continue, and his friend, the lay preacher, also joined
them:[35]

> I felt I had to comply with the wishes of one who had shown
> so much kindness to me, so I turned back, gave out another
> hymn, and preached from Romans 8:18. My soul was deeply
> moved, the vast audience caught the fire, and before the
> close of the sermon the whole congregation was on its feet,
> shouting 'Glory' and 'Amen'.

Even when allowance is made for natural sympathy with a
young lad, this occasion was remarkable. There was fire in the
bones of the preacher, and his natural talent of speech was
inspired and intensified by supernatural power, that power
which Griffith John sought throughout his ministry. The text,
and the one on the previous occasion, are also significant,
bringing out the good news of the gospel and its eternal
dimension. To the lad of sixteen years of age heaven was real.
Although at this tender age the 'present sufferings' were not
burdensome, this dimension was an integral part of the salvation that he had received and that was clearly taught at
Ebenezer; besides this, of course, his mother had died, and her

son sincerely believed that she had gone to heaven. His simple faith grasped that profound truth. Indeed, whether in terms of the gospel or in terms of circumstances, Griffith John was to know that eternity was always breaking in upon him.

There were strong reactions to the young man's desire to preach and prepare himself for the Christian ministry. At first John Williams, Onllwyn, dissuaded him, but on seeing the determination of the young preacher he supported him. A number of people, including some ministers, did not think that college education would benefit him, because a bias against ministerial training still lingered in the country. Elijah Jacob, however, welcomed the news, and was glad when Griffith John returned to Swansea in 1848. The pastor agreed to prepare the boy for further study:[36]

> I commenced November 12th/48. Everything went on very comfortably until August the 11th 1849 when my poor father died of the Cholera that was raging in the town at the time. He was taken ill in the morning and died in the evening about 10 o'clock. This was a dreadful blow.

The blow could not have come at a worse time, just as the young man was ready to open a new chapter in his life. Friends and family rallied round him; his aunt, who kept a shop in Llangyfelach Street, gave him a home, and Elijah Jacob continued to teach him free of charge.[37]

The situation in Swansea was quite serious, although not as serious as in Merthyr Tydfil, where 573 people had died between 25 May and 17 August. Proximity to the harbour and the presence of dirty streets and wells quickened the spread of cholera in Swansea. In 1843 there were only eight men and four carts employed to clean some five miles of streets. Of the 176 houses in Back Street, 64 were without privies. The drawing place for water for Greenhill on Nant Glandŵr was 'situated 20 feet downstream from a privy, which spanned the stream and ejected its ardure into it'.[38] From 16 July, when cholera broke out in the town, an average of two a day were dying. Different sources give different numbers of the deaths that occurred. The *Cambrian* tended to minimise the suffering; one source mentioned 139 and another 241; but a dependable figure is 152 for three months.[39] During one week, 21 to 27 August, 6 people died in the town and 14 in the country.[40]

Griffith John could not understand what was happening to his mother when she died, but now he had the bitter experience of seeing his father suffering. The son had to look on the pain and the vomiting, and watch the sufferer turning blue in colour. His father was beyond help. Those who were unable to pay for medical relief were authorised to go to a qualified doctor, who would be compensated 10s-6d for each case. It is not known whether the Johns did so.

During this time, numerous services were held in English and Welsh, and collections taken to help the suffering and bereaved families. Father Kavanagh, 'one of Swansea's memorable priests',[41] showed remarkable commitment to the sufferers. He performed menial services as he washed the victims, made their beds and combed their hair. During a period of weeks he laid out one hundred and seventy bodies, after which he was exhausted.[42]

With the dark cloud of cholera came the refreshing showers of revival. Ebenezer, and Swansea, had experienced such visitations in the immediate past, in 1807, 1828, and in 1839, when the work of the American revivalist Charles Finney was popularised by the translations of Evan Griffiths, the deacon at Ebenezer and Griffith John's friend.[43] Cholera and revival had an impact on Ebenezer. Members were lost through death and gained through revival. Some who had been converted from the world lapsed; but the majority, from amongst Sunday school scholars and hearers, persevered.

It is possible to make exaggerated claims for the Revival, but it is also possible to make sweeping, critical remarks, like those made by E. T. Davies. He tends to take Evan Price's description as being typical of the whole of Wales, but it is not possible to justify his claim that lack of preaching, falling membership and chapel quarrels were evident throughout Wales. Even the claim E. T. Davies makes concerning the county of Monmouth is misleading. He says, 'Every Welsh Independent church in Monmouthshire which appeared in the Association's report showed a substantial fall in membership by 1852, although most had added to the membership in the current year.'[44] A number of comments should be made. Where there

was a decrease, it was 'substantial' in only four or five cases
out of thirteen. The decrease was very small in four cases, and
in three cases there was an increase. For the figures for a whole
county to be meaningful, many more statistics would be
needed, and also evidence of the nature of the decrease: that is,
the number which lapsed, the number which left by letter to
another chapel, and how many emigrated during this period.

Figures are available for Ebenezer, Swansea, for 1850 and
1852:[45]

1850:	Number received last year	87
	Membership	405
1852:	Received by letter and restored	36
	Left by letter or dismissed	22
	Membership	419

Another important factor is the number of hearers, those who
attended but were not members. There must have been a good
number at Ebenezer, for the average attendance at the evening
service in 1851 was 550. This figure can be accepted as exact,
for Elijah Jacob, the minister, commented on it to the commissioners of 1846. It had been said that there were 800 present,
but the pastor corrected the figure to 550.[46]

A sympathetic pastor, revival blessing, a large, lively congregation and close family ties were some of the comforts for
Griffith John during this time of loss and suffering. He contin-
ued his studies with his pastor, and a study of the Greek language was added. It was now time for the student to choose a
place for further study, and he decided on Brecon Congregational College, which could trace its origin to the early
Academy of 1695.[47] Griffith John, with David Evans, Josiah
Jones and Evan Harries, passed the entrance examination in
June 1850, were admitted in September and fully admitted in
December.[48] There were two tutors, Henry Griffiths and
Edward Davies, son-in-law of Dr George Lewis, minister,
author and former head of the College. Griffith John himself
refers to them:[49]

Here I spent about three years and a quarter under the
tuition of Messrs Griffiths and Davies, to whom I feel
greatly indebted in many respects, *especially* to the former.

His comments are of interest because, whereas the students generally regarded Edward Davies as being more popular and sociable, the young student from Swansea was attracted to Griffiths. The former was the classical tutor, and his 'portion of food was good' but 'insipid'. Professor Griffiths was responsible for theology, mathematics, science and philosophy, subjects which reveal the educational tradition of the Nonconformist Academy, although changes were introduced a little later in 1869, when the course was divided into three, with more emphasis on theological training. Henry Griffiths, regarded as being detached from the students, could inspire as well as inform, and the new student took to him immediately. 'I had not been in the College a week before I began to feel the Professor's inspiring influence.'[50] The student also settled down in a place of worship, and joined the other students in attending Plough chapel, which was a Welsh cause, while the College used English as the means of instruction: 'As the ground bridge over the gulf between the English and Welsh mind, the institution is invaluable.'[51]

Griffith John settled down to hard work, and could easily have qualified for the University of London, Brecon College having been authorised in 1852 to prepare students for that University. By that time he had spent two years in College, excelled as a student, and become most popular as a preacher. A strong conviction was forming in his mind that he should be a missionary overseas. He felt a divine persuasion, and on one occasion believed that God was speaking to him personally through the words of the prophet Isaiah, 'Whom shall I send?' The student's response was, 'Here am I; send me.'[2] The other specific reference to the call is connected with the visit of the Rev. David Griffiths to the College. The former missionary to Madagascar pressed the claims of that country, and Griffith John was moved to commit himself to work there. When he shared his conviction with his friends, many of them tried to dissuade him from taking such a step, while others thought that he was beside himself. One student, however, did enter into covenant with him, pledging his support to the venture.[53] Even Professor Griffiths was reluctant to lose such a student to a foreign country, but when he realised the depth of the student's conviction he soon gave his unqualified support.

Griffith John offered his services to the LMS on 18 March 1853.[54] The die was cast, but it was not a gamble, because the teaching at Ebenezer and his own experience assured him that God is a God of providence, dealing personally with his people and ruling every aspect of the life of the universe. The transcendent God is immanent in his world, and active in the affairs of men and women.

Further preparation and long-awaited destination

In his application to the LMS in March, Griffith John expressed three desires: to obey the commission of Christ (Matthew 28); to do so by going to the heathen, who were in a terrible state; and, if at all possible, to realise the first two desires in Madagascar.[55] That country appealed to him because of its close connections with Wales; also, he knew David Griffiths personally, and no one could be in his company without hearing about Madagascar. The country, however, was closed to missionaries, and the Christians there had been suffering bitterly since 1835. In spite of this obstacle Griffith John and Professor Griffiths were optimistic, and the tutor wrote a glowing tribute to the student as 'a strangely winning and affectionate little creature, overflowing with kindness and sociableness and an universal favourite'. Academically he was at the head of his class, in terms of preaching the most popular of all the students, and there was one chapel which had already extended a call to him. He had the virtues of perseverance and inventiveness, and the professor added, 'altogether just the kind of person I should like to see sent to a place like Madagascar'.[56]

Apart from being recommended by others, Griffith John had to answer a series of questions, including one regarding his doctrinal position. It is fairly brief compared with some others, but it does reveal his theological framework:[57]

I believe that there is only one and true God the Creator and Sovereign over all things, the supreme object of religious adoration who is represented as revealing himself to us in the person of the father, the Son and the Holy Ghost. I believe that Jesus Christ is the Son of God, coexistent with the father, before all things, but was manifested in human flesh, and appointed by the father to be the Mediator between God and Man. I believe in the Scripture doctrine of atonement that the mediation of Christ is necessary to rescue us from the ruin of the fall. I believe in the necessity of the Divine influence to enlighten and sanctify the soul. I believe the present life to be a state of discipline and moral responsibility, preparatory to a future state where rewards and punishments will be administered to all men according to their work.

The statement ascribes primacy in all things to God the Father, is strictly Trinitarian, and has the atonement accomplished by the God-man at its centre. It is the prerogative of the Holy Spirit to work a change in the heart of the sinner, and all men will have to give an account of themselves to their Maker. Griffith John proclaimed the eternal consequences of our life on earth, and that at a time when the eternity of punishment was being questioned. It was only in 1846 that Edward White had published his *Life of Christ*, in which he had criticised the orthodox teaching on the matter.

In order to be better equipped for the work Griffith John entered Bedford College, leaving Brecon on 26 January 1854, and arriving at Bedford the following day. During his stay at the College his instruction was undertaken by Edward Jukes and Richard Alliott. One of his fellow students was James Duthie, who went to India as a missionary, and the two were attracted to each other immediately.[58] During the same period the Welsh student had an opportunity to visit Woodbridge, Suffolk, where the Rev. David Griffiths was working with the Rev. T. Meller on the revision of the Malagasy Bible for the British and Foreign Bible Society.[59] As the months passed by it became evident that there was no possibility of going to Madagascar. The Directors suggested China to him, and on 15 September 1854 the applicant agreed to the request. The agreement was confirmed by the LMS secretary on behalf of the Society. The change was accepted rather stoically—'I cannot say I was sorry; I cannot say I was glad'[60]—but Griffith John believed that the Directors knew what they were doing and that they were being guided by God.

Griffith John himself summarises the next important events in his life:[61]

I left Bedford the 26th for Swansea. Was ordained at
Ebenezer on the 6th of April. Was married on the 13th at
Moddfey by Mr Jacob of Swansea.

There was a meeting at Ebenezer on the evening of the fifth of
April, and an afternoon and evening meeting on the sixth, but
the ordination service took place that Easter Friday morning,
the same day that 250 Mormons left Swansea harbour for their
paradise in Salt Lake City.[62] The Rev. Evan Griffiths, the printer,
read and prayed; an address was given by the Rev. W. Fair-
brother, former missionary in China; the Rev. W. James asked
the relevant questions (and by this time the congregation was
bathed in tears); the ordination prayer was offered by the Rev.
Elijah Jacob and the sermon preached by the Rev. E. Davies,
Brecon College.[63] A farewell meeting had already been held on
24 March at the College in Brecon,[64] and another followed at
Ebenezer on the Wednesday after the ordination. At that meeting a gift of £20 was presented to Griffith John, but the main
feature of the service was the sermon which he himself delivered.[65]

On Friday 13 April, the ordained minister and prospective
missionary married Margaret Jane, daughter of the Rev. David
Griffiths, formerly of Madagascar, and the one who had so
influenced the student while he was at Brecon.[66] During that
period David Griffiths was at Hay on Wye, very close to the
College, and the two lovers must have met during that time.
Most probably they also met when David Griffiths moved for
a brief period to Woodbridge and when Griffith John was at
Bedford. Margaret Jane had been born in Madagascar and was
acutely aware of the pioneering days and the following period
of persecution. Her father and David Jones carried on the work
started by Jones and Thomas Bevan, who died soon after arriving on the island. David Jones had to leave because of ill
health, and David Griffiths because of persecution. He was
allowed back for a short time, and while there reported the
death of one who was very dear to the Griffiths family. She
was Raminhay (the caring one), who had nursed Margaret
Jane when she was a baby. With a heavy heart David Griffiths
wrote in his diary, 'Raminhay-Flora has died a martyr 9th July
1840.'[67] At the time her husband David was being educated in

England, and did not know of his wife's death until he returned to Madagascar.

Having such a background Margaret Jane was singularly suited to be the wife of a missionary, and indeed to be a missionary herself, although she must have been disappointed at not going to Madagascar. Before leaving, the newly married couple had to visit Mrs Griffiths' mother at Machynlleth. They drove there majestically, being provided with a pony and trap by David Griffiths' brother who farmed the Beili in Llangadock.[68] Further farewell meetings were held, including one at Woodbridge chaired by David Griffiths, and one on the Quay attended by friends from Beaumont Chapel.[69] Griffith John and his wife, accompanied by the Rev. A. Williamson and his wife, sailed from Gravesend in the *Hamilla Mitchell* on 21 May 1855.

Occasionally the four were 'poorly', but they experienced no serious illness on the voyage. Indeed, on 1 August Griffith John recorded in his Journal, 'We have had nothing hitherto to impede our progress.'[70] Many aspects of the voyage thrilled him—the rushing, swelling and breaking of the waves, one moment like large mountains ready to bury the ship, and the other moment striking its side until the ship danced again. The main cause for amazement was the sunset. According to Griffith John it was worth coming from Wales to see the beautiful sunset of a fine evening: 'I have not witnessed anything worthy of being compared with it in point of sublime grandeur.'[71] There was one main cause of grievance: 'I enjoy the Sunday less than anything else on the voyage.'[72]

The last thing Griffith John wanted to do was to waste time. The entry for 6 June reads:[73]

> Commenced a regular course of study—portions of the Hebrew Scriptures and of the Greek Testament, also study Mathematics, Natural Philosophy, animal and Vegetable Physiology, Chemistry.

He elaborated on this theme in a letter to Elijah Jacob:[74]

> I read nearly the whole series of the Congregational Lectures, so that I have a pretty good stock of theology in my brains, Henry Rogers' Essays in three volumes, Macaulay's

Essays in two volumes, Barnes' Notes on the Revelation, Herschel on Astronomy, Mitchell on Astronomy, a large volume on the steam-engine, Carpenter's Physiology, books on chemistry, electricity, magnetism, mechanics, and other branches of science. Several other books of a lighter character I read.

Not only did Griffith John give a reading list, but he would also comment on some of the works mentioned, and at the same time refer to others. His comments can be summarised:[75]

25 June	I have finished Gilbert's on the Atonement today. I have not yet read anything that coincides so completely and thoroughly with my own views on this great theme.
8 July	(Reading Book of Revelation)
9 July	(Payne on Original Sin.) The Dr's arguments are not always conclusive.
3 Aug.	I have finished Dr Alexander on the connexion between the Old and New Testaments. This book has done me some good.
4 Aug.	I have just got over Barnes' Notes on the Book of Revelation, and have been very much pleased with them on the whole.

It is obvious that Griffith John made full use of his time. The journey to a foreign country afforded the opportunity to study. It was during such a journey that many missionaries settled down to learn the language of a particular people. Griffith John does not refer to this aspect of his work, but does mention working at Hebrew and Greek, studies he had started at Swansea and Brecon and which would be so important to him later in the task of translating the Scriptures.

Apart from the language study, the biblical studies deepened Griffith John's knowledge and understanding of Scripture, which he regarded as fundamental for a minister working at home or abroad. The study of the Book of Revelation would open up his mind to God's great purposes in history to be fulfilled eschatologically. Barnes on Revelation was becoming popular at this time, and one of the men responsible for introducing his work to Wales was the Rev. Thomas Rees while he ministered in Llanelli; a future minister of Ebenezer, Swansea, he was regarded by Griffith John as a friend. One clear theme in his theological reading was the Atonement, which as a student he had regarded as so central to the Christian faith. He had a personal interest in the scientific works and was fascinated by them, but they were also a means to an end. The Welshman knew of the ability of the Chinese to deal with matters like mathematics and astronomy. He had to be prepared to meet with them: 'A missionary need not forget the civilisation of the people among whom he labours.'[76] It was in this frame of mind that Griffith John was looking forward to his arrival at Shanghai.

The four missionaries arrived at their destination on 24 September 1855, tired but in good health.[77] The boy preacher, who had swayed large congregations in Swansea and other parts of Wales and Britain, had set his foot on the threshold of a vast empire. Undaunted, Griffith John was ready to occupy this great land of China. Was he naive, optimistic, ambitious, or foolish? He himself would say that he was moving in the realm of faith, which is the assurance of things hoped for and the conviction of things not seen. There was no closed door that faith could not open. He also knew that when there is an open door there are many adversaries.

'All I can do is to lay myself on the altar and say: "Lord Jesus, take me as I am, and use me as Thou wilt."'

Griffith John, *The Reason Why*

'I could not turn back without guilt on my soul.'

William Carey
quoted by Griffith John, *A Voice from China*, 111

2

Shanghai: an open door and many adversaries

1855-1861

The Treaty of Nanking, 1842, opened up Canton, Amoy, Foochow, Ningpo and Shanghai to foreign residence and trade. Nothing specific was said regarding religious toleration, but the ports were open and presented a new challenge to the missionaries.[1] It is true that the privileges gained were the outcome of a war that resulted in the thrusting of opium upon China, but the missionaries, deploring the opium trade, believed that they had to take advantage of what had happened. This was the attitude of Catholics and Protestants: 'In both Catholic and Protestant circles the treaties were welcomed as marking a new era in missions and advantage was at once taken of them.'[2] A welcome provision was the clause that allowed foreigners to be tried under their own laws and by their own officials. Travel outside the ports mentioned was not allowed, but the application of the law varied from province to province, depending very often on the attitude of the local officials. In Shanghai, British, American and French Consulates were set up, many foreign companies were established, and soon there was an influx of sailors. Indeed, seamen could outnumber residents by ten to one.[3]

On 7 September 1853, two years before Griffith John arrived, the city was captured by the Triads, a secret society whose members appealed on oath to Heaven, Earth and Moon, the trinity of powers in the Chinese universe. Politically they opposed the rule of the Manchu dynasty, socially they acted on the principle of robbing the rich to give to the poor, and religiously they functioned as dissenting religious groups.[4] Imperial soldiers surrounded the city in a bid to recapture it, but it was not relieved until February 1855, a few months

35

before Griffith John's arrival. The fighters and civilians in the city were treated harshly, ears and heads being cut off, and the city was left in a miserable state. To complicate matters, refugees from neighbouring provinces poured into the city, increasing poverty, gambling, prostitution and thieving.

The city was still in turmoil when the Johns and the Williamsons arrived on 24 September 1855. The two men were of one heart as far as the work was concerned, but physically they contrasted sharply. Griffith John was not much over five feet tall, broad-shouldered, with a large head, dark hair and brown twinkling eyes, while Williamson was six feet four inches tall with large ears and hands.[5] The four newcomers, like Hudson Taylor, were struck by the noise and the smells of Shanghai. Even Sunday—so strange to the Welshman—was like every other day, full of noise, tumult and impiety. Griffith John was appalled at the dirt: 'The city of Shanghai is one of the filthiest in the world. I have seen nothing to be compared to it in dirt and filth, it surpasses everything.'[6] The smells were 'abominable with garlic predominating'.[7] Looking at the city it was possible to say that it was a 'superb settlement', the centre of commerce and gaiety. On the other hand, considering its narrow, busy streets with their shouting, toiling people, it was 'a mean place'.[8]

On their arrival the Johns stayed with Walter Medhurst, the LMS printer, while their home was being prepared for them. The house allocated to the new missionaries had been occupied by John Burdon, CMS, and then rented to Hudson Taylor, who sub-let part of it to Dr Jenkins, the American missionary. Hudson Taylor had been glad of a temporary home, as he was finding it difficult to provide shelter for himself and his co-workers, the Parkers. The 'sword of Damocles fell' when the Johns arrived at their new home on 1 October.[9] Dr Jenkins moved out ready to build a house for himself, and Hudson Taylor found a home near the south gate. The Johns' home was next door to that of Alexander Wylie, a renowned Chinese scholar highly regarded by Griffith John: 'Alexander Wylie was one of the most remarkable men I have ever met, whether in or out of China.'[10] Another fellow missionary referred to him as a 'very pleasant, quiet person, and of superior qualities'.[11] Other members of the group were Dr Lockhart, whose hospital had played a crucial role during the Triad trouble, William Muirhead, 'bold as a lion',[12] author and outstanding evangelist, and Joseph Edkins, a great sinologue: 'Between Edkins and myself the closest friendship grew up at once.'[13]

Spying out the land and first attacks

The first task for Griffith John was to tackle the language. He knew that 'The language is a colossus', but he was not deterred in any way.[14] Learning the language was a challenge, an obstacle to overcome, like the challenge of an unclimbed mountain to a mountaineer; but it was also the means of communicating with the Chinese. He was determined to reach the top, however high the peak seemed to be, and there is no doubt that it was high, as many Europeans had found out. Only a few of them had really mastered the language. There were altogether 40,000 characters, 6,000 of them in constant use: 'Chinese is written with curious-looking characters. They are not the symbols of sounds, like ours, but of ideas; the sounds, or names of them, change with every variation of dialect; but the ideas they represent never alter.'[15] It was possible for people who spoke different dialects to understand the same book, but it would be impossible for them to exchange ideas by speech. The Chinese marvelled at the simplicity of the English alphabet with its twenty-six characters which could be learnt at one sitting.

Griffith John did not expect great difficulty with the Shanghai dialect, however: 'Nothing but a thorough acquaintance with the language will satisfy me.'[16] Apart from the help of fellow missionaries it was essential to have a native teacher, and Griffith John acquired one immediately. Throughout his career he was going to depend heavily on such a person. Another way to establish good relationships with the Chinese and hear the language spoken was to show them scientific experiments. Electricity was a popular subject: '22 February 1856. To day Dr Medhurst brought a Mandarin in followed by about a dozen men to see some experiments in Electricity.'[17] The newcomer acknowledged the scientific bent of the Chinese mind, and how advanced they were in many fields of learning. Griffith John had Herschel on the subject of astronomy, a work which was being translated into Chinese by Alexander Wylie.[18] While

John had a personal interest in scientific matters, Wylie was a specialist and could write with authority on such subjects as astronomy, geometry and calculus. When good relationships were established it was possible to present the gospel to the people.

Griffith John would observe others at work and was 'trying various experiments myself'.[19] As he learned and observed, he was eager to go out to preach the gospel. He made a start before the end of his first year in Shanghai. On 2 March 1856 he ventured out with Williamson to the villages:

Thus we had an opportunity of speaking a few words to those who are in utter ignorance of the truths that concern their eternal welfare.

The following day he went out with his teacher:

Went in the afternoon with my teacher to the city to preach. We had a first-rate congregation.[20]

During the same month he went on two short journeys, one with Muirhead and the other with Edkins. After only six months in Shanghai, Griffith John was out preaching the gospel to the people in their own language. Working from Shanghai he took a sweeping look at the country within a radius of a hundred and fifty miles. Here was territory to be occupied. Fifty miles distant was the large city of Sungkiang. Having gained confidence in the work he felt ready to go to that city because the examination day was approaching. The examination system was all-important for promotion in China. Those who did well in the annual examinations arranged by the government would have the best jobs, and it is no surprise, therefore, that large numbers would sit them.

Griffith John visited Sungkiang alone, that is, without a fellow missionary: 'I have now ventured for the first time to go alone, with the intention of spending the chief part of the winter in itinerating, in penetrating the country in every direction from Shanghai, for the purpose of proclaiming the one true and living God and Jesus Christ whom He sent.'[21] At Sungkiang:[22]

Hundreds if not thousands of students will be present. I have in the boat two large bags full of books consisting of the New Testament and various tracts. We have anchored within four miles of the City, the darkness of the night preventing from proceeding any further.

Early next morning he entered the city:[23]

After breakfast, Wong, the colporteur, and myself proceeded to the place where the examination was held. We took along with us a good supply of books. We had glorious opportunities of preaching, which we availed ourselves of, and of satisfactorily distributing our books. These were eagerly sought and gladly received.

The two men were busy for two days, and enjoyed a good reception. The Chinese respected the written word, and would be reluctant to destroy a book even if they disagreed with its contents. The two were surprised, therefore, when one person who had accepted a book tore it in pieces. The action made Wong very angry, and he rebuked the man for not returning the book if he did not like it. The people around the two told them that they should not be surprised because the man was a Roman Catholic.

Soochow was one of the richest and most beautiful cities in China. The Chinese would say: 'That to be happy on earth, one must be born in Su-Cheu, live in Canton and die in Tien-Cheu, for in the first are the handsomest people, in the second the richest luxuries, and in the third the best coffins'.[24] No foreigner had visited the place without a disguise, but Griffith John and Edkins made the attempt. Once inside the gate they were met by an official, who sent for another official of high rank. He told the two intruders that they could not enter, for to allow them to do so would be 'contrary to treaty, contrary to custom and contrary to everything'. The two, therefore, decided to try the water gate, and told the boatman to turn the boat in that direction, and 'fortunately got in safely, though I must confess clandestinely'.[25] They walked about in every direction, visited places of interest and preached to a large number of people. On the second day the two missionaries went in to the centre of the city where they distributed several hundred copies of the New Testament. They regarded the visit with pleasure, not only in terms of their distribution, but also feeling that they had done a little to break down the prejudice against foreigners.

It was in the company of William Muirhead that Griffith John took a journey on 21-22 September 1857. They visited a number of places, and as usual were very busy, even before breakfast, but the method they adopted was a little different this time. [In summary:][26]

We spent the greatest part of our time in going from house to house and speaking to each face to face of the way of salvation. We were received very kindly by all. I don't remember being repulsed by more than one—who told me that he was a Confucianist and did not want to hear what I had to say. I intend giving myself to this work during the whole of the ensuing winter.

The shops were included in the visiting, and early on 22 September they entered every shop in Neaziang, where they shared the gospel and distributed tracts.

In order to pioneer and consolidate the work already begun, Williamson settled in Sungkiang for a brief period, and Griffith John in Pinghu. He and the family left Shanghai on 29 March 1858, arriving on the 31st. They chose the best way to travel, by boat, as all the main rivers were connected to canals. The boat in which the Johns travelled measured 25 feet by 6 feet and, apart from a space of a few feet, was enclosed and partitioned into sections. The outer cabin led into the central compartment, which had windows for light and seats for comfort. It was here that passengers could eat, sleep and relax. Astern of the central cabin was a small room for the servant; here he would sleep by night and cook by day.[27] The travellers passed the city of Sungkiang, and noticed that each side of the river was lined with the mulberry tree. When they arrived at Pinghu they moved into the house that Griffith John had rented. The following day John was ready to preach to the people, but could not open the door of the room because of 'some pecuniary difficulties' which were not specified.[28] Probably some financial gain was expected by someone for opening the door, because the preacher did make the comment that there was no end to Chinese intrigue, even in the smallest matters.

Griffith John had no intention of settling down in Pinghu, but he did not leave immediately because he believed that if a lasting work was to be established in any place a prolonged stay was called for. It was pointless paying flying visits to a place and expecting the work to last. After staying at Pinghu for a few months he left the work in the care of two national teachers, satisfied that they had the ability to look after it. His eye was on Sungkiang, and he visited the place on 16 June 1858. He failed to rent a house there on 21 July, and did not succeed until 4 August, when he obtained a place at the North Gate, outside the city walls.[29] The hired room was used as a preaching centre, and Griffith John made full use of it when visiting the city, which he did at least three times before the end of 1858, on 6 and 18 November and 3 December.

The first of these visits was made during a journey along the Grand Canal, when Soochow was also visited.[30] By this time the Treaty of Tientsin had been signed (26 July 1858), although all the clauses were not implemented until 1860.[31] Nine additional ports were opened to foreigners, and the right given to them to travel and trade throughout the Empire. Three further centres, Hankow amongst them, were to be opened once peace was established. Toleration for Christianity was guaranteed. As far as missionaries were concerned their sphere of labour was significantly enlarged, and they and other foreigners could venture to buy property in the interior. It is true that there was no specific clause concerning this latter privilege, but neither was there a clause prohibiting foreigners from buying property. Chinese Christians were placed under the protection of foreign powers, who were to act as protectors of the faith: 'Many Chinese, seeing the advantage to be obtained from powerful foreign backing, feigned conversion.'[32] This was one of the dangers inherent in the Treaty, but Griffith John had no doubt at all of its advantages, and that the missionaries had played an important part in securing the changes.

Griffith John's optimism was rekindled, and he expressed an almost haughty attitude towards the Chinese. The inferiority of the Chinese Empire had been revealed: 'The force of European character has been wholesomely felt, and the superior science of the heretofore despised barbarian is beginning to be acknowledged in many quarters.'[33] It was time to go on with confidence. It was in such a spirit that John, Lea, Burdon, Aitchin and Wong journeyed to the Grand Canal. They left on 5 October 1858, having two aims in mind, to proclaim the gospel and to ascertain the impact of the Treaty on the interior. They travelled by boat again, because the rivers flowing into the Grand Canal formed a water communication almost complete from Peking to Canton.

The change of attitude was evident when they approached the custom house at Hutzguan. This was usually avoided by foreigners, but on this occasion the boat which guarded the river swung around and allowed the missionaries to proceed immediately.[34] There was a brief delay at Chang-cheu-fu, but the travellers could understand why, because the custom-house authorities had been thrown into confusion by the sudden appearance of the foreigners and could not believe that they wanted to cross the Yangtze. At Tanyang two military mandarins tried to dissuade the company from continuing because the journey was so dangerous, but when they saw the missionaries' determination they gave them all possible help. Many places were visited for the very first time by Protestant missionaries, and when they visited Soochow the change was remarkable. Just eighteen months previously Edkins and John had to enter the place secretly, but this time the Christian workers had no difficulty at all in going in openly and preaching the gospel. They arrived back in Shanghai on 8 November.[35]

Opposition was still experienced, especially when the missionaries travelled deeper into the interior. There were expressions of hatred when Griffith John and Muirhead went on a visit to the Yellow River, leaving Shanghai on 2 June 1859. They made a point of stopping at populous places like the city temples at Soochow. Every afternoon hundreds of people, if not thousands, would gather together to enjoy a cup of tea and share news, and every person did his utmost 'to excel his neighbour in verbosity'.[36] With the appearance of the missionaries the talk ceased, and all attention was given to the strangers. They grasped the opportunity to preach to them and had a good hearing. Another way to promote the work, if at all possible, was to rent a house, but for foreigners to do this was almost out of the question. In Soochow the problem was overcome by renting a house in the name of the national workers supervised by Griffith John and others. The two missionaries were glad to meet with a number of inquirers who were meeting regularly with the national Christians.

On 8 June the two men arrived at the district city of Kiangyin. It was examination time and no less than three thousand students were gathered together. When John addressed some of them, one candidate adopted a threatening attitude and tried to excite the others to turn against the speaker. Griffith John turned to them, and 'I told them that I was an Englishman, which word uttered with considerable emphasis, and I may say national pride, made some of them turn pale.'[37] The preacher thought there was 'magic' in that word 'Englishman'. It was not the only occasion when the Welshman took this particular shield to defend himself.

Thousands of people were present at Kiangyin, and here Griffith John met a Chinese colporteur who was devoted to his books, anxious to teach his fellow Chinese, yet seeking for more truth to satisfy his spiritual desires. He was attracted to Buddhism and Confucianism but was willing to consider the claims of the Christian faith. Griffith John believed that the light which the colporteur had would eventually lead him on to seek greater light, and to find it in the Lord Jesus Christ. The Christian missionary was always encouraged when he came across a sincere inquirer after the truth. In many places during the journey the travellers were reminded of the troubled times by the imperialistic camps and the presence of refugees. At Shau-puh, for example, which they visited on 14 June, there must have been four to five thousand soldiers in possession of powerful guns. The refugees were numerous and lived in mud- straw houses near the canal.

There was a long delay at Tsingkiangpu because of the suspicion of the people and the delaying tactics of the authorities. Eventually the deserted bed of the Yellow River was reached:[38]

We did not only cross it dry-shod, but converted it into a temporary pulpit. Where but a few years ago the turbid waters of the Hwang rolled majestically—the common

dread of the inhabitants of the plain—there now cottages
are built, gardens are planted, carriages pass to and fro,
the grass is beginning to grow, and sheep are browsing at
their ease. Here and there pools of water may be seen, but
no continued stream. At this place the bed is nearly as
high as the banks, and the surface deposit is of the finest
sand.

The authorities in the area were suspicious of the intruders,
and when they continued on their journey the following day
they were watched closely until they reached their boat again.

When Griffith John returned to Shanghai he immediately
sensed a change of mood, recording on 13 July 1859: 'Reached
Shanghai this morning and found the people as I expected
very much cast down by reason of the late disaster at the
Peiho.'[39] The reason for such a change was the temporary victory of the Chinese over the foreign allies during the opium
war. Half the imperial force had been killed or wounded
immediately. 'The rest floundered back to their boats and the
desperately bungled operation ended with four hundred and
sixty killed or wounded and six gunboats out of action.'[40]
Shanghai was so unsettled that Griffith John and the other missionaries did not enter the city for a few days; but he decided
to do so on 5 August, and again the next day, when he was
accompanied by William Muirhead. They did not escape abuse
but were not physically attacked, although one of them had
water-melon thrown over him. In the evening, however,
restraint was withdrawn:[41]

> On this said saturday night, a mob collected about our large
> Chapel and broke the doors, windows, benches and pulpit
> to atoms, and stole all the things belonging to the door-
> keeper, poor man. he came to us early sunday morning with
> only his trousers on very much frighten. (*sic*)

That was Mrs John's reference to the event. Her husband adds
some more details:[42]

> On the night of the 6 ultimo, about a hundred or hundred
> and fifty men broke into our chapel in Shanghai and

smashed everything to pieces, with the exception of a few benches. Then they proceeded into another, but ere they had finished the work of destruction there, the native soldiers were on the spot and the crowd was immediately dispersed. I have no doubt that they fully intended proceeding from chapel to chapel and doing to them all they so effectually did to ours. The only reason they assigned for their conduct was that the missionaries had returned into the city after a week's absence.

By the beginning of September the city was more settled, but the missionaries had to be careful, as 'the least provocation would be followed by another tremendous explosion'.[43]

Much work had been accomplished in a number of centres, including Shanghai, Soochow, Sungkiang and Pinghu. One of the many problems facing the missionaries was uncertainty, as they were never sure how the local authorities would respond. The work at Hangchow is a good illustration of the problem. In October 1858 Griffith John had preached openly there, and in 1859 had distributed 4,000 copies of the New Testament, but in 1860 the city was closed to foreign and native Christian workers. Not only were the authorities unpredictable, but the attitude of the people generally could change quickly: 'The people, who but three months ago were as harmless as doves and very respectful, are now as bold as lions and often intolerably impudent.'[44] The work was making progress slowly but surely, and it is time to survey what had been accomplished between 1855 and 1859.

Methods and message
Griffith John did not expect the gospel to spread like wildfire through Shanghai and district, but he was expecting a measure of success, as he believed in the power of the gospel to change the lives of men, women and children. Preaching the gospel was a 'glorious task':[45]

But O, how difficult it is to impress the minds of this people with the importance of it; their hearts seem to be altogether impenetrable. Nothing but almighty power can break their strong hearts.

Two days later he expressed the same feeling: 'I am finding that I am preaching to stones.'[46] The missionary could not ascribe the hardness to God, for he loved the world and had given his only begotten Son as an expression of it. Griffith John knew that there was hardness in the very nature of the Chinese, but he also blamed himself for not being earnest and prayerful enough: 'I sometimes fear that ideas touching the conversion of the world partake rather too much of the romantic.'[47] He was making a general statement, but he was also, possibly, acknowledging that he had entertained such a notion.

It was not romantic to concentrate on preaching, but it was Griffith John's basic conviction that he should do so. He was always busy distributing literature, but never regarded this as more important than preaching. The method was new in China. The people were not used to being addressed in this way, and, of course, the missionary preached in order to bring about conversion, which would mean a radical change of life for the people. The consequences could be quite serious, for a Chinese convert could be turned out by his family and would not be welcomed by the villagers. This concentration on preaching was in marked contrast to the Roman Catholic method, which did not emphasise the proclaimed word, but endeavoured to win the people by distributing literature and only instructing inquirers in the faith. That would always be in the context of the church, that is, of bringing people into it as an institution. The Roman Catholics would also try to help the people with their personal and domestic problems, especially those of a legal nature. Their emphasis was on membership in the church as an institution, while the Protestant missionaries emphasised response to the preached word. In making preaching central Griffith John was of one mind with such men as Hudson Taylor of the China Inland Mission, and the Wesleyan, David Hill. Another marked difference between the Protestant and Roman Catholic approach was the readiness of the former to give the Bible to the people, while the latter would keep it from them. The Protestants spread the Scriptures, and the converts would be thoroughly instructed in them. As far as the Roman Catholic was concerned the Bible was the book of the priest and not of the people.

Griffith John had no doubt at all as to the content of the

message: it was 'the great and glorious doctrine of the cross', a
message which was a stumbling block to the Jews, folly to the
Greeks, and both to the Chinese.[48] A hearer had told Muirhead
that he could preach Jesus, but not his death on the cross, and
Griffith John commented: 'Then the [hearer] was directed to
the first chapter of the first Epistle to the Corinthians, and then
acknowledged that the doctrine of the Cross was an insepar-
able and main element of Christianity.'[49] The death of the sinless Christ atoned for the sin of the world, which death was,
according to Griffith John, the only basis of reconciliation
between God and man. Such a message was in direct conflict
with all the religious traditions of China. The Christian preacher
was conscious of idolatry, although according to Griffith John
it was influencing the Chinese only in a superficial way. Much
more serious was the influence of Confucius, 'as it penetrates
the very depths of their soul, entwines itself around all their
thoughts and affections, and holds them with a tenacious
grasp'.[50] The worst aspect mentioned by the missionary is that
of ancestor worship, which involved living children sacrificing
to their dead parents. For the Confucian, knowledge was
always accompanied by action, making it impossible for him
to accept the doctrine of justification by faith alone. The
Buddhist ignored the individual as an entity, desiring a
Nirvana where the unity of all would be realised. He wanted
to cancel out the consciousness of self, while the Christian faith
aimed at conquering the sinful self, which would enable man
to be what God intended him to be.[51]

With the cross at the centre of his message, Griffith John proclaimed the grace of God towards sinful man, but he had to
preach to a people who were adamantly refusing to think of
sin in the terms proclaimed by the Christian preacher. Griffith
John was appalled by the pride and impenitence of the heathen in general and the Chinese people in particular: 'I have
never met a heathen who seemed to be troubled with a sense
of sin, or appeared to have the least desire to be delivered from
its dominion.'[52] Consequently, there was a great need for
patience and perseverance. No lasting work was to be accomplished quickly.

As far as the *method* of preaching was concerned, the Welshman followed the traditional pattern of proclaiming without

interruption, an exercise that could take an hour or even longer. The sermon, however, was not always long, as Griffith John could preach short discourses, 'embracing a simple enunciation of Gospel truth, and an earnest, affectionate appeal to the consciences of our hearers'.[53] He would also vary his method: 'I often invite discussion, for the obvious reason that it is an excellent way of explaining, adapting, and enforcing the truth that we have to teach.'[54] Griffith John was aiming at winning the Chinese to the Christian faith, but his method also shows respect for them. He was aware of the fact that the Chinese were not only a reading people, but also a thinking people:[55]

> The man who can do them real good is he who is able and willing to enter into the endless labyrinths of their own speculations—sympathise with them and with all that is true and noble in their system—point out plainly but kindly their grievous errors and defects—and then open up to their minds the inexhaustible treasury of that system which is infinitely true and perfect.

In no way would the preacher compromise the Christian gospel, but at the same time he sensitively appreciated the best things in Chinese life and thought.

Preaching had to be carried on in all possible places, on the street, in the chapel, on the bed of a river or on a boat. As many people as possible should be reached, because the gospel is for all classes of society, but Griffith John was convinced that a special effort should be made to reach the poor. He explained himself in more detail in one of his letters to the Directors:[56]

> The more I have to do with the people the more profoundly convinced I become of the absurdity of the old standing idea that China must be worked upon from above—and that *here* we must commence with the wise, the rich and the noble, and descend from them to the lower classes.—If we would convert China we must begin with the common people, and devote our energies principally to their enlightenment.

To justify his approach, he quoted a Roman Catholic for

support, and pointed out that the same emphasis is found in the ministry of the Lord Jesus Christ. The poor people heard him gladly. This approach was so different from that of Alexander Duff in India and, later, of Richard Allen and Timothy Richard in China. Duff, for example, concentrated on the more learned and taught through the medium of English.[57]

Connected with the 'old standing idea' was another 'false impression'. So many people believed 'that none but men of high mental endowments and profound erudition will do as Missionaries for China'.[58] It was proper that some learned missionaries should spend some time with the learned in China, but Griffith John knew from experience that most of his time had to be spent with the illiterate poor. He made a plea for less educated men, intelligent, of course, having had some education and with a willingness to learn the essentials of the language, but not of necessity learned or academic. They could work hand in hand with the national workers. What was needed was 'a good staff of native agents, and a large reinforcement from home'.[59] John wanted to safeguard the two aspects, that is, give as much responsibility as possible to the nationals, but, as they lacked 'prudence and method', a foreign teacher was necessary as a supervisor. The object Griffith John had in mind was to establish as many stations as possible where the national assistants could function as supervisors. Adopting such a plan it would be possible to open up the interior, and the Welsh missionary had no doubt of success, whatever might be the outcome of Lord Elgin's effort to open up the country. The future was in the hand of the missionary, not that of the military leader or politician.

Progress was slow, but there were encouragements, even numerically. Writing from Shanghai early in October 1857, Griffith John was glad to report that their female servant and her two children had been baptised a few months previously. When she started working for the John family she was utterly ignorant of the Christian faith, but Mrs John had made it a point to instruct the servant personally and when present at evening family worship.[60] The initial effort to establish a station in Pinghu failed, but Griffith John's concentrated effort from April to June 1858 was fruitful. The afternoons had been spent in preaching, usually from 2 o'clock until 5 or 6 in the evening, Griffith John and his national assistant giving the message alternately. A Bible class was held twice a week for those who were inquiring about the Christian faith, and six members of the class had been baptised, all of them as far as the preacher could ascertain 'walking worthy of their profession'. Apart from preaching and the Bible class there was another feature of the work at Pinghu:[61]

> Opened a society today similar to what we have in Wales, for Church members and candidates for membership. This is something definite and will prove quite as useful I believe as immediate baptism. I don't like to administer that ordinance to those who are ignorant of the truth and prefer waiting until they are instructed, at least, in the essential truths of the gospel. In our society today there were present Mrs John, woman servant, Wong the native assistant, myself, and two candidates for church membership—my teacher and a son of my landlady.

There was a clearer experiential emphasis in the society, and Griffith John could draw on the tradition of the Methodist society and the Dissenting preparatory meeting. Griffith John's teacher, and two other nationals were baptised a few weeks later, an event which was full of emotion for the missionary: 'My feelings were very intense on the occasion. They are my first.'[62]

Although Griffith John and his co-workers were concentrating on the poor people, the other classes were not neglected. Indeed, Griffith John enjoyed discussing and arguing with the scholars and prominent literary men. Those who belonged to the young church at Pinghu included two literary graduates, two tradesmen, a shopkeeper and a silk merchant.[63] Whatever their social standing, all inquirers had to apply for membership. There were three phases: candidature, baptism and membership. A candidate's application would be considered in detail, and very often his baptism and membership would be postponed for a period of time. There was general agreement amongst the missionaries that membership should be on the basis of a personal, credible profession of faith. If there was an obvious lack of understanding or lack of fruit in terms of conduct, the application for membership would be delayed. Becoming a member called for moral courage, and Griffith John refused to accept one person because he had not told his father, 'fearing that, should his father object, he might retrace his steps'.[64]

A serious problem in this context was drug-taking. As early as 1856 Griffith John had expressed revulsion at this habit: 'I saw to day for the first time opium smoking. This is the very bane of China. To see men under the influence of this cursed stuff is sickening and heart rending.'[65] Deterioration could be rapid. Once a person became a habitual smoker he could be destroyed in ten years. Not only did the opium smoker himself suffer, but his family as well, as he would not be in a condition to work. It had further social implications in that the Chinese would grow poppy instead of rice, creating economic instability. Before the end of the century it was said that on many of the Szechwan roads 'opium houses are as common as gin shops in our London slums'.[66] Griffith John was appalled that Britain could make capital of such a trade, as the Chinese were paying Britain £14 million to £16 million per annum for 'the destructive poison'.[67] The Chinese people were being robbed and their life was being destroyed. The action of the British Government was taken as the standard of Christian morality, and this hindered the work of the missionaries in China.

In the context of the church the Christian leaders were agreed on procedure. Griffith John interviewed a candidate who had cut down the amount of smoking by half and was making an effort to stop completely, but he applied in vain: 'As we admit none—even as candidates—who smoke opium, we spoke to him to that effect.'[68]

There was more disagreement concerning another serious matter, that of polygamy. There was a general conviction that no polygamist, heathen or Christian, should be a member of the church. Griffith John and Alexander Wylie differed from this view. They agreed that no one who is a member of a Christian church should take a wife in addition to the one he had, but a person who had taken two wives during his life in heathenism, if worthy in all other respects, should be admitted to the fellowship of the church.[69] Griffith John was trying to avoid the extreme of being too rigid, and demanding near perfection from the candidates. The basic principle was acceptance on the basis of a credible confession of faith.

This principle could clearly be applied to adult believers, but the Welsh Congregationalist argued that sincere inquirers and children should be included. He was facing an unresolved tension, as he was arguing that infants who could not exercise faith, and adults who could do so, should belong to the church. The Congregationalist presented his case concerning infant baptism with confidence. He had read Halley on the subject, and agreed with him that all who are instructed by the church should be baptised. It initiated a person as a disciple and learner of Christian doctrine. That was his first line of argument in a detailed defence of infant baptism. He developed the theme in his second point:[70]

This position is maintained:

1. The great commission to disciple all nations.
2. That no restriction of the terms of the commission to any class of persons can be found in any part of the New Testament.
3. That this unrestricted commission was given to the Jews whose rites of decipling [sic] were uniformly administered to children of proselytes together with their parents.
4. That Jesus had taught them that little children were members of the Kingdom, into which none could enter without being born of water.
5. That the apostles baptized persons when they had previously known nothing on the day in which they heard the gospel.
6. That they baptized some whose unfitness through ignorance if faith and piety had been qualifications might have been easily detected, e.g. Simon Magus.
7. That no qualification (such as faith and repentance) is prescribed in Scripture, and therefore no man has a right to impose one.
8. That neither the refusal nor delay of baptism can be justified by any Scriptural example.
9. That for a thousand years, no person of any party among Christians can be found not having received Baptism in infancy, if his parents were themselves baptized.

The last section of the defence confirmed most of the arguments mentioned, adding a few others, such as the reference to New Testament teachers baptising on their own individual authority, and the language of Scripture that baptism is 'unto' not 'on account of' forgiveness. Not only was there a theological tension here directly concerned with baptism, but tension also between gospel and denomination. The gospel was common to all denominations, but why relate it to a particular form of denominationalism from the West? The original missionaries of the LMS had gone out to different countries, not to establish denominations but to preach the glorious gospel of God. There was always the danger of making denominationalism an essential aspect of the Christian message.

The newly established churches and the pioneering work in the interior had to be supplied with literature. Immediately after arriving in Shanghai, Griffith John had done everything possible to help in this area. The printing press was already there, and the newcomer was largely responsible for keeping it busy. It was essential to have Bibles and parts of Scripture, but Griffith John contributed a number of works published in leaves, including *Strait Gate*. As in so many other countries the missionaries in China translated *Pilgrim's Progress* into the language of the people. The work experienced a setback in 1856: 'The normal routine of the printing office has experienced temporary interruption during the past half year on account of the recent fire which entirely consumed one of the buildings and its contents.'[71] It was not too difficult to reprint the smaller pamphlets, but it was a much harder task to reprint a large portion of the New Testament which was in the course of completion.

The Taiping rebels

Griffith John had arrived in Shanghai in the shadow of the Triad's attack on the city, and from then on until 1860 lived in the sound of Taiping activity, the strongest and most notorious of revolutionary societies. Their attacks, uprisings and clashes with imperial troops devastated some of the richest and most prosperous provinces of China, with a loss, by 1860, of fifteen to twenty million lives. At the head of the movement was Hung Xin-quan (Hung Hsin-ch'uan), or the Heavenly King.

While in Canton he had listened to a missionary (probably the American, Edward Stevenson) and was also given a work by Liang A-fa (1789-1855), *Good Words to exhort the age*.[72] The author had been in contact with Robert Morrison and William Milne of the LMS, and had been baptised as a Protestant.

Good Words was vaguely evangelical, had some echoes of Christian standards, like the equality of all men and the injustice of exploitation, but was confused regarding the heavenly and earthly kingdoms. Hung obtained a Bible in 1847, helped by Medhurst and Gutzlaff, the able and unpredictable missionary. Hung obtained further instruction in the Christian faith from Issacher Roberts, 'the uncouth and eccentric American Baptist',[73] who described Hung in 1846: 'He is a man of ordinary appearance, about five feet four or five inches high; well built, round faced, regularly featured, rather handsome, about middle age, and gentlemanly in manners.'[74]

By the time Griffith John came into close contact with the Taipings, the central authority of the movement had been challenged by younger leaders, but Hung regained control and in 1859 appointed his cousin Hung Jen-kan/Hung Jin as Shield King or Kan Wang. He had also been in contact with missionaries, especially James Legge of the LMS.[75] The military strategist of the movement was the Chung Wang (Zhong Wang), the Loyal Prince, who enjoyed temporary success before his defeat in 1863. There was no end to the number of Wangs or Kings, and prominent, apart from the three mentioned, were the Eastern and Western Kings. Names were also won because of feats in battle, such as Yellow Tiger, One-eyed Dog and Cock Eye.

Griffith John knew the characteristics of the movement. It was anti-foreign, wanted social reform that would benefit the Chinese people generally, and was strongly religious with some Christian influences. The leaders were convinced that these aims could not be realised without getting rid of the Manchu rulers.[76] Griffith John was not satisfied, however, with considering the movement from a distance. He wanted to meet the leaders to discuss their doctrine and plan for China.

The Welsh optimist visited rebel country during April 1860. At that time the great city of Soochow had escaped rebel attack, but in less than a month this city, with its six principal

gates and a population greater by several times than that of
Shanghai, was devastated by the rebels. The Welsh enthusiast
and Alexander Wylie visited Hangchow during May, only to
see the havoc created by the Taipings: 'The city gate was
opened to let them in and they found some of the fairest parts
of this heavenly jewel of China in charred ruins, and the whole
of the west suburb. A mass grave holding a thousand bodies
was only a drop in the ocean of misery.'[77] It was difficult for
Griffith John to accept the fact that the rebels were responsible
for such devastation, and this made him more determined
than ever to meet the leaders.

A small company comprised of Griffith John, Joseph Edkins,
Macgowan and Hall left Shanghai for rebel territory in July
1860: *'The week we spent in the insurgents' territory is by far the
most eventful in my history.* In fact, it is the experience of a
twelvemonth condensed into that of a week.'[78] The fourth
night of the journey was spent among dead bodies floating on
the canal: 'For two or three hundred yards our boats had actually to push through heaps of bodies, in an advanced state of
decomposition. Many of these had been killed by the insurgents, but by far the majority were cases of suicide.'[79] At
Wukiang the party was welcomed by the chief in command,
and after a brief interview the four passed on to Soochow, to
the palace of the Chung Wang. After a long delay they were
allowed into his presence between a train of nearly a hundred
officers and servants. A salute of six shots was fired, and music
played with gong beating. The missionaries were conducted to
the right of the Chung Wang:[80]

The hall of audience was carpeted in red. Large lanthorns
were held between the officers who stood on each side. They
all wore robes and caps of red and yellow silk. The only
man seated was the Chung Wang himself. He is a man of
small, keen features, wears spectacles, and appears in a rich
yellow robe and gold embroidered hat after some ancient
model.

The Chung Wang behaved in a most friendly manner, and
discussed different aspects of the troubled situation with the
visitors.

There were three clear aspects to what the Chung Wang declared in the interview. First of all, the appeal to nationalism. The greatness of China could only be restored by overcoming the Manchu domination. Secondly, there was an attempt to realise an agricultural utopia. Land would be apportioned according to the size of a family. During a time of famine, surplus in one area would be moved to a needy area. Great care would be taken with the planting of mulberry trees. Thirdly, the Wang's thinking was deeply religious but syncretistic. Some of the religious aspects appealed to the missionaries. Contrary to so much in Chinese philosophy, the insurgent believed in the personality of God; contrary to popular pantheism, he accepted the unity of God, and in opposition to fatalism (as in Buddhism) he believed in Providence. Not only the Chung Wang, but many of the leaders respected the Christian Scriptures. Regular prayer meetings were held, with a Christian ring to them, while offerings and sacrifices were presented in a way which was reminiscent of Confucianist custom.

A central tenet in the Christian faith is the teaching that Christ is the God-man. The Chung Wang expressed his belief that Jesus Christ was not divine, and he regarded himself as Christ's brother. This was a matter of serious concern for the missionaries, and it was the first point mentioned in a theological statement prepared by Edkins and John for the consideration of the Chung Wang: 'We first spoke on the Trinity, especially on the Divinity of Christ, and His perfect equality with the Father, and also the Personality of the Holy Spirit.'[81] A few months later Griffith John summarised what he thought were the characteristics of the chief's beliefs:[82]

1. He believes in one God the Father.
2. That the son is a mere man—the *first* begotten of the Father.
3. He believes the Holy Spirit is identical with the Father.
4. He believes in the O. and N. Testaments as revelation from God to man. But unfortunately believes in his own visions.
5. He says that Christ had three sons and two daughters.

6. He believes that he himself is the visible head of the kingdom of heaven and that all nations ought to acknowledge
him as supreme lord.

The points in Griffith John's summary were either implicit
or explicit during the interview at the beginning of July, but he
continued to hope that the Christian elements would become
more prominent. He wanted to share ideas not only with the
Chung Wang but with the Kan Wang as well (Hung Jin).
Griffith John and Joseph Edkins wrote to Hung, and his response, supported by the Chung Wang, was to invite the two
missionaries to Soochow. They started on their way on 30 July,
travelling through territory which, in the opinion of the missionaries, had been plundered more by imperial troops than
by the insurgents.[83] On arrival on 2 August they had an audience with the Kan Wang, who conducted the first part of the
discussion dressed in his rich robe and crown of gold. After
discussing the progress of the gospel in China, he took off his
robe and crown and continued the conversation in an infor-
mal, relaxed manner. He opened his heart to the missionaries,
confessing that he was happier as a native assistant to the missionaries than in his present position. He still had high hopes
that the Christian gospel would make good progress in China.
Before eating together the Kan Wang insisted on singing a
hymn and praying: 'Having selected one of Dr Medhurst's
hymns, he himself started the tune, and sang with remarkable
correctness, warmth and energy. After a short prayer offered
by Mr Edkins we sat at table.'[84]

Another meeting was held on the second day when Christian beliefs were again discussed and also the character of the
Heavenly King. On this occasion again a hymn was sung and
the Kan Wang led in prayer. The missionaries were escorted to
their boat, and received presents of a goat and some fowls sent
from the Kan Wang. The missionaries were pleased with the
response of the Kan Wang, the main sources of hope being the
spiritual devotion of the chief and his belief in the Bible as
being inspired. On the other hand the Christian leaders were
grieved that the chief had given in on the matter of polygamy.[85]

For a while there was cause for concern, especially during
August 1860, when the insurgents attacked Shanghai, but they

were driven back by the combined force of the imperialists, the British and the French.[86] This event marked the beginning of foreign intervention in the affair, infuriating the insurgents and causing grief to many of the missionaries, including Griffith John. The attitude of Britain did not prevent him from making further efforts to meet with the insurgents. He and Hendrick Kloekers, from the Netherlands,[87] and two national workers left Shanghai on 6 November 1860.[88] They had three aims in mind—to inquire into the state of the country, what possibilities there were for missionary work, and eventually to reach Nanking to ask for a declaration of religious liberty for the Christians. As the small company proceeded on their journey they soon saw rebel boats passing them on the river. Conflicting reports were received at Sungkiang, but the four soon witnessed the scars of fighting in the area. At one point of the journey they 'could hardly pass along on account of the vast number of boats that were lying on the creek together with the wreck of houses and furniture'.[89] In Soochow, Liu, who was in command there, told Griffith John that the Celestial King had promoted Issacher Roberts to the third rank under the King and, according to John, 'I believe he is much respected, and is regarded as a great mind by the Insurgents.'[90]

Before meeting Liu, an American named Lested had told Griffith John that the chief had three bona fide wives and thirty concubines, but the missionary did not know whether to believe the American or not. When he did enter the chief's room the visitor was encouraged: 'I was glad however on my entering the room to find on Liu's sofa a copy of the N.T., the delegates version and the Old Testament history, both open.'[91] When they moved to another room, Griffith John recognised the Bible which he had given to him on a previous occasion. He expressed his belief in one God, 'But he does not seem extremely anxious to know much about religion'.[92] The party anchored nearby in the wealthiest suburb with a population not less than that of the whole of Shanghai: 'Now it is in ruins.'[93]

It was the same story as they continued on their way; numerous villages and towns had been deserted by the inhabitants and were now garrisoned by the Taipings. Occasionally groups of women, mainly, would appear bringing their fruit, vegetables, bean cake and pork to sell to the soldiers. The four reached Tanyang, where they were told that the chief had gone to Nanking, but they were received by his deputy, 'a stout, strong, robust looking man', with whom they had a long conversation on religious matters.[94] On 16 November the company left Tanyang for Nanking. Many villagers were afraid to shelter them, but they were welcomed eventually in a three-roomed house, one being the kitchen and bedroom, one a storeroom, and the other used for various purposes such as weaving and spinning. All the visitors had to sleep on straw: 'In such a house I had never slept before.'[95] The pilgrims were up at 3 o'clock in the morning continuing on their way to the insurgents' capital. As they drew near to Nanking thousands were coming out of the city, and thousands going in.[96]

The company entered the capital on the 18th and stayed until the 26th. Because he was leaving for a while the Kan Wang had told his officers to take the visitors to see Issacher Roberts. The missionaries had a discussion with him concerning the troubled situation and, before they left, Roberts led in prayer. While waiting to see the Kan Wang, Griffith John invited a few people to come together to read the Scriptures and pray. He expounded a part of chapter 1 of John's Gospel pointing out that Christ was the source of all light, and that he was the Son of God.[97] When they did enter the presence of the Kan Wang, the Person of Christ was again one of the main topics of discussion. The other important matter that demanded attention was the possibility of missionary work in the area. The Wang was confused concerning the Person of Christ and was reluctant to allow missionary work for the time being. Griffith John and his friends left, grieved and puzzled because of such an attitude, as was Issacher Roberts when the report was given to him in the evening.[98]

The following day the visitors were invited to have breakfast with the Chung Wang. They received a warm welcome, but a marked difference of opinion appeared as soon as they started discussing religion and missionary matters. After breakfast he supplied them with five horses in order to ride around to see Nanking and district. One place they visited was the palace built by the Chung Wang, 'which is by far the most beautiful building I have seen in Nanking. Mr Roberts tells me that the Chung Wang had offered it to him.'[99] In the evening the missionaries discussed with Roberts a letter sent to him by Liu Wang, which they believed contained blasphemous statements as far as the Christian faith was concerned: 'It is a remarkable one and puts the question of his blasphemous pretensions beyond doubt.'[100]

In spite of all doubts and tensions there was a change of attitude and the leaders in Nanking gave the missionaries permission to travel the country and guaranteed their safety. All the Wangs (kings) were informed 'that they must act lovingly and harmoniously towards these men, and by no means engender contention and strife—and these [missionaries] be treated exceedingly well'.[101] The missionaries paid another visit to the Kan Wang on 22 November, visited the city the following day and held an English service on the 24th, the insurgents having worshipped on the Saturday. The visitors left Nanking about 10 o'clock on Monday morning, 26 November. Four chairs were prepared for them, eight men for each chair, a number of men to carry their luggage and two more to act as guides.[102] A great deal of travelling was done by night because the terms of the edict would not be known generally. They called at Soochow, where they showed the edict, travelled all night on December 1, and arrived in Shanghai the following day.[103] The visit gave fresh fuel to Griffith John's optimism. He was convinced that the leaders at Nanking were determined to uproot idolatry and establish Christianity in its place, or, at least, acknowledge it officially.

Although optimistic, Griffith John did desire at times to move to new territory. At the end of 1860 he considered going to Hankow, but an opportunity came to work with Joseph Edkins in Shantung province, concentrating on Chefoo. They were the first missionaries to travel this province with its population of nearly twenty-nine million, including the teeming crowds on the banks of the Yangtze. The country with its bays, hills and mountains reminded Griffith John of Wales. The district city of Fuh Shan was visited early in January 1861, where the Mandarin allowed them to rent a house for the purpose of preaching.[104] The work was hampered a little by the weather as snow fell for a number of days, and Edkins' ill health made it impossible for him to join his co-worker. Riding on their ponies they reached Tung Cheu-fu and passed on to Hwang-hieu, the luggage following carried by mules. In his zeal Griffith John could aim too high, not only in terms of distribution and preaching, but also in terms of travelling. After a two-day journey he was exhausted: 'The sixty miles of this day, and the forty of the previous, were rather too many for both the pony and myself.'[105] The average was usually thirty miles a day. On their journeys the two heard that the insurgents were within thirty miles of the provincial capital—another sign of the coming defeat of the imperial forces: 'The Manchus might as well attempt to blow the sun out of the heavens, as to quench the flame, which their folly and tyranny have kindled.'[106] The news also created in Griffith John a desire to meet with the leaders of the rebels once again.

The opportunity to visit Nanking came in April 1861, and Griffith John set out with his colleague Robert Wilson on the 9th.[107] When they boarded the ship they found that some of the family of the Kan Wang were on board, and they were delighted to hear that the missionaries were going to Nanking. The ship left Shanghai at 2 a.m., anchored at U Sung until daylight, experienced difficulties in two places because of the tide, but arrived safely on the 14th. During his previous visit Griffith John had seen the streets crowded with people, shops open and a brisk trade being carried on. Now, however, the people had been forced to leave the city and no trade was being carried on. Any disobedience was dealt with immediately. When a few people dared to remain within the city they were beheaded. When a woman accidentally set a hut on fire, her hands were tied together, she was thrown down on her face and her head cut off by the continual chopping of a sword. Inevitably, as shops closed and the people were forced out of the city, poverty increased and some were even dying of starvation.[108]

The Celestial King himself was demanding, and receiving, more and more honour. Schools were opened, and he laid down what was to be taught in them. Many of the books contained central Christian truths, like God the Creator, and some aspects of the life and death of Jesus Christ, but 'mixed up with a great deal of error'.[109] As the brother of Christ, the king was asserting his authority and claiming a divine commission to correct many things in the Old and New Testaments. The authority was based not on what the ear had heard, which could be the experience of missionaries, but on what is seen, the visions granted to him—and 'the seeing of eye is solid'. Heaven had revealed to him the fixed number of wives for the respective kings and officers, six being the number for the former, three for the highest officers, two for the middle officers and one for the lowest rank. This was a bitter disappointment for Griffith John: 'I had no idea that he had sunk so deep. He is either a great impostor or insane.'[110] John believed it was the former. Before leaving, the missionary heard that the Tien Wang (Heavenly King) had sent a letter to the brother of the Kan Wang, promoting the Welshman to the rank fourth below the king. He responded strongly, 'He is a silly old fellow to suppose that I would take an office from him or anybody else.'[111]

Griffith John expressed deep sympathy with the insurgents because, as Chinese, they were fighting to guard what they believed to be the better traditions of their country. They were fighting against an unjust and cruel dynasty, and Griffith John, like so many other missionaries, would be pleased to see that iron yoke broken. He was also critical of the foreign support given to the imperialists and was angry when the troops intervened on 18 August 1860 and again in April 1861. Referring to the first intervention the missionary asserted that 'it was in direct violation of the principle of non-intervention'.[112] It did not worry Griffith John that this was going against public opinion in Britain, and that it was contrary to the belief of a prominent person like Sir John Bowring, orientalist, plenipotentiary for Britain and author of the hymn 'In the Cross of Christ I glory'. He was pro-Manchu and was also critical of missionaries.[113]

It is difficult, therefore, to understand some comments that have been made concerning missionaries during this period. A. E. Hughes says, 'Missionaries of all denominations took their colour from official suggestions and believed the propaganda which was passed on to them from Manchu sources.'[114] In no way, not by any stretch of the imagination, could such an attitude be attributed to Griffith John. His inclination was to believe the insurgents and not the imperialists. It is quite surprising that he continued in sympathy with the insurgents for such a long time. It seems that he was closing his eyes to the confusion of errors and the excesses of the rebels. The leaders were taking to themselves the praise and honour due to a divine being, especially Hung Xin-quan. Making such claims for himself, he denied that Jesus Christ was the Son of God, a tenet so basic to the Christian faith. Hung's praise was sung while he lived in luxury in his magnificent home. Outside the city walls of Nanking many were starving to death and he would not lift a finger to help them. It is true that Griffith John's optimism was shaken on a number of occasions, but it was not until 1861 that he really abandoned his sympathy with the insurgents, although they had been plundering the country since 1853. Even if their aims were honourable, their methods could not be justified.

The situation in Nanking was deteriorating, and there was strife in and around Shanghai. Once again Griffith John had to think of moving to another area. Once more his mind turned to Hankow.

'Enjoyment! God has not called us to a life of ease and enjoyment, but to a life of self-renunciation, self-crucifixion, and entire devotion to His will and redemptive purposes.'

A Voice from China, 64.

'The missionary must have more than a tremendous conscience in dealing with converts; he must have a big heart and deep human sympathies. He must have the quenchless love of Christ.'

A Voice from China, 119.

3
Hankow:
the heart of the Empire
1861-1873

Because there was trouble in rebel territory Griffith John looked to other directions for further openings. He had already drawn the attention of the Directors to Hankow in December 1860. That place was now open, and the rebels had left. Here was an opportunity for the pioneer, 'the irrepressible and intrepid Welshman'.[1] Pioneering work gave him much joy, and whenever he was engaged in it his heart was at rest. Griffith John and his colleague Robert Wilson left Shanghai on 9 June 1861, soon reaching unknown territory, stopping only at one place, Kiukiang.[2] As they travelled, the two missionaries thought they were on the sea, as the Yangtze had burst her banks, drowning many villages of mud and straw: 'Sometimes the tops of trees and the roofs of these miserable huts are to be seen just peeping out of their watery grave.'[3] There was plenty of remarkable scenery to attract their attention, especially the grandeur of Wild Boar Hills which they passed on the afternoon of the 15th. They arrived on 21 June, but did not enter the city until half past six the following morning. On that morning they ascended Hanyang Hill to view the three cities of Hankow, Wuchang and Hanyang:[4]

Han Kow is itself dead flat, and at present completely surrounded by water. The town forms a rectangle, the Yang-tsi forming one side, and the river Han the other. I am told by the natives that the principal street, which runs along the banks of the two rivers, was in former times from ten to twelve miles in length. The shops are high, deep and wide. The population is large, even now; there is a vast amount of life about the place.

Griffith John had pinpointed two of the characteristics of Hankow, the rivers and the shops.

It has been said that 'The glory of Hankow, as well as its terror, is the magnificent Yangtze.'[5] It must have been a glorious scene to see it flowing majestically a mile wide, although Hankow was almost seven hundred miles from the sea. Even the Han, a tributary of the great river, was a waterway for three hundred miles from Hankow, with so much traffic that Griffith John thought he was looking at a forest of masts.[6] When the two rivers overflowed their banks the destruction could be frightening. The roadways in the city were bad, but the principal street was paved; here shops were found, almost on top of each other, so that it seemed to Griffith John that he was looking at one great shop.[7] There was trade in oil, idol-making, drugs, tea, silk, and characteristic of the life of the city were the itinerant barber and coffin shops.[8] Even during this period of unrest it had the largest mart in China. The poorer people lived on the river bank, those more fortunate than others in ramshackle buildings supported by poles, while below them lived 'the very lowest dregs' of the population, including the beggars, the blind and the lepers.[9]

Hanyang was regarded as being of no importance, but Wuchang, the capital of the province, was 'very prettily situated'. Griffith John was immediately drawn to it: 'I have seen but few places in China that I should like to reside in better than in this city.'[10] He was convinced that the LMS should establish a work in all three places. Not only was it important to start a work in them, but also from this area it would be possible to penetrate the Empire.

Planting and watering

Griffith John and Robert Wilson immediately faced the task of preaching and distributing tracts on the streets, but they found it most difficult to rent a house for preaching.[11] In August the Welshman went back to Shanghai for his family, returning to Hankow on 12 September, John himself being responsible for the arrangements without any cost to the Missionary Society. They rented a small native house 'in a narrow lane in an evil smelling and crowded quarter of the great heathen city',[12] which 'defied all sanitary laws'.[13] The situation became desperate:[14]

.Two families and a chapel are contained now in the same
native house. I dread the very idea of spending another
summer in a native home, as the summer heat is excessive. I
believe building will be cheap in Hankow.

The heat and the rain posed real problems for Hankow. The
temperature reached 90° in summer, and although this was not
exceptionally high compared with 110° in Cairo, there was
intense humidity. The rain came with the heat, falling in blind-
ing sheets; the annual rainfall was 51.4 inches, compared with
1.1 in Cairo and 24.5 in London. The Yangtze would surge
down from the melting snows of Tibet, creating mist and
floods.[15]

In the city itself the situation improved quickly. Rapid
strides were made in rebuilding. On the sites of miserable
shanties, even of filthy pigsties, houses were being built, many
of them remarkable for their size. Merchants could be reck-
oned by the hundreds, but there was only a handful of
Christian workers. The people were anxious to develop the
material resources of the area, but workers were not available
to develop the spiritual lives of the needy. Griffith John felt sad
that the church at home was so slow in responding to the work
overseas and, making use of William Carey's words, expressed
the view that the church expected great things from God, but
was not ready to attempt great things for God.[16] He himself
attempted what seemed to be superhuman. He must have felt
lonely in the crowded streets, but a little later, in January 1864,
he was able to say, 'Since my arrival the gospel has been
preached daily to all who might desire to hear it.'[17] The services were conducted in his house, and the hall was usually
full. In spite of its smallness and its inconvenient location, the
preacher spent many a pleasant hour because he was coming
into closer contact with many Chinese people.

A tension was created in Griffith John's life when he was
asked to take English services in Hankow. This was an opportunity for further ministry which could benefit those who had
no other spiritual provision. On the other hand, the preacher
was afraid of being distracted from his main work, which was
reaching the Chinese people with the gospel. He agreed to the
proposal in the hope that a chaplain would arrive to relieve

him of this work. He first ministered to the foreign residents
on Sunday 17 November 1861.[18] Though there were about forty
foreigners present in the city, only six gentlemen turned up. It
seemed that the Chinese were more anxious to hear the gospel
than the foreigners. The fact that he had accepted this ministry
made Griffith John doubly zealous in his care for the Chinese;
he was determined not to neglect them. Such care soon bore
fruit when he baptised the first convert in Hankow on Sunday
16 March 1862: 'I had the privilege of baptising the first
Protestant convert at Hankow, this afternoon. It is a cause of
much thanksgiving to me that *one* has been enabled to make a
public profession of faith at this important place.'[19] The convert
could read well, and was, according to Griffith John, of an
inquisitive, independent turn of mind.

Apart from the one baptism there were a number of inquirers. A few lost interest completely, and some had the wrong
motives in coming to the missionary, expecting financial gain
or a daily portion of rice. When there was doubt about a person's sincerity Griffith John would ask the national worker to
inquire about the past history of that inquirer.[20] The information received would very often help the minister in his assess-
ment of a candidate. There were also three or four catechu-
mens who were soon to be added to the fellowship. Six were
received into membership in June and two in August, bringing
the number in the fellowship to eleven, nine nationals and two
Welsh people, while there were others attending some meetings.[21]

The small group of worshippers were continually looking
for a place of their own. After much searching they succeeded
at last, and with much joy Griffith John recorded the event in
his Journal on 19 July 1863:[22]

We opened our chapel on the 19th July, and from that day
until this, it has been opened everyday for public services. It
is in one of the best thoroughfares in Han Kow, as near to
the centre of the town as possible. A better site it would be
difficult to find. In the style of architecture, the Chinese taste
has to a certain extent been consulted, and on the whole
they seem much pleased with it. The only fault to be found
is its smallness. This, however, could not be avoided, as the

ground would not admit of a larger building. It will seat about a hundred and fifty people.

The small chapel was full every day, with many listening outside. Those attending would be given some Christian literature; many would read it and come back for more material.

A few months after the opening of the chapel Griffith John expressed satisfaction with the work. He believed that the Church was 'waxing strong'. By the end of 1863 twenty-two adults and six children had been baptised; one died and another was excommunicated for immorality, but three were added from the church at Shanghai, making a total of twenty-three members.[23] To support the work financially the pastor introduced monthly subscriptions, which realised 30 dollars during the first year. He was convinced that the members should be taught in this matter of giving, and they 'seem to be learning the lesson slowly'.[24] He also took time to instruct those suitable for leadership, as he thought that national agency was essential to the success of the work, although the general supervision was in the hands of the missionaries. The most important step towards national leadership was taken on 1 February 1863: 'This morning two deacons were set apart. I preached to them from 1 Timothy 3 chapter.'[25] Another real encouragement was the holding of the first Chinese Christian wedding on 30 November 1863.[26]

Soon there were other firsts. The first school was opened on 26 February 1864: 'We opened the first school today—about 20 scholars present.' The school was built through the liberality of 'certain friends of this community'.[27] Griffith John had established friendly relations with the foreigners in Hankow and was quite happy to solicit their financial help when there was a particular need. Within a few months two more schools were opened, making a total attendance of sixty to seventy children. The test of progress was not simply how many could read and write, but how many had learned the catechism and portions of Scripture. The aim was that the children would learn by heart, be influenced by the gospel and relate what they had received at school in their homes. Learning was important, but the school was also a means for evangelism. It could be an effective means, in that it could lead some of the children to faith in Christ, and they could influence their parents. On the other hand, the parents' interest lay in securing better opportunities for their children, and it was possible for the children to learn a great deal by heart without having any real interest in the Christian faith. The situation in the country could be difficult at times, too. Rumours were spread abroad concerning the imperialists. It was stated that they would come down and set upon the foreigners and all nationals connected with them. According to another rumour, the object of the schools was to poison the minds of the children with foreign ideas in order to kidnap them and send them away to other countries; this same rumour had been spread earlier in Shanghai. Consequently, the school numbers decreased suddenly, and the workers had to wait for months to re-establish the work.[28]

The first hospital was opened on 3 September 1866. This had a distinctive contribution to make to the city of Hankow, but was also related to the work of preaching the gospel. Griffith John himself was happy with such a relationship, and was one of the people responsible for ensuring it. He had suggested a larger preaching hall, and 'I mentioned this to two or three of my mercantile friends with the view of obtaining some pecuniary assistance from the community'.[29] Many of the foreigners were most willing to help, and it was suggested that a hospital could be built as well, with the possibility of help from Dr Reid, the physician of the foreign community. He himself was quite enthusiastic about the venture because he had been learning Chinese in order to come into closer contact with the people. On being made aware of this Griffith John was delighted, and he made the project known to as many as possible. Within three days the sum of £300 was received. There was an exceptional response. The largest part of the sum donated by the middle of August 1866 had come from members of the foreign community; the Chinese people were next in line, and a substantial sum had been received from the Governor of the Province. He was responding to kindness shown him by Dr Reid. Having suffered from a bad foot for about eleven years, he had been advised to see Dr Reid, who was able to solve his problem.[30]

The building itself was strong and commodious, situated

behind the preaching hall. The dispensary and consulting rooms were immediately behind the hall, and behind them again two large rooms in which fifteen to twenty indoor patients could be accommodated. Along the west side there was a veranda providing shelter in wet weather. Griffith John believed that it was 'the most compact and best looking building' that he had seen in the country.[31] In this venture again, as with the school, the missionary worked hand in hand with members of the foreign community. Unlike some of his colleagues, Griffith John was happy to act in this way, but the different outlook did create tensions at times. Dr Reid, the physician for the foreign community, agreed to give two days a week gratuitously to the hospital. The work was established on a firm foundation and was handed over to Dr Shearer in 1868, but he only stayed for a very short time, leaving when Dr Reid returned. Dr Reid was highly regarded by his own profession and stood high in the estimation of the foreigners in Hankow. He was followed by Dr Mackenzie.[32]

Some notable national workers

As soon as possible Griffith John prepared national workers to help in the church. In Hankow there were two Chinese preachers, and others were sent as evangelists to other stations. When Alexander Wylie visited Hankow, arrangements were also made for another member to be a colporteur.[33] One promising Christian was transferred to the Wesleyans. He was Chu Shao An, who was born in Anhui in 1836. His family had suffered during the Taiping rising, and his wife was so afraid that she committed suicide. Soon afterwards he lost his children and moved with his mother to Hankow, but she died on the way. In Hankow, Chu heard the gospel preached by Griffith John, experienced conversion and was baptised. The Wesleyans needed a worker, and it was arranged for Chu to work with Josiah Cox. When David Hill arrived, Chu became his language teacher. This was a most important contribution to the Wesleyan mission. In 1880 Chu was ordained a Methodist minister at Wuchang.[34]

It is proper to sketch the life and contribution of a few of these national workers. Shen Tsi-sing, Griffith John's principal national assistant, was born in Nanking. His parents, anxious to see their son receiving honour as a man of letters, educated him thoroughly from the age of four. He did not become as eminent as his parents had hoped, but he did settle for a while in his native city as an ordinary teacher. Like Chu, Shen was disturbed by the Taiping trouble and decided to drown himself, but the concern of his mother and dreams of the future greatness of the Empire prevented him from ending his life.[35]

Shen and his family managed to escape from Nanking. For a few months he joined up with the imperialist forces but, unsettled, travelled five provinces before reaching Shanghai. It was here that he heard the 'new doctrine' of the missionaries. His feelings changed from contempt to doubt and to interest. He entered into more and more discussion with the missionaries and became their language teacher. In considering the Christian faith, what struck him most was the doctrine of sin, and this led to a deep conviction of his guilt before God: 'My sin appeared to me as a mighty sea.'[36] He had no answer, but found relief when the missionaries explained to him the doctrine of atonement, that sin was covered by Christ's death on the cross. One of the missionaries in Shanghai was Griffith John, and he was involved in considering Shen's application for church membership, which was readily accepted. Shen became Griffith John's teacher, and the pupil was so pleased that he decided to take his teacher with him wherever he went. Unfortunately, when the time came for John to move to Hankow, family matters made it impossible for Shen to leave; but within a few months the situation changed, enabling him to join Griffith John in Hankow.[37]

In one of his letters John gave an insight into the nature of Shen's work. Every day, from about half past eight in the morning, he would be in Griffith John's study, spending all the morning reading, translating and writing. At one o'clock he dined. At half past two he would be at the chapel, taking part in preaching, talking and debating, and continuing in this until five o'clock. Notices posted in different parts of the city made it known that Shen would be in the vestry behind the chapel from six o'clock until nine to converse on Christian subjects. On Sunday he always took part in the services, and when Griffith John was away the arrangements for the whole day were in his hands.[38]

Lo Hiang-Yung was a native of Wuchang district, and although he had little education compared with Shen, he could read and write. At the age of twenty-seven, because of a sense of sin and what he thought to be coming vengeance, he became a committed Buddhist. This led to the neglect of his family. Consequently they turned against him, and after much tension Lo left for Hankow where he lived as an ascetic. When Griffith John and his workers arrived, they presented the gospel to him, and Lo believed and was received into the fellowship of the church: 'His consecration seemed to us whole soul consecration, and his earnestness was a novel, and a very pleasing spectacle.'[39] Griffith John wanted a coolie at the time (the lowest of servants in China) and Lo was glad of the work; he was paid fourteen shillings a month, the sum he had received from his Chinese employer. Now, however, his circumstances were more agreeable and he had opportunity to grow as a Christian believer. As a Christian he was anxious to be reconciled to his family, but it was only at the second attempt that he succeeded. Even then the family made it clear that they were accepting him and not his religion. As Lo developed mentally and spiritually, the pastor could see in him a future leader. The first step in that development was for him to do some pioneer work in Tsaitien.

While at Hankow, Lo welcomed another inquirer after truth, Yii Ki-Fang.[40] He had listened to the daily preaching of the gospel, and in conversation with him Lo realised that the newcomer had believed in Christ for salvation. Yii was encouraged to attend the Sunday services; this he did, and was accepted into membership.

His story reveals some of the characteristics of Chinese life. In his early teens Yii became addicted to gambling and 'soon after' his father gave him a wife, but she did not want any female children because a girl was regarded as inferior to a boy. Their first child was a daughter and the mother insisted on putting her to death. When Yii tried to prevent her, the wife said that she would either kill the baby or take her own life. The little one was drowned by holding her head under water. Infanticide was 'fearfully common in China'. The next child was a boy, but he died when nine years of age, followed by the mother two or three years later. For nearly thirty years Yii lived an aimless, immoral life, until he arrived in Hankow, where he became a changed man. The national believers welcomed him wholeheartedly, showing a confidence in him that is not easily expressed in relationships between Chinese. Yii committed himself to the work of the church, inviting people to the services, discussing the faith with them and, as he had a little money, sharing some of it with the needy. He still had material needs, and Griffith John paid the worker twelve shillings a month, with clothing. His discussion of the faith soon led to preaching, which was always appreciated by the congregation. Griffith John commended it because it was full of Christ, and he was attracted to Yii himself: 'I love this venerable old man, and hope to spend a happy eternity with him when our labours are ended.'[41]

Another person, different from the other three, was Pau Ting Chang, a prosperous merchant from Wuchang.[42] After his conversion Pau and his wife became zealous personal workers, meeting people on a one-to-one basis. The husband also preached, while the wife met with the women for discussion. These are only samples of the national workers who were so important in Griffith John's plans. He had an eye for leaders, and the patience to encourage them. Griffith John encouraged all the members, not just the leaders, to be personal workers. Many of those attending the meetings would be there as a result of personal contact. During this early period of the church, one member was responsible for bringing seven of his friends to a meeting.[43]

Doubt and assurance

Griffith John was an active man, but he did take time to reflect on the situation and on his own life. When he arrived in Hankow he had been six years in China, long enough for his optimism to be tested. The country was vast, and John must have felt frustrated that success was so slow. He had now realised how difficult it was to reach the Chinese. On the one hand, they would agree with the preacher out of politeness, but on the other hand, their heart would be far removed from the truth. External politeness often concealed inner resentment. Griffith John himself was of a serious disposition, and though he could give the impression of being an extrovert, he felt everything deeply. During this early period in Hankow he reveals more of his heart, allowing us a glimpse into his inner being. Not only was he trying to break the heart of China, but his own heart was being assaulted by many adversaries.

Besides the cultural and religious obstacles he faced, Griffith John believed strongly that there was another dimension, that of the supernatural. Behind the human activity and earthly opposition was the realm of the spirits. An awareness of such a realm was a weight on the missionary's mind. It was in the light of Paul's Letter to the Galatians, chapter 6, that the preacher considered his work. The spirits could influence people and even possess them, making human beings in-human—an aspect that is clearly revealed in the life of Pastor Hsi.[44] Griffith John himself felt quite inadequate to deal with this new and strange situation. At times he felt impotent.

To complicate matters there were personal and domestic difficulties. The main cause of these was the arrival of death. When reviewing the year 1861 Griffith John expressed his feelings in this entry in his Journal: 'The past year is one which will never be forgotten by me, as the first in which death has visited my family.'[45] He was referring to the death of his infant son. On returning from the funeral he received a second blow, hearing of the death of his friend, Joseph Edkins' wife. His grief could well have been intensified by childhood memories of the death of his parents. During this period death was a regular visitor: another infant son died in 1862, John's closest friend Robert Wilson in 1863, a friend's daughter in the same year, and Dr Wells in 1864.[46] A little later there were other deaths, an infant son in 1867 and an infant daughter in 1870.[47]

Griffith John's faith was being assailed by circumstances, and he felt their impact upon him. Sometimes an arrow would pierce him: at other times he felt as if a cannon had been fired. Something of his sorrow is revealed in his words after the first two deaths: 'Heavy did we feel those strokes to be.'[48] On hearing of the death of Dr Wells he had to cry out, 'Why? Why? Why? This everlasting Why? keeps ringing in my ears.'[49] A problem that was very real to the Psalmist was very real to Griffith John too. He could see the wicked prospering and

active, while the good men were taken. He expressed his feelings again that same year:[50]

> The truths of the gospel seemed to be losing their grasp on
> my *heart*. My heart was becoming as hard as stone. Whilst
> logically assenting to the truths which I preach, my heart
> seemed to repel as fire, the lie to them all.

The preacher still had an intellectual grasp of the truth but had
lost the joy of his salvation and the thrill of proclaiming it to
others.

How did he respond in such a situation? He realised that his
own resilience was not enough, and even his faith was being
shaken, it seemed. He believed, however, that faith is 'heaven-
born' and, if tested, will eventually be strengthened.[51] Although
he found it difficult at times he had to acknowledge the wisdom and love of God. When doubting God's wisdom Griffith
John would think of what would happen if the government of
the world were on the shoulders of man. It is folly for finite
man, he concluded, to try to fathom the infinite mind of God.
Not only is God wise, he is also loving. When his faith was
revived the missionary's heart was softened to see the loveli-
ness of the Saviour. John knew that he had been bruised, but
twice he quoted the line, 'Tis love that bruises me', and on one
of the occasions the preceding line of the couplet too:

> I bow beneath thy chastening rod;
> 'Tis love that bruises me.[52]

In such an experience Griffith John realised again the supernatural nature of faith and the sufficiency of grace in all situations. That faith, grounded in grace, Griffith John related to
eternity. Indeed our life here is a kind of probation: 'Looking
on the present as a state of probation, of moral and spiritual
training, I cannot but thank God for bringing me here.'[53] He
received added consolation in 1866 when Evan Bryant arrived,
not just another missionary but a fellow Welshman,[54] who was
to be connected with the Hankow Mission until 1880. He had
come just in time to be of help to Griffith John personally, and
also to confirm the work which had already been pioneered
outside Hankow.

Reaching out from Hankow

The first attempt at establishing a work in Wuchang was made on 27 February 1862, when Griffith John sent Li, the national assistant, to stay there for a few days.[55] He preached in the streets and distributed tracts without being molested in any way. Encouraged by the response Griffith John took the next step of trying to rent a house in the city, but was faced with real difficulty as the people were afraid to rent without the permission of the mandarin. The missionary, with Josiah Cox, visited the Governor General of the two provinces, Hupeh and Hunan, and presented to him the advantages of forging links between China and people of other countries.[56] The Governor responded by asking them their opinion of Confucius. They replied by acknowledging the greatness of Confucius as a philosopher, but pointed out that he confined his teaching to time and space, neglecting important matters such as the nature of God and the eternal state. Those aspects, according to the Governor, were treated by Buddhism and Taoism; but according to the missionaries these two religions were the fruit of man's imagination, not a revelation from God. At the centre of that revelation was the Lord Jesus Christ, God incarnate in the flesh.[57]

It was impossible to find any agreement regarding doctrinal matters; yet, despite this, the Governor was sympathetic when they discussed the renting of a house. Griffith John had high hopes that Josiah Cox would soon settle there, and that the room could be used by John himself and Robert Wilson. But having to deal with the mandarins was a different story; they even ignored the fact that the Governor was sympathetic towards the Christian workers. So they failed to find a room, and did not succeed until the beginning of 1864:[58]

> I have bought a piece of ground in the city of Wu Chang for the Society. The ground is on one of the principal streets and is about 60 feet wide and 160 feet deep. On this I hope to be able to put up suitable buildings after the festivities of the new year are over.

There were, however, many obstacles to overcome. The land-owner was summoned to appear before the magistrate of the department, accused of selling land to a foreigner, which was not strictly true because it was in the name of the national worker. The court allowed him to keep the house, but for his private use only.[59]

Griffith John sent a letter to the magistrate, describing himself as an 'Englishman and Missionary of the Religion of Jesus'.[60] He appealed to the right of British subjects in a treaty port, the fact of religious toleration, the presence of Roman Catholics, and the promise of support given by word of mouth by the Governor. The magistrate responded sympathetically, but he was in a difficult position because opposition was growing in the city, from the people, the mandarins and the Roman Catholics. The opposition to Griffith John could be quite frightening, as is evident from this account:[61]

> About two or three hundred of them would go in a body and besiege the mandarin's office, and entreat his honour not to permit me to enter the city with my pernicious doctrine, to poison the minds of the people and subvert their customs. Placards were posted upon the city wall reprobating my attempt to build in the city of Wu Chang—calling upon the people to resist it with all their might—threatening any natives who might assist with vengeance—and swearing that they would pull the buildings down as soon as they were up. They were, probably, instigated to this by the mandarins.

A settlement was achieved when Griffith John agreed to return the deeds on the first plot which he had bought, and accepted another piece of land in another part of the city. The new deed was drawn up by the magistrates, transferred to the LMS, and registered at the British Consulate in Hankow.[62]

This was a trying hour for Griffith John, and even more so for the Chinese evangelist and deacon, who would visit Griffith John, sometimes at midnight, for consolation. They knew, however, that they had to persevere, because to open up Wuchang meant opening up the province. Griffith John's belief in providence was still strong, but he was also ready to acknowledge the place of second causes within God's plan. The missionary mentioned in particular the help given by the British Consulate.

Buildings were erected: a chapel, two rooms, a house for the evangelist and two schoolrooms. Half the ground was left open in order to build a hospital or dispensary. The cost was enormous, amounting to £500, but once again Griffith John appealed to the liberality of his friends and the money was forthcoming.[63] Collecting money in this way enabled John to act quickly, without depending too much on the LMS. The Directors could take a long time to respond and very often they were short of money. By developing the work quickly the missionary leader could also give more and more opportunities to the national workers. Realising that there were great opportunities in the city, Griffith John was anxious to spend time there rather than making an occasional visit. On 22 January 1867 there was an entry in his Journal:[64]

Slept in Wu Chang last night. The first time Protestant missionaries have slept over a night in Wu Chang. Though the work has been going on there for two years.

Considering the opposition Griffith John believed that the workers were making remarkable progress.

The work in Wuchang afforded an opportunity to work with Evan Bryant, Alexander Wylie, Dr Mackenzie, Thomas Bryson, and the Wesleyan, David Hill. Bryson settled in Wuchang in the room behind the church—not the most comfortable of places but better than the accommodation Griffith John and his wife had when they settled in Hankow. He was single and therefore, according to John, should be able to put up with many inconveniences.[65] Evan Bryant took on more responsibility in Hankow, and this meant that Griffith John could supervise the new work. Soon, however, they faced an added difficulty when a controversy in *The Times* stirred up parliamentary opinion, and that of the people to some extent, against foreign involvement in mission work.[66] In the opinion of the LMS Directors it would be wise to withdraw from Wuchang, but when Griffith John was informed of this he could not understand how they could even contemplate such a move. His independent spirit was quickened, and he expressed to the Directors in strong terms his conviction that Wuchang should definitely be kept open. It was inconceivable that they should leave such an important centre with its 2–300,000 inhabitants. It had been opened by LMS agents and they, including himself, had been involved in a hard, prolonged battle to establish the work there. As a result of this pioneering work, 'We have met here with an encouraging measure of success and, in every respect, have made considerable advance in forming a missionary settlement.'[67] The LMS had been first in the field and the place should not be abandoned lightly. The Directors decided not to take the threatened, retrograde step.

In missionary terms the third important city was Hanyang, a city of more consequence commercially than Hankow. Griffith John was anxious to occupy it and complete the triangle of Hankow, Wuchang and Hanyang. He succeeded in renting a house there on 19 April 1867: 'Rented a house at Hanyang today.'[68] National workers settled down there, supported by fellow believers: 'I fully concur with the opinion that the station ought to be made self-supporting as soon as possible.'[69] The triangle was complete.

Other ventures, however, were not so successful. The Chinese assistant at Tsaitien was seized and sent back to Hankow as a prisoner in the custody of a policeman. His testimony and that of the other witnesses contradicted each other and it was soon evident that there was no case to be brought against him. Before the end of 1864, however, the missionary could report that there were three converts in Tsaitien.[70] The station at Kingkow had to be abandoned as it was of an experimental nature. John believed that it was a mistake to form stations as an experiment. There were no Chinese believers there and, therefore, it was impossible to establish a church. The correct procedure would be to evangelise, gather a company of believers and leave them, as soon as possible, in the care of national leaders. Such an approach was according to 'Apostolic example and the dictates of common sense'.[71]

The work was confirmed in Hankow, Wuchang and Hanyang. Thompson pinpoints one characteristic of the work: 'One happy result of the consolidation and development of the church was seen in the gathering of women into membership.'[72] During the early years the men were reached, in the preaching halls especially, and received into membership. It was one of Griffith John's difficult tasks to convince converted husbands that they should bring their wives to the meetings, because Chinese custom was against it. In 1868, however, John was able to report that out of 51 members, 13 were women and 11 of the 13 were wives of converts.[73] Three years later it was estimated that there were six or seven thousand communicants connected with the missionary societies in China, of whom two thousand at least were women. Griffith John cried out, 'Give us the mothers and daughters of China, and China must soon become Christ's.'[74] As the number of converts increased slowly, they were supervised by Europeans, making it possible for John to be away for longer periods.

A remarkable journey
As opportunities arose, Griffith John and his workers ventured into the interior, and in 1868 prepared to go beyond Hupeh province. He arranged a journey with Alexander Wylie of the British and Foreign Bible Society, which was described by Wylie as 'one of the longest, and, in some respects, the most interesting Missionary journeys that has ever been made in China in modern times'.[75] A Bible Society report referred to it as 'almost if not quite unprecedented in the experience of Europeans'.[76] Their aim was to travel along the Yangtze, reach Szechwan, cross the hills to the river Han, following it down to Hankow. Detailed preparations were made for the journey. Griffith John's people gathered together in prayer for the two men and prepared what was necessary for travelling. Alexander Wylie arrived from Shanghai on 31 March 1868 with a supply of New Testaments from Hong Kong. The men were joined by two Bible workers and two servants, and when they left on 3 April they had twenty-six boxes of Scriptures to distribute on the way.[77]

The first part of the journey was familiar to the travellers as they aimed for Lake Tungting. They passed the places where coal had just been discovered, but what really attracted their attention was the water. One stream had opened up into a sheet of water almost fifty miles in length. Two days later they came across two lakes, one thirty-five and the other twenty-four miles in length.[78] The scenery changed for about two hundred miles to extensive mud flats, with occasional ranges to break the monotony. The six tired men had a welcome stop at

Heachang, 'a very busy town marked by a small pagoda on the left bank', before moving on to the district city of Hwaywng.[79] On their way the travellers noticed the great traffic in reeds, which were essential for fuel, fencing and roofing. Many workers were busy in the fields taking care of the barley, rice and beans.

Early on the morning of 23 April the important city of Shashi was reached, 'a centre of confluence for a number of lines of traffic, with an assemblage of junks'.[80] It also had a most striking pagoda. As the foreigners tried to enter through the gate, a guard's dirty hands brought them to a halt, and he took them to a miserable lodge until an officer should come to question them. Before they reached the lodge a curious crowd had gathered, and the guard had to use his whip to pass through them. Two officers arrived and were reluctant to allow the visitors to go into the city, but they changed their minds when the Christian workers produced the necessary document from the Viceroy.[81] After a short stay they passed many populous villages and were glad to arrive at Shasze, where their stay proved most fruitful because they sold 155 New Testaments and 1968 Scripture portions.[82] Wylie's comment, however, at the end of the month was, 'progress slow'.[83]

When the company reached Ichang, crammed with boats, they realised that their boat was too light for the next part of the journey and managed to buy another at a reasonable price. As they continued towards Chengtu they could see a mountain chain dividing the eastern and western provinces and, approaching it, were very conscious that the venture was 'difficult, hazardous and expensive'.[84] Alexander Wylie described this part of the journey vividly:[85]

The scenery is grand in the extreme. Instead of six or eight men, as in the former boat, our crew is now increased to sixteen, a dozen of whom are trackers, engaged in dragging the boat along by a bamboo line; but in ascending the rapids the number has occasionally to be increased to forty or fifty. Men are always in attendance for this service. They are a strange set of beings. Scant indeed are the nether garments of those who are most generously clad, but some of them go absolutely naked. When the towing-path at times comes to a terminus, or is swamped by the rising waters, these plunge into the stream like water dogs, carrying the line from one point to another, till the whole team are again yoked to the work. Nothing seems to be an obstacle to their progress, high up on the most precipitous rocks, or wading up to their middle in water. At one time you may trace them on some almost inaccessible ledge, and, before you have time to wonder how they will ever make their escape from such a position, the foremost of the party are seen rounding some peak, or emerging from a crevice further on.

Once again the travellers had occasion to praise the providence of God, that providence which had overruled through the natural and developed abilities of the trackers.

The difficulties continued. On 5 May the current was so strong that it was fortunate they had a load to steady the boat. The seventh day of the month was spent in rapids, while their experience the following day was even more frightening. Gigantic granite boulders projected on each side, narrowing the passage of the boat and increasing the power of the water. Their boat was in a queue of nine or ten boats, so the foreigners could watch the procedure for passing this part of the river. About two hundred Chinese had to help each boat, tied to a bamboo line four or five hundred yards long with sixty or seventy men attached to it. When the passengers were ready they sounded a drum as a signal to the men to pull on the bamboo line. It was a most precarious exercise. Wylie, John and their co-workers had to wait nearly two hours for their turn, and were much relieved to continue on their journey safely.[86] High peaks came into view, some of them as high as three thousand feet, and many of them forming perpendicular walls dropping into the water. These were the 'rarest pieces of mountain scenery' that the viewers had witnessed, and with the eye of the naturalist Alexander Wylie noticed a bed of green poppies, the only one they had seen on their journey.[87]

When the boat anchored at Wushan, the first city in Szechwan province, the pioneers ventured into the city. Here, unlike most other places, the people just ignored them at first, but they became more interested when they saw the New Testaments and heard the preaching: 'Our sales were small;

but we had excellent congregations, and the people listened with great attention to Mr John's preaching.'[88] The following day they passed the picturesque Wind-box gorge, and reached the city of Kwei-chow on 15 May. When they arrived in the district city of Wan the visitors witnessed the first signs of real business since leaving Ichang on 2 May. At Wan 'we had a very fair sale of books', and a few days later at Foo 'had a good sale during the day'.[89]

During their stay at Chungking the workers faced added difficulties because of the presence of Roman Catholics. Two of them did call on the Protestants and had a friendly discussion, but the general attitude of the estimated ten thousand Roman Catholics in the city was strongly opposed to the selling of Scriptures. On the other hand, the Chinese, who were very suspicious of the Roman Catholics, spread the rumour that it was the books of their Church that were being sold by the Protestants. It was a difficult situation, but the Protestants stayed on from 5 to 9 June, walking the streets and selling Scriptures every day but Sunday, having good success even with some Roman Catholics.[90] Occasional comments were made by Wylie concerning the progress of the work: 'tolerable success' at Keang-tsin and 'receiving much encouragement' at Loo, where they were delayed an extra day because of the boat race being held there.[91] After a 'very good sale of books' at Keanggan, the workers reached Nanke on 29 June, where Griffith John had to rest for a while because he was feeling unwell.[92] They were able to leave the next morning and by midday on 1 July they had reached the confluence of the two rivers Keang and Min. They were now leaving the great Yangtze and anchored in the Min, but they were not welcomed by either the Prefect or the Mayor, both returning the visitors' cards, although the Mayor accepted a New Testament.[93]

There was danger once again on the river as the boat approached Taon-sze-kwan. Here, because of the strength of the rapids, it was customary to tie a rope from the boat to a hook on one of the rocks to enable it to pass safely. The captain, however, thought that his men could manage without the rope, and Alexander Wylie described the moments of terror that followed:[94]

The boat got unmanageable, and we were sucked into a boil-
ing eddy. The head of the boat was swirled swiftly round
under an overhanging cliff, and, had it struck, I believe we
must have inevitably gone down. It was a critical moment,
and I can scarcely think of it without a shudder. The men
dropped their oars instantaneously, and all crouched flat
down on the deck; not a word was spoken, all expecting the
next instant to be in the water; but we were mercifully pre-
served, for the boat just cleared the rock by about two inches.

They quickly calmed their emotions and continued on their
journey, selling several New Testaments at Chuh-kan-tau,
where they visited some of the hundreds of salt wells in the
area. The sale of books was still 'tolerable', and occasionally
'very good'.[95]

A significant date was 21 July when the travellers left the
mountainous region and made for Chengtu, seeing on the way
the first bridge on their journey, its nine arches built of red
sandstone.[96] Here was the political centre of Szechwan and in
Alexander Wylie's opinion, 'It is decidedly the finest city I
have seen in China.'[97] It was one of Griffith John's life ambi-
tions to start a work for Christ there, 'where I thought I could
die in peace knowing that my grave at that great city would
stimulate others to come and occupy it in the name of the
Lord'.[98]

That dream was not realised, but John and his co-workers
did spend some time there, in spite of the fact that a plague
was raging in the city claiming an average of eighty lives a
day. Apart from selling books and talking to the people, the
travellers had to map their journey back to Hankow. Since
leaving Ichang on 2 May, the workers had sold 71 Old
Testaments, 935 New Testaments and 9059 portions of
Scripture.[99] The group left the river and started on their way by
land, travelling by 'sedan' in a heat which was at times so
oppressive that it soon tired the travellers. It was much cooler,
however, when they reached the Han for the last stage of the
journey to Hankow. They reached home on 4 September, having travelled over two thousand miles. They had learned a
great deal about the people of different regions, collected valuable information for other missionary workers, witnessed

glorious scenery and sold 15,062 items of literature in 153 districts.[100] In the long term they had been prepared to think of possible stations, especially in parts of Szechwan.

By this time many doors had been opened, especially in the three main cities, but there had been many adversaries as well. Before the end of the decade Mrs John's health was quite poor and her husband was forced to think of the possibility of returning to Britain. This he did reluctantly, because he believed, like James Chalmers, that furloughs should be avoided.[101] They were unsettling and could make the missionaries too ready to leave difficult situations. Husband and wife had to leave on 26 July 1870, reaching England on 30 September. They met their two sons in London, which was a bitter-sweet experience as the boys did not know their parents. The furlough gave the missionaries an opportunity to visit friends and relatives at Gwynfe, Machynlleth and Swansea, and Griffith John was able to take meetings in different parts of the country. He would have preferred to concentrate on England, but agreed to do most of the work in Wales, as the people in his own country were not so well-informed on missionary matters as the people over the border.[102] He made two visits to North Wales, Carmarthen, Llanelli, Aberdare in South Wales, and Edinburgh in Scotland, where he had good meetings but did not see any of the enthusiasm he had experienced in Bristol.[103] In the LMS meetings for 1871 he gave a remarkable address dealing with missionary principles and vindicating the work of the Society in China.[104] Later the same year he addressed a congregation of about three thousand in the Music Hall in Swansea when the Congregational Union held its meetings in his home town: 'It was spoken of as the most marvellous and thrilling missionary speech which had ever been heard.'[105]

Not only was his wife unwell, but Griffith John himself was feeling the strain of a long period of hard work: 'I believe I need absolute rest for some months, and that unless I get it I shall break down.'[106] His memory was not functioning properly and he was not eating well. He believed that his problem was mental, and that it had been coming on during the last two years. He would have liked to be fluent in his native tongue again, but the mental strain made it strenuously difficult: 'It cost me a desperate effort to get the old language back, so I have really had no rest.'[107] He did have a brief respite, but soon he was travelling the country again. The illness of them both forced Griffith John to think seriously of his future plans. His strongest desire was to return to China, but his wife's continuing ill health persisted and many of his friends urged him not to go back. Another possibility was to go to Germany for a brief period to study, following a trend which had already started in Wales, men like J. Harris Jones and G. P. Davies having received part of their education there.[108]

His wife's health had not really improved, but the call of China was so strong that Griffith John decided to return to that country. They left Liverpool on 8 February 1873, in sorrow because they had to leave the children behind, anxious because of the state of Mrs John's health, yet eager to see China once again. The desire to serve Christ in China had not been weakened by the trials he had experienced; they had, rather, strengthened his determination to spend his life in that country. China was his only parish.

'The brightest day in a man's life is the day on which the revelation of God as Father becomes a reality to his soul. Is God my Father? Then I know that there is no poison in the cup which He gives me to drink. It may be bitter, very bitter; but there is no poison in it, there is nothing in it to hurt me. Is God my Father? Then, though nailed to a cross, I *can* trust Him, and *will* trust Him.'

A Voice from China, 92-3.

'We are here, not to develop the resources of the country, not for the advancement of civilisation; but to do battle with the powers of darkness, to save men from sin, and conquer China for Christ.'

From Griffith John's address
at the Shanghai conference, 1877.

4
Hankow:
city and interior
1873–1883

Margaret John's health did not improve; indeed her condition grew worse during the voyage back to China. She, her husband and her friends on board soon realised that there would be no recovery. She died at Singapore on 24 March 1873, and Bishop Russell officiated at her burial.[1] Griffith John's faith was being tested again. As he watched his wife's burial, he thought that, for many, the word 'hope' would be too strong on such an occasion, but he was convinced that the proper word was 'certainty'. The certainty of the Christian hope was sustaining him as he faced the uncertainties of life. It was, however, a hard blow for the missionary, and he also meditated on the irony of the situation: that his wife was being buried at the very place where she had caught cold on the way to England. The dedicated Welsh wife, born in Madagascar and having worked in China, now lay buried in Singapore.

There were moving scenes when Griffith John arrived in Hankow on 26 April, especially when the national converts looked at a photograph of Mrs John. The feeling was even more intense during a communion service at the beginning of May, when the women from Wuchang and Hanyang joined the church at Hankow. Before partaking of the elements three of the Chinese members spoke; two of them broke down completely and 'the whole congregation was bathed in tears'.[2] The emotion was more overflowing than at Griffith John's ordination in Swansea in 1855. His own response was to give himself anew to the work:[3]

Believing that work is *the* balm for me at present, I have

plunged into it with all the energy I can command. The language is as fluent as ever, and I am able to enter fully into every department of the work. How I shall get on without my dear wife, I know not. For eighteen years she was to me a loving, devoted, self-sacrificing, and efficient helpmate. We have a goodly number of women in our little Church in Central China, and this is to be ascribed in a great measure to her exertions and influence.

'Occupational therapy' was the missionary's prescription for himself. Work for his shoulders was rest for his soul.

Church work and personal faith

Griffith John, like Evan Bryant, was a staunch Congregationalist, anxious to safeguard the autonomy of the local congregation. There could be tensions in this context, especially in the relationship between the District Committee and the local church. To what extent should the Committee interfere in the life of the church? What was the responsibility and authority of the Committee in the matter of ordination?[4] Griffith John was confident that he and Bryant could keep the peace in Hankow. Another matter of concern was the delay in receiving replies from the Directors in London. Very often Griffith John was frustrated, and would report what he had done rather than ask permission for a particular project. A good example would be his collecting of money from the foreigners of Hankow. He was convinced that there was an immediate need to extend the work and rebuild.[5] A small beginning was made at the end of 1872, when a new mission house was built, and a list of buildings was included in a report at the beginning of 1876:[6]

1. 2 houses built in 1873, for John and Bryant.
2. Hospital, boys school, girls school, erected 1874.
3. Chapel of 1863 for native assistant and school house.
4. Old hospital and former school house let for purpose of smelting silver.

Progress had been made in a fairly short time, enabling the missionaries to work more efficiently.

Whatever aspect of the work was discussed, Griffith John had strong convictions. He wanted to see the medical work developing, but hand in hand with the evangelistic work. The medical men should be missionaries.[7] He readily acknowledged that the women had an important part to play in the life of the church. They could conduct classes for female converts, visit heathen women in their homes, teach in schools for girls and be employed as Bible women. These aspects of the mission could be carried on by national and foreign women, but the burden of the work should fall on the shoulders of the missionaries' wives.[8] On no account, he argued, should unmarried female workers be sent to a mission constituted exclusively of men, adding the comment, 'You will probably conclude from the tone of this letter that I am not a strong believer in unmarried Female Agents for China.'[9] This was in opposition to Edkins within the LMS, and contrary to the view of Hudson Taylor of the China Inland Mission. During the early seventies the work of the CIM had spread quickly, and by 1876 their workers numbered almost a fifth of the Protestant missionaries in China. The Society was encouraged to make use of more women, and from 1878 Hudson Taylor even sent them alone into the interior.[10] This does not mean that Griffith John was inflexible at all times. The converts in Hankow arranged open-air services at night, and when he attended one of these in 1873 the missionary thought it would be a good idea to open the chapel for night services.[11] The response was most encouraging, many people attending who would not consider doing so during the day. The preacher was helped by seven or eight nationals who had some experience of taking services in the hospital; they gave their services gratuitously, paying also for the oil and candles which lighted the church. This pattern was followed successfully by other missionary societies.

Griffith John was continually drawing attention to the need for new workers to enter new areas. He described clearly the kind of men he had in mind. They should be 'young, energetic and godly' and 'full of the missionary spirit like Mr Taylor's men', but not of necessity university men:[12]

Give us men possessing a good English education, sound common sense, a warm heart, an intimate acquaintance with the Bible, a fair knowledge of Theology, a simple aim, an intense earnestness—give us men of this stamp, and we will give them a glorious work to do in China.

New workers did come slowly, including the Welshman William Owen, the kind of man that would fit Griffith John's description. Others came who were well educated and even scholarly, including Arnold Foster and Kenneth Mackenzie.[13]

Nothing was too much for Griffith John to do for the national workers. There were four assistants, Shen, the senior man, being paid £2-8-0 per month, and the other three £1-5-0 per month. When the Directors ventured to suggest a decrease in their wages, Griffith John responded angrily. He felt ashamed that the suggestion had been made, and reminded the Directors of Shen's age and tireless devotion to the work. Although he did not really want this, the missionary would prefer to see a reduction in the salary of the foreign staff, so that more money would be available for the national workers. Apart from the four assistants there were seven evangelists, five of them paid by the Society, one by the national church and the other a volunteer. The converts, most of them poor, were expected to contribute towards the upkeep of the building and the needs of the very poor in their midst. The Directors had given a little more money but had also cut down on some of the usual grants. Whatever the difficulties, Griffith John knew exactly what he would do: 'I intend, however, to go on with the payment of the native assistants as heretofore, hoping that the Directors will continue the old grant. If they refuse, I will pay the difference myself.'[14]

Besides facing the demands of the work and dealing with the Directors in London, Griffith John had to look to himself. Following the assurance of hope, even during the funeral of his wife, doubts returned and even the shadow of spiritual depression. However, his second marriage enabled the missionary to gain strength and new hope. He had known Mrs Jenkins, the widow of an American missionary, since 1855 in Shanghai. When he lost his first wife, Jeannette Jenkins comforted him and was a source of strength during that time of deep sorrow. She was, according to her husband, 'a remarkable woman in every respect'.[15] She was firm and gracious, and had a notable gift of winning the friendship of others. Her burning desire was to make the love of God in Christ known to the Chinese.

His wife's spiritual experience during this period helped significantly to renew Griffith John's faith and hope. After the death of her first husband, she had returned to America for a while, and in conversation with Christian friends came to the conclusion that there were greater experiences for them as believers. She had deep longings for that perfect life in Christ, to live on a higher plane and enjoy victory over sin. Seeking such an experience, 'The Heavenly Dove descended upon her as a spirit of sanctity and power.'[16] Griffith John entered into a similar experience. He himself refers to it as having a full vision of Christ. Previously he had a degree of love, power and holiness, but now he felt that he was full of them. The passage of Scripture relevant to him was Ephesians 3:16-20, where Paul deals with the breadth, length, height and depth of Christ's love, a comprehension of which can lead the believer on to know the fullness of God. The one who had opened his heart in this way to the flow of God's love was the Holy Spirit:[17]

> It is the Holy Ghost in us that is everything, and the Father is willing to bestow Him upon the weakest if he will but ask in the spirit of implicit faith and entire self-surrender. My cry these days is for a Pentecost, first on myself and my missionary brethren, and then on the native Church, and then on the heathen at large.

The blessing he sought came to him after he had been wrestling with God in prayer. The following day he was going out to preach but had no specific text in mind. God, however, opened his lips and endowed him with exceptional power, such power that he had no doubt as to its divine origin. It was a baptism of the Holy Spirit of God. Griffith John could see the significance of this experience in the context of personal holiness and service, but the work of the Holy Spirit was also related to the Church, locally and worldwide. He believed that the Spirit could come in an exceptional way and reveal that power made known on the day of Pentecost, a power not unknown in Wales, which had experienced so many revivals.

During this period many believers in America, Britain, South America and France were taken up with different ideas about the work of the Holy Spirit and the nature of sanctification. The National Holiness Movement was formed in America in 1867, and those prominent in it, including Walter and Phoebe Palmer and W. E. Boardman (1810-86), quickened interest in the doctrine of holiness in Britain. This was channelled by such agencies as the Ira Sankey and D. L. Moody meetings, the Salvation Army and the Keswick Convention.[18] The titles of the works published during this period are significant, all pointing to the higher Christian life. Boardman's book *The Higher Christian Life* appeared in America in 1858, and two years later it was published in England. One person who was influenced by it was Robert Pearsall Smith (1827-98), who joined with Evan Hopkins (1837-1919) and others to produce *The Christian's Pathway to Power* (1874). Hanna Whitall Smith, Pearsall Smith's wife, produced an influential book entitled *The Christian's Secret of a Happy Life* (1875). Evan Hopkins' contribution was *The Law of Liberty in the Spiritual Life* (1884).

These works, and the Keswick Convention, proclaimed the gospel of the fullness of the Spirit. In receiving this fullness the believer would be enabled to live a victorious life which could be spent in committed service to the Lord Jesus Christ. According to the holiness teaching, although a believer has received forgiveness from God, this does not mean that he has received the necessary power for service. This power he can receive through the Holy Spirit. All authors and speakers on the subject agreed that that experience was God's will for all Christians, but they did not all agree on how the Spirit was to be received. The experience would lead on to a continued rest in Christ: 'It is the function of Keswick, Evan Hopkins would say, to lead the struggling soul, and the clinging soul, on to the trust of the resting soul. Only a soul who thus rests in Christ's sufficiency for himself has liberty to toil for Him among his fellows.'[19] It was essential, according to this teaching, to start with character, because it is only when that is formed that the fruit will appear. Christian character cannot be fully developed without the fullness of the Spirit, and when the believer is filled it is possible for the Spirit to flow from him to others.

That same message was carried to China by the CIM missionaries and their leader Hudson Taylor. The latter was present at the Brighton meeting in 1875 which prepared the way for the first Keswick meeting in July of that year, at which he was also present. A little earlier, in 1869, he had entered into a more intimate relationship with his Saviour, referred to as the 'exchanged life'. Instead of living a struggling, defeated Christian life, Taylor explained that he had found rest in Christ. This was made possible by realising, through the power of the Holy Spirit, that he was united to Christ as the branch in the vine: 'As I thought of the Vine and branches what light the blessed Spirit poured direct into my soul.'[20] When, therefore, he met with the group in Brighton he was one with them, and more than ready to promote the higher Christian life. His experience and Griffith John's corresponded closely, but, unlike Taylor, John did not have a close link with Keswick, although he did contribute to *The Life of Faith* which was an official organ of the Keswick Movement. Both Hudson Taylor himself and all the prominent CIM leaders were connected with the Keswick Movement; but although individuals within the LMS accepted its teaching, it was not a characteristic of the Society as a whole.

The strength of this teaching was its emphasis on holiness, urging believers to seek it, knowing that without that work of grace it is impossible to see God. Character must be formed in order to bear fruit in service, and the missionary impact on the CIM especially was outstanding. It created a renewed interest in the doctrine and experience of the Holy Spirit, which led on to a desire for revival. It was also the means of bringing together Christians of different denominations.

There were weaknesses in this teaching as well as strengths. There was the danger of dividing Christians into two classes: those living a struggling life, and those living the life of victory entered into by an act of faith. This is clearly seen in its teaching on Romans 7–8: chapter 7 describes one kind of life, and chapter 8 what the normal Christian life should be. This is contrary to the Calvinistic interpretation of these chapters. According to that tradition, chapter 7 describes the struggle of the believer in the process of sanctification, but a measure of victory is always possible. The Keswick emphasis tends to

concentrate on personal holiness, or rather to confine holiness
to that realm, without applying Christian principles to every
aspect of life, socially, politically and culturally. Many of the
leaders in America and England tied the concept of holiness to
that of revival. This particular teaching of holiness was regarded
as the path of blessing, leading on to revival. There was a tendency to lay down conditions, and to argue that if these were
fulfilled God would bless his servants with revival. The influence of John Wesley and Charles Finney was strong within
Keswick circles.

Griffith John was influenced to some extent by the Keswick
teaching, but he never adhered strictly to it. His desire for holiness is expressed, very often, in similar terms. He did not,
however, describe his actual experience in Keswick terms, that
is, as gift, crisis and process. He had a crisis experience but
never thought of it as a once-for-all event which had guaranteed sanctification for him. The Welshman was concerned with
the inward change in the nature of the believer, but knew that
this could not develop without the quickening work of the
Spirit of God. He was concerned with holiness for believers
and the conversion of unbelievers, not in ones and twos but
in great numbers. A manifestation of the Spirit of God was
needed to accomplish such a work. A God-sent revival would
establish holiness, justice and love in a whole community, and
even in a great nation like China.

It is not easy to attach a label to Griffith John in this context
of holiness. Failure to do this would not have worried him,
because he was always of an independent mind. Although he
had a good theological mind, his emphasis was on applying
doctrine; he never worked out the different branches of theology in any detail, but he had no doubt whatsoever as to the
change the fresh experience of God's love had accomplished in
his life. It made a definite impact on his personal life. His affections were quickened and set on the Lord Jesus Christ. Griffith
John knew that it was the work of the Holy Spirit because he
had a 'full vision of Christ'.[21]

There was also an impact upon his service for Christ,
because new power had been given to rededicate himself to
the work of mission. In his human weakness supernatural
power had been given to him. Consequently there was a

difference in his preaching. His method had been that of teaching and enlightening. The preacher had been content to take his time and patiently wait upon God that he might bless the word to the heart of the hearers. The surge of new life throughout his being led Griffith John to preach more directly and to expect immediate conviction and conversion.[22] Almost immediately a difference was felt in the life of the whole church in Hankow. When the pastor experienced the love of God in an unusual manner he began to pray for the congregation that they might know that love in the same way. Having that deep desire on 21 April 1875, the preacher decided on the following day to preach on Acts 1:2. He felt much freedom in his spirit to proclaim the message, and at the close of the service suggested that they should have a prayer meeting in the afternoon. While the believers were praying fervently in that meeting, Griffith John felt constrained to hold prayer meetings each day for the following week, and the nature of those meetings soon convinced him that he had come to the right decision. The Chinese were not easily moved to tears, but in these meetings the whole congregation cried and groaned under the guilt of sin, and this turned to rejoicing in salvation. Prayer continued for long periods without interruption, people crying to God for the conversion of individuals and families.[23] Griffith John had not seen anything like it in China, and was reminded of revival meetings in Wales.[24]

During 1875 there was a high number of baptisms, due to the faithful testimony of the members and the fresh experience of the Holy Spirit. In Hankow itself twenty-three men, nine women and two children were baptised. The strong manifestation of the work of the Spirit had an impact also on some of the national workers, who were regarded as crucial for the work at Hankow and for going out into the interior. One who was to become a national worker was Liu, who had heard Griffith John preaching on a theme 'which had become clothed with a new and powerful significance to my own mind, namely Christ's power to save from *sin*'.[25] Liu was an opium smoker, drunkard and gambler, but sincerely seeking deliverance from such practices. He had spent fourteen years as a soldier, and liked to boast of his physical strength. During one period of rebellion he had killed thirty rebels with his own hands. When he asked Griffith John if Jesus Christ could save him, the preacher answered immediately 'Yes'. After further explanation of Christ's power to save from sin, he confessed faith in the Saviour and became a changed man. Although he was a sawyer by trade, he was given the work of a cook in the hospital because, unlike Englishmen, 'all the inhabitants of the Celestial Empire without exception are gifted with a remarkable aptitude for Cookery'.[26] Being in the hospital also gave him the opportunity to work with opium addicts. His past experience and new life made him a most suitable person to counsel such people. Liu also worked in his home village, and through his testimony and support of a few faithful believers the village experienced what the church at Hankow had known as a powerful manifestation of the working of the Holy Spirit. The fire spread to Wei village near Hiaukan, which was the centre of LMS activity in that division of the District.

Hupeh and Hunan
Active in the Hiaukan district was Wei, who had been converted under Griffith John's ministry in Hankow.[27] As a result of his faithful work in the city thirteen members were added to the church. A characteristic of his life and experience was a strong emphasis on the power of the Holy Spirit, which pleased Griffith John very much. Having gained experience in Hankow he was appointed evangelist in his native district, where he met with some success and bitter opposition. Afraid of what could happen he hurried to Hankow to report to Griffith John that their place of meeting had been attacked and pulled down to the ground. Wei wanted John to have the information because he had promised to visit the district early in 1876. The news made the missionary more determined than ever and he made the necessary preparations to leave for Hiaukan. On 31 January 1876 the party set off, comprising Griffith John, Kenneth Mackenzie, Sian the hospital evangelist, Chia, Wei and his brother.[28]

The meaning of the name Wei Kia Wan was 'the village of the family', as all the inhabitants belonged to the same clan. Wei himself had a position of influence amongst them. Consequently, the missionaries were assured of a warm welcome, but they were uncertain as to what would happen in

some other parts they intended visiting. They were the first
foreigners to visit some of the areas and they were eyed with
excitement. In some villages they were allowed to preach
openly and share tea with the people. The outlook seemed
very promising, and this made the travellers' steps a little
lighter.

When the missionaries were within two miles of Wei village
there was a sudden change. They experienced a violence
Griffith John had not known since his arrival in China. A
whole village seemed to combine to prevent the foreigners
from entering and continuing on their way. It started with
hooting and yelling; then the mob became more violent and
took to throwing lumps of clay at the intruders. Griffith John
remonstrated with them, expecting success as on similar occasions in the past, but this time his arguments only intensified
the villagers' opposition. Dr Mackenzie was struck scores of
times; Griffith John received 'two cuts' according to his own
account, but Robson added in his report:[29]

> Mr John was struck on the mouth with a hard lump of clay,
> which made the blood flow freely, and almost caused him to
> faint, and soon after another piece cut his scalp at the back
> of the head.

The cries of the mob grew louder and louder: 'Beat the foreigners!'; 'Kill the foreigners!'; 'Back with them to Hankow!' Many
of the attackers looked like fiends, one having a large club in
his hand and another a rapier.[30]

The Christian workers wanted to cross a creek about a mile
away in order to reach their destination. They knew they
would be followed by the mob but made their way cautiously
to the bridge; here they were met by about a thousand villagers, so that they were now threatened both from behind and
in front. As soon as Griffith John set foot on the bridge he was
showered with lumps of mud. He and his friends scrambled
back on to the bank realising that if they attempted to cross the
bridge they would be murdered. The only path open to them
was to ask the mob for permission to return to Hankow, and to
the surprise of Griffith John he obtained it. Darkness overtook
them, but the home of one of the national converts was close at

hand and he was glad to receive the tired travellers. He prepared a good meal for them and the best available bedroom—a barn where the company slept on straw. The following day they made their way back to Hankow, and their host, who received no payment for the hospitality, insisted on helping the travellers to the boat which was eight miles distant from his home.

Mackenzie records in some detail the last part of the journey and Griffith John's response to what had happened at Wei village. When they left the boat they had a long walk to Hankow across a muddy plain and it was pouring with rain: 'I can truly say I never had such a walk before in my life.'[31] When they arrived at the north gate it was locked and they had to use their powers of persuasion to get the official to open up for them. Griffith John decided to report the incident to the English Consul, and also discussed it with the head magistrate of Hiaukan who was in Hankow at the time. In three weeks time the missionaries were able to return to Hiaukan in peace. This was surprisingly quick action by the authorities.

The foreign missionaries admired the courage of the national workers in this situation. Griffith John asked one of them how he felt at the time and he replied: 'Never better. Our hearts are full of peace and joy. God has honoured us in thus permitting us to suffer for His name and cause.' One of them insisted on walking with Griffith John and was exposed to many blows. One expressed the desire to be taken so that the pastor might be saved, while another, when seized by an aggressive attacker, held him firmly and explained to him the secret of Christian conduct. The members of the group, he declared, were Christians, taught to overcome evil by good. He declared boldly to his attacker that all he could do was to 'eat this body of mine, but you cannot eat my soul'. Wei's character, according to Griffith John, 'shone out beautifully'. He walked like a prince in the midst of trouble, knowing that God would enable them to face the trial and benefit from it. He was convinced that nothing could 'Knock the religion of Jesus into nothing. Impossible. Ten thousand times impossible.'[32]

Wei continued faithfully in the work and was set apart by the church, officially, to be an evangelist.[33] His method was to travel continually, and not to settle down in one place for more than two or three nights. He would diligently visit every house in an area and discuss the gospel with the people. His own congregation and Griffith John had complete confidence in him. The other worker, Sian, visited Hankow in November 1878 giving a most encouraging account of the work in Hiaukan. Griffith John decided to visit the area again and left with Sian on 27 November. The first three days were spent with Wei and Sian, given up 'to incessant talking and preaching'. On the third day, a Sunday, Griffith John baptised thirteen adults and eleven children. When he visited Wen village the next day he baptised a young man, the son of one of the oldest converts there, and in Wei village, the same day, the missionary baptised four adults and four children.[34]

The next stop was at Liu village. Early on Wednesday morning Griffith John entered the village, and was joined by Evan Bryant, who had arrived from Hankow. They spent two days together, talking, preaching and exhorting. Four adults and two boys were baptised, while many were told to postpone their baptism; the reason was not given, but probably it was the lack of credible faith. Nine families joined the church; over their doors red slips of paper had been posted bearing the inscription, *Je Su Sheng Kiau* (The Holy Religion of Jesus).[35] The village was made up of sixty to seventy families, all belonging to one clan. On the one hand this made it easier to present the gospel, but on the other there was a danger that many would accept the message superficially because others were doing so, anxious that all members of the clan should behave in the same way. Griffith John, however, was optimistic, believing that in a short time every family would have accepted the Christian faith. He thought that the children had a crucial role to play, as they visited huts, reciting Scripture passages and singing the gospel songs they had been taught.

An open-air service was held on the Wednesday evening, a little distance from the village. It was a beautiful moonlight night, and a large congregation gathered and listened attentively to Griffith John preaching for an hour. They left the following day, and John reported a significant development that had taken place in the village:[36]

Before we left, a part of Liu's house was converted into a

Chapel. The room was cleared of all encumbrances, the old family shrine was taken down and cast out, and a tablet was put up over the door bearing the inscription, 'Huh-yin-hwei-tang', The Gospel Hall.

Griffith John had no doubt that the work had a good root. It was a work of the Spirit of God without the lure of financial gain. There is a suggestion in his report that not only were the Chinese looking for such gain, but that money was being misused in Christian work in China: 'Money has been a real curse to the missionary work in China, and when it is introduced, however small the sum may be, a certain amount of rottenness must follow.'[37]

Griffith John had his eye in another direction. To the south were the provinces of Kiangsi and hostile Hunan. John Archibald of the National Bible Society of Scotland had arrived in 1878, and the two Celts had become firm friends. They set out on a journey together at the end of December 1879, making their way to the south.[38] First of all they entered Kiangsi and followed the usual pattern, preaching, selling books and talking to the people. When they saw a pedlar selling peanuts, John Archibald challenged his friend to get the Chinaman to give them some peanuts. It was generally accepted that this was impossible; a pedlar would rather lose his blood than give something away for nothing. After half an hour of eloquence the two missionaries received some peanuts. Archibald commented, 'I used to say he could make a Chinaman do anything he pleased, if he set his mind to it, and he was something of the same opinion himself.'[39]

The two entered an area famous for its porcelain, where the air was thick with smoke. The workers, thousands of them, were noisy and quarrelsome, but Griffith John revealed his usual mastery of the crowd that gathered around. They moved from street to street and eventually managed to sell five thousand items. 'This was the biggest end-on sale I was ever engaged in.'[40] They approached Nanchang, knowing that missionaries had previously been refused entrance to the capital of the province. The only welcome they received was to drink tea with the guards; they were then told to come back another day. Griffith John, however, insisted on seeing the magistrates.

When they arrived they pointed out to the missionaries the danger of entering the capital and advised that it would be better for them to pass on: 'Their powers of persuasion were of no mean order, but in Dr John they met their match.'[41] The two Christian workers were allowed to enter, and the incident opened up the way for other foreigners to visit the city.

The opposition in Hunan was even stronger. The missionaries went on shore from their boat, hoping to enter Siangtan, but some officials persuaded them to enter a gunboat and discuss the possibility with the authorities. Permission was given to go on shore, Griffith John overhearing one of the officials telling his men that the missionaries were to be escorted to the town, and if they were beaten at all they were not to be killed. When they were ready to leave the boat, they heard a fire gong signalling a mock fire. This brought out crowds of people who began shouting, 'Beat the foreign devils! Kill the foreign devils!'[42] Wisely, John and Archibald decided to stay in the boat, thinking they would be safe there. But soon they faced a new danger:[43]

> Before the lapse of many minutes another tremendous shout greeted our ears. We went out to see what it meant and, to our unspeakable horror, we saw a big junk sweeping down upon us, filled with buckets containing unmentionable filth, and with men well armed with long-handled ladles. It was not difficult to take in the situation. It was their intention to pour this filth into our boat, and dose us with it as well, this being one of the methods prescribed by the Hunan scholars and gentry to keep foreigners out of the province. That was an enemy with which we could not fight; so without a second thought we got up both anchor and sail and hurried away as fast as the wind and current could take us.

Undaunted, Griffith John and John Archibald tried to enter Changsha and Yochow, but failed in both places. It was only 'heart comfort' that they had, that is, the possibility of entering at some later date.[44] They were used to such a response and knew that they had to persevere.

Immediately after arriving in Hankow Griffith John made arrangements to visit Hiaukan again. A national called Tung had become a believer through reading Christian literature. He visited Griffith John at Wuchang during the examinations in 1879, when he was admitted into fellowship by baptism in the presence of a large congregation.[45] Tung returned to his home district and early in 1880 sent a plea for help, to which Griffith John responded by sending Chang, an evangelist, to join him. The missionary wanted to see how the work was progressing in Hiaukan generally, and desired to visit Tung in particular, whose home was in the district of Kingshan about a hundred miles west of Hankow. Griffith John started out on 13 April 1880, travelling through populous villages. The journey on the river was rather uncomfortable as the boat was narrow, low and open at both ends, and it was difficult even to sit in it without stooping. When night came, the traveller had a cup of tea, spread out his bedding, hung his overcoat up as protection from the wind and tried to sleep. He called at the home of Sian, the national evangelist, but had to stay indoors for a whole day because of the heavy rain. Visiting Hiaukan with Sian, Griffith John commented on the change that had taken place there. It had been a centre of opposition, but now the Christian men worked there openly, and as peacefully as in Hankow.[46]

On the fourth day of the tour Griffith John, his coolie and Sian started out overland to Kingshan. When they arrived at the little town of Kepootan they were ready for a meal, but had to move on because the people were so boisterous and insolent. They spent the night in a small mud hut and would have slept 'if the rats had been more disciplined'.[47] Early on the morning of the fifth day they walked six miles before having a breakfast of fine white rice, three kinds of vegetables and abundance of indifferent tea, for the cost of four pence. Their place of rest was Ying-cheng, where the three met with a Roman Catholic priest, and once again the differences between Roman Catholics and Protestant missionaries were noticeable. The former was busy baptising dying children, posing as a doctor, and dealing with lawsuits concerning property in the hope of gaining converts.[48] When talking to the priest Griffith John was struck by his ignorance of the New Testament, especially as compared with the knowledge of the LMS national assistants, who were thoroughly acquainted with the Scriptures. The priest had no gospel to preach, according to

John, and he was sure that he was the first to make known the good news in that place.

On leaving the city, the gypsum and salt wells came into sight, and hundreds of horses, mules, oxen and children were passing the missionaries, taking gypsum to the city to be shipped to different parts of the province and other places further afield. The salt was worked by shafts and drawn up as natural brine in buckets. Gypsum was used as medicine, for cosmetics, and also as pulse-curd, 'which with rice, was for the Chinese what bread and butter is for the people of Britain'.[49] The people of the area would have it for every meal. A village was attached to the works, giving the friends an opportunity to spread the gospel by preaching and distributing tracts. A few men approached Griffith John because they had seen him before on his preaching tours, and others told him that they had been to the hospital in Hankow. The foreign missionary was being accepted over a wide area.

After a tiring journey of thirty miles, Griffith John arrived to a warm welcome at the home of Tung, who had gathered together a number of Christians from different villages. Many of them had been taught by Tung and, though sincere believers, were rather timid in coming forward to make a public profession in baptism. There were a number of reasons for that timidity. Although they had accepted the Christian faith, the rite of baptism seemed strange and mysterious to them. Some of them were afraid of opposition from families and friends, and a possible war with Russia created uncertainty as to the future. Such a conflict could lead to the expulsion of foreigners, therefore it would be unwise to associate too closely with them for the time being. Tung, however, in Griffith John's estimation was a sincere, enlightened and respected believer. It was customary in China to display posters outside the house, and Tung made use of this custom to convey such gospel messages as 'Ye must be born again' and 'Repent'. The family gods had been cleared from the home and the ten commandments written on a chest in one of the rooms. There were also private rooms, a study, a guest room and a chapel with many of the doors covered with writing, including the Beatitudes written over the chapel door.[50]

The following day, a Sunday, was in John's opinion one of

the most remarkable spent in China. Tung had arranged a platform and benches outside the house as he expected many to
attend that day. They started coming before the 11 o'clock service:[51]

> Whilst we were preaching Tung himself attended to the
> audience, leading them to their seats and serving them with
> tea. In the midst of the service a number of scholars made
> their appearance, and they were led to their seats in front of
> the platform, where they sat for about an hour, listening
> with attention to the Gospel as preached by us. At the close
> of the service I was introduced to them and was told that
> they were some literary friends, whom he had invited to
> come, and meet me, and hear the Gospel from my lips.

Griffith John dined with the scholars, and discussed with them
aspects of the Christian faith. Although it was his aim to concentrate on the common people, he was quite at home with the
scholars.

Villagers continued to come during the day. If the preacher
was not present when they arrived they would call for him to
start preaching again. He found it difficult to have a quiet
time; if he went to his bedroom, or went for a walk, the people
would flock after him wanting to hear a sermon. Indeed they
would plead with him to resume preaching. Tung helped a little as he would also take his turn at preaching. During one ses-
sion he was rudely interrupted by his uncle, who was angry
that his nephew had accepted the foreign religion, but the
national believer ignored the opposition and continued to proclaim the gospel. There was no end to the activity until 10
o'clock in the evening, when the small group of believers went
into the chapel to hold a brief service; this was crowned at
midnight when Griffith John baptised Tung's mother, a wife
and two children, and a young man from another village.
Griffith John and Sian left the following day, called at Hiaukan,
where they baptised for the first time within the city walls, and
arrived at Hankow after a ten-day journey. 'One of the most
satisfactory journeys I have ever made in this land', he wrote.[52]

The work in Hiaukan had a prominent place in Griffith
John's report for 1880. Developments in that area had provided

him with an opportunity to advocate once again the principle of self-help. There was need for church buildings, but the Society could not help financially.[53] Griffith John convinced the national believers that it was their responsibility to find the land and build the chapels. He promised that if they accepted this responsibility, he would present the need to the church at Hankow and try and get some help from them. Two pieces of land were obtained, and the church members at Hankow responded willingly: 'The consequence is, that two little sanctuaries, with a prophet's room attached to each, are being built in Hiau Kan by the natives themselves, the missionaries helping only as members of the church according to their private means.' This arrangement pleased Griffith John: 'This is the first time that this has been done in these parts, and so far as our Mission is concerned, it is likely to be taken as a precedent by the converts.'[54]

Relationships

Within the LMS circle Griffith John worked with the Chinese believers and other missionaries, including Evan Bryant, William Owen and T. Bryson, but he made an effort to co-operate with others as well. He had been in contact with Hudson Taylor, CIM, since the Shanghai days, and after moving to Hankow related well to the Wesleyan, David Hill. The Bible Societies were close to his heart. He had high regard for Alexander Wylie, who became an agent of the British and Foreign Bible Society, and it was with him that he made the memorable journey of 1868. He also had strong links with the National Bible Society of Scotland, supervised the work of John Wilson for two years, was friendly with John Archibald, and worked with Alexander Williamson.[55] One thing which made co-operation impossible was proselytising. When American Episcopal Church missionaries received into their church a few believers who had been converted under Griffith John's ministry, and that without his knowledge, he expressed his disappointment and displeasure in a printed pamphlet.[56]

One area which called for co-operation was tract work. Griffith John had been busy writing tracts since he arrived in Shanghai in 1855. He, and others doing the same work, carried on each in his own way, paying their own costs.[57] In 1875 the

missionaries in Hankow and Wuchang formed the Hankow
Tract Society, made possible by a grant of £50 from the Religious Tract Society in London. At the end of the first year it
was reported that 9,000 publications had been circulated. As
the channels for distributing tracts increased, the demand for
them also increased.[58]

There were differences amongst the missionaries. Deciding
on the best Chinese term to use for 'God' created a heated controversy, and pamphlets and articles flowed from the press.
Criticisms were levelled at societies for concentrating on itinerant evangelism, carried out very often by uneducated men, the
CIM according to some missionaries being the main culprits.
There was a feeling within missionary circles that a conference
should be called to discuss matters of common interest, and to
further better relationships between the different societies. It
was decided to hold one at Shanghai in 1877.

In preparation for that event Hudson Taylor, Griffith John,
13 others from the CIM, 5 others from the LMS, 6 Wesleyans
and 1 from the American Episcopal Church came together at
Wuchang. They met for discussion, preaching and prayer.
Much time was spent in prayer and Bible exposition. When the
CIM missionaries related their experiences Griffith John could
not hide his delight. It was the kind of itinerant work which
was so close to his heart. He himself preached from Acts 1, the
very chapter which had been so important to him in 1875. It
was an opportunity for the preacher to emphasise again the
need for the power of the Holy Spirit, arguing that they should
wait upon God to receive the Spirit. Without his power the
preacher believed that he and his fellow preachers would be
working like atheists. On the final day all present met for a
communion service in which further grace was given to break
down barriers. Having rested physically and been refreshed
spiritually, they felt better equipped to go to Shanghai.[59]

Twenty societies were represented at Shanghai in a conference which lasted from 10 to 24 May.[60] Throughout its duration
there was a strong emphasis on preaching and evangelism,
which was to be expected with such men as Hudson Taylor,
Griffith John, Alexander Wylie, William Muirhead and David
Hill being present. When it was Griffith John's turn to preach it
was no surprise that his theme was the work of the Holy

Spirit. This time he took Luke 11:13 as his text, dealing with 'The Holy Spirit and Mission'. This verse was foundational for the belief in the extraordinary work of the Spirit in the life of the believer and the Church. The Spirit was at work, but the believers were also exhorted to ask for the Spirit. John's emphasis reveals his conviction that the well-being of the Church depends on supernatural power which is made manifest by the coming of the Holy Spirit. The experience of 1875 was still spurring him on, and this was not only his personal conviction but was also in keeping with the tone set on the first day. 'First day of the Conference was reserved for devotional services; morning, noon and night its members met to seek for the baptism of the Holy Ghost and to consecrate themselves afresh to the work to which God had called them.'[61]

The topics discussed at the Conference ranged from Confucianism and the work of the Holy Spirit to the place of women in mission work and foot-binding, the cruel habit of deforming the feet of girls to increase their beauty.[62] W. A. P. Martin and Young Allen argued for the introduction of Western literature and science in order to change the people of China, but this was opposed after Griffith John and Hudson Taylor had spoken strongly against the idea. The chairman, Carstairs Douglas, whom Griffith John knew from Shanghai days, wanted to discourage uneducated men from coming to China, but once again the Welshman was the counsel for the defence. He championed the not-so-educated missionaries in general and those of the CIM in particular. He confessed that in the past he had thought like the chairman, but had changed his mind. The kind of men needed were those of strong physique, mental vigour, good common sense, a fair education, a thorough knowledge of the Bible and, above everything else, consecration to God. A man is not inferior because of the lack of formal training, and an educated man could be inferior as a missionary. He admitted that he could not accept every aspect of the policy of the CIM (the role of women would be one of those aspects), but was convinced that its leader had been guided by God in the choice of men who had come to China. 'I should rejoice to see hundreds and thousands of such men come out to China.'[63]

There was disagreement when the matter of including notes

with translations was discussed, but the sharing did make future developments possible. The National Bible Society of Scotland decided to include them in 1883, the year when Griffith John started working for that Society. There was a strong emphasis on preaching, in the actual proclamation of the word and in discussion. Hudson Taylor read one of two papers on 'Itineration', on which there was agreement as to the principle but some disagreement as to method. It was generally felt that the best approach was to concentrate on a limited area and cover it well, rather than travel too far and work superficially. There was more disagreement when colportage and preaching were dealt with, one group arguing that the living word should always precede the written word, while another group responded by saying that no law should be laid down. Attention was also given to medical mission, education and literature.[64] Hudson Taylor believed that the Conference was 'the most important step China missions have yet taken'.[65] The degree of agreement was unexpected; as Latourette comments, it was an 'unexpected success'.[66]

It was not always easy to maintain good relationships within the narrow confines of the LMS compound. Harmony was essential for confirming the work already started and for pioneering in other areas. Strained personal relationships could hamper progress seriously. Griffith John himself would claim that he had lived in peace with his colleagues, but often when there were tensions he was expected to take sides.[67] From about the middle of 1877 many of the workers were 'keeping up appearances'.[68] He believed that without his presence Evan Bryant and Dr Mackenzie would not last six months together. They were just managing to co-exist.[69] There was no doubt according to John that the doctor could make a significant contribution to the work of the LMS in China, but he was too much under the influence of his wife: 'She is without exception the worst specimen of human nature I have known, and her influence over the doctor himself is utterly debasing.'[70] She would not join the others for worship, and while Griffith John was conducting a service at his home, Mrs Mackenzie could be heard playing on her harmonium. Mrs Bryant was not without blame, and she was, according to Dr Mackenzie, poisoning his wife's mind against Mrs John.[71]

Griffith John showed much wisdom in this painful crisis, although it must have been difficult for him to be objective when his own wife was involved. He believed that Dr Mackenzie's resignation could be avoided, but the doctor was determined to leave. When he did go his place was taken by Dr Mawbey. John dreaded the thought of another medical missionary joining the compound. 'I do not believe this appointment is of God.'[72] Mawbey, however, settled down and did his work admirably for a while, but tensions soon emerged once again. He disagreed with Griffith John regarding the medium of instruction in the hospital, arguing that Chinese was not suitable for medical work. Although John disagreed with this view, he eventually gave in, but reluctantly. Mawbey also disagreed with Lockhart concerning Mrs John's health.[73] She had been away for a while, and while Lockhart thought that she was well enough to return, Mawbey believed otherwise. It is difficult to say whether he was thinking in purely medical terms or whether his mind was coloured by a small dose of personal prejudice.[74]

His wife's health was a matter of concern for her husband and clouded his life for a while in spite of some encouragements. Another fellow Welshman, William Owen, had arrived, and his examination results at the end of the first year were satisfactory.[75] He was ready to take on more responsibility with Mawbey, Arnold Foster, Bryson and Griffith John. The work at Hankow was well cared for, and William Owen was appointed to be responsible for the work in Wuchang. Consequently Griffith John was able to give more attention to his wife's needs. She was so ill early in 1881 that it was arranged for her to leave for America.[76]

Looking back over 1880 must have encouraged Griffith John during this time of anxiety. It had been a good year in the church at Hankow, where 87 had been baptised during twelve months[77] and a new hospital had been built. This was opened by the national worker Tung, whom Griffith John admired as a Christian and whose father was amongst the first group of twelve baptised by the missionary in Hankow in 1862.

After his wife's departure Griffith John left for Hiaukan because the chapel in Wei village was ready to be opened. 'This little sanctuary is the first that has ever been erected in

Central China by the natives themselves.'[78] The pretty little
building, situated on a low hill, could be seen for miles around.
During his visit Griffith John presided at a meeting in which
forty to fifty believers partook of communion, four deacons
were appointed, and two adults and eleven children were
baptised.[79]

In a few weeks the news was received from America that
Griffith John's wife would have to face an operation. Her husband made arrangements to join her and reached New York on
9 March. The operation took place, but the doctors discovered
that the tumour was not malignant.[80] She was given time to
recover and Griffith John had opportunity to enjoy the fellowship of his host, the Rev. Ll. D. Bevan, another illustrious son
of Wales.[81] There was opportunity too to hear some of the outstanding preachers of America. When Griffith John heard D. L.
Moody he was 'greatly impressed', but that was not his experience when he heard Talmage: 'I never in my life listened to
anything which pained or disappointed me more.'[82] Jeannette
John's health improved slowly and her husband thought that
she was strong enough to go on to England before returning to
China. They sailed on the *City of Berlin* on 2 July 1881.[83]

During their stay in Britain it was Griffith John's preaching
that impressed the people, especially his eloquent message
during the Jubilee Meetings of the Congregational Union of
England and Wales in Manchester, October 1881. He informed
the congregation of the situation in China, pleaded for help
and proclaimed the power of the gospel to change the country,
while Buddhism, Taoism and Confucianism were failing to do
so. R. W. Dale, minister of Carr's Lane, Birmingham, was present and commented, 'Such earnestness I have rarely listened
to.'[84]

Griffith and Jeannette John visited friends in different parts
of the country, and he attended a good number of meetings.
Both were anxious to return to China, and as soon as possible
made arrangements to do so. A number of farewell meetings
were held, including three in London. In the Valedictory
Meeting held in the Weigh House Chapel, 2 January 1882,
Griffith John spoke passionately on behalf of China. There
were two strings to his bow, the importance of prayer and the
need for strong men to go to China. He appealed to the home

churches to meet for prayer. 'I would suggest that special attention be given to the missionary prayer meeting.'[85] It was here, the preacher was persuaded, that the fire would be kindled. This prayerful spirit would then lead on to sacrificial giving. He challenged the young men of the Universities and young men of independent means to go out to China. He called upon fathers and mothers to give up their sons and daughters to the service of the gospel in that country. In the meeting held on 14 February 1882, A. J. Wookey and his wife were present, ready to return to Africa.[86] He had been brought up in Wales, and contributed to many aspects of the work in Africa, especially translation. Just as he was looking forward to returning to that country, so Griffith John was looking forward to going back to China—that country which he regarded as 'grand' and 'wretched', but with tremendous opportunities for the Christian missionary.[87]

'Let us not dread the multiplication of versions, but rather dread the indifference, or the indolence, which would lead the missionaries to accept as final anything less than the very best version that can be secured in the age in which they live.'

A Voice from China, 151.

'We drill our converts in the Bible, and try by every means to make them genuine Bible Christians.'

A Voice from China, 156.

5
Hankow:
increased activity
1883-1890

To some extent Griffith John had been renewed physically and spiritually during his furlough. He settled down quickly to tackle the existing problems and to face new challenges.

Tensions and compensations
On his return Griffith John had to grapple with personal relationships once again. He had to involve himself in the disagreement between Mawbey and the others, which was becoming serious. Mawbey was attending to European private patients, but John argued strongly against such a practice. If the doctor had spare time it should be devoted to evangelism and personal counselling, and the Welshman quoted Dr Gould of the English Presbyterian Mission at Swatow to support his argument.[1] Mawbey had also been appointed medical adviser to the British Consulate, but the fact that the fee received was donated to the hospital did not change Griffith John's attitude to medical missionary work.

He sent detailed letters to the Directors explaining his standpoint. Mawbey's position was not compatible with the true spirit of the medical missionary. 'Its tendency is to create a divided heart, and lead away from the line of direct missionary work.'[2] Although, at the moment, Mawbey was thinking in terms of small numbers, there was the temptation to take on more and more cases, and the added temptation of working for his own benefit. He should have considered others as well, especially the practitioners in the ports. They had ventured out at their own expense, while the medical missionary had been sent out at the expense of the Society and provided with a

115

house and salary. In Hankow itself the Society would suffer, because some would support Mawbey and others Dr Begg who, with his friends, 'form the great bulk of the community'.[3] In any case Mawbey had enough work to do apart from taking private patients, and there was still work to be done on the language. Financially, Griffith John believed that ultimately the Society would suffer, because Mawbey's position created uncertainty. The Consulate could change, and the community could withdraw its support. The present position was encouraging, and the hospital was in need, so the best plan surely was to keep to the pattern agreed upon initially. 'Hitherto we have managed very well, and I don't see why we would not be able to get along in the future as we have done in the past on the old lines.'[4]

Griffith John believed that the situation was creating uncertainty in the minds of the Chinese and Europeans, as it placed the doctor in a false position before them.[5] In any case Dr Begg was practising amongst the Europeans, and if Mawbey continued to work with them the relationship between the two would be very strained. Such was Griffith John's conviction that he informed the Directors that it was not possible for him 'to be the colleague of any medical missionary who would go in for foreign practice either for his own benefit or that of the Society. I would infinitely prefer to see the Hospital closed at once than have it carried on in these circumstances.'[6] Griffith John was afraid that Mawbey's action would harm the medical work, the missionary work and personal relationships in Hankow. No solution was found and Dr Mawbey resigned in 1883.[7]

During the same period the missionary had to bear the burden of his wife's continuing illness. Jeannette John had to leave for America in July 1882 and did not return until October 1883.[8] More uncertainty was caused by the threat of a secret society; this created a 'fearful panic', driving the people of Hankow 'almost daft with terror'.[9] No attack took place, but the authorities reacted harshly against those who had caused the evil scene and began 'to chop off people's heads'.[10] Peace was restored within a few days, but not before half the population of Hankow had left to look for hiding places.

There were, however, compensations which were most precious. William Owen was settling down well, and two new workers arrived, Dr Gillison and the Rev. A. Bonsey. In 1884, Griffith John's daughter Mary arrived, followed in 1885 by C. G. Sparham, who was later to marry Mary. Thompson refers to the company—Arnold Foster, Dr Gillison, Arthur Bonsey, C. G. Sparham and Griffith John—as 'associates in a delightful intimate fellowship of service'.[11] It must have been a great thrill for John to have Mary with him, especially during this trying time in his life.

Griffith John lost no time in visiting the new stations in order to confirm the work, but he was also looking for areas that could be pioneered. He was interested in areas in Hupeh and Szechwan (where he had travelled with Alexander Wylie in 1868) and also hostile Hunan, and he even drew the attention of the Directors to the needs of Korea.[12] The more difficult the challenge, the greater his eagerness to respond. This was especially true of Hunan, where he and John Archibald had experienced bitter opposition in 1880. The two men made another attempt to work there in 1883.[13] When they reached Yochow they were greeted with cries of 'beat' and 'kill', and then the pelting started, forcing them to run to the boat to hide. They crossed the lake to Lungyang where everything seemed peaceful, but soon the placards appeared inflaming the crowds against the foreigners. One of the men with a placard caught hold of Griffith John and dragged him by the coat—an act which attracted a large crowd. After much argument the missionaries were allowed to go and look for the magistrate's office. When they found it they had to wait a long time before seeing the official, and when they did he denied the fact that a despatch had been sent to him from Yochow introducing the workers. His attitude changed, however, when he realised that the two visitors were not connected with the Roman Catholic Church or with the priest who had been in Lungyang for a few days. The missionaries had no doubt as to the cause of the opposition: 'In fact the entire plot had been hatched in the Yamen by the gentry with the magistrate himself at their head.'[14] It was an example of well-to-do leaders making use of the crowd to further their own ends, while hiding in the background to avoid the consequences of the disturbance.

Even though the magistrate had changed his mind, getting back to the boat was a problem because the crowd had not calmed down. When the missionaries entered the square outside the magistrate's office, they were faced with an angry mob. Realising the danger, the magistrate arranged for guards to escort them back to the boat. Even then it was not easy:[15]

> Even with the strong guard we escaped with difficulty. One strong fellow, a perfect cut-throat in appearance, made a rush at me in the street, and would have laid me prostrate in the gutter but for the intervention of the braves in charge. He had a stout iron bar in his right hand, and this he tried to bring down on my head twice. The braves, however, were on the alert, and the blows were warded off. The boat was reached at last, and we left the place at once.

They left for Changteh, and here they encountered more opposition.[16] Indeed the official refused to meet with the missionaries, and the Prefect informed them by letter that he would not protect them. So the workers had to return to Hankow, realising afresh what an enormous task it would be to establish a work in Hunan. It was clear that foreign workers could not settle there at present, but Griffith John believed that a national colporteur or evangelist could visit some parts of the province.

The care of the churches in Hupeh
It was absolutely essential to confirm the work in Hankow, not only in order to make further progress in the city, but also for the sake of the outlying stations and churches. Failure or success in Hankow would soon have an impact on a wide area. The work in Hankow had been started in order to conquer as much territory as possible, and from the very beginning Griffith John had considered the city as a runway to distant areas.

The place of worship in Hankow was the Kia Kiai chapel. For twenty years this had been the centre of Christian activity. Here the people met for worship, for Bible study, and to hear the preaching of the gospel. Preaching took place not only on Sunday but every day of the week. Thousands of people must have heard the Christian message as they passed through the city. The building was rather small, and there was an immediate need for a new and larger place. Griffith John toured

Hankow to find the best possible location. As chairman of the Hankow Committee he reported that he had found a piece of land leading from the Foreign Settlement to the Chapel in the centre of the city. The cost would be £700, much higher than he had anticipated, but he felt that they should go ahead with the project. That, however, was only the first estimate, and eventually the cost was £1,000, which for the work in China was unusually high.[17]

Griffith John also reported that he would inform some friends of this particular need, and one of them, a Mr Rogers from Clapham, London, was asked to collect £100.[18] Griffith John had a few such friends in Britain. Other money was available from gifts received by the missionaries when visiting Britain. John was convinced that the work would be completed and costs covered. 'Our dear old building' was coming down in March 1885, and work on the new chapel was progressing satisfactorily.[19] The building was erected and the chapel opened on Sunday 27 June 1886. Morning worship was followed by an afternoon meeting in which the Rev David Hill, the Wesleyan missionary, preached from Genesis 28:17 to a congregation of 450 Christians.[20]

David Hill's text in the afternoon service drew the attention of the hearers to the awesomeness of God's presence, and the wonder of entering into that presence. The purpose of having a building was to meet with him, but the building itself was something startling for the nationals:[21]

> It had never been their lot to worship God in such a place as that; and the arched and ornamental roof, the graceful pointed windows with their diamond-coloured panes, the prettily-carved platform, and the general appearance, which had been specially designed to please Chinese taste, produced a very gratifying effect on the converts. Some of them have since said that during those opening services God became to them higher, grander and worthier of praise.

It was the largest and most beautiful Protestant place of worship in Central China.

Outside the chapel there was a courtyard, having at its entrance a bookshop looked after by the keeper of the chapel.

Several features of the building were visible reminders of benefactors. One window commemorated the gifts of friends in Westminster Chapel, London, and another was in memory of the late John Kemp Welch. The cost of the platform had been met by Dr John Thomas and his people at Liverpool. There was another courtyard at the back of the chapel, neat and tidy with flowers and plants. Beyond the courtyard was a 'large vestry or guest hall furnished in good Chinese style'.[22] At the back of the vestry was the six-roomed house of deacon Tseng and his wife. Beyond their home was the Girls School which was supervised by Mrs Arnold Foster. There is no doubt that this was a remarkable building, and although the cost seems high and the architecture extravagant, the new development greatly enhanced the reputation of the LMS, while it acknowledged the fact that the building was erected in China, not in England. It was possible now to meet many more people and present the gospel to them.

One other window in the new chapel must be mentioned. It was in memory of Griffith John's wife.[23] She had looked forward to the chapel's opening, but she did not live to see that day. She had suffered terribly: 'For six years she had scarcely enjoyed one day of perfect freedom from pain. For about three months before her death even her indifferent health was below par. Still we apprehended no evil until the Christmas Day.'[24] That was Christmas Day 1885, and in the night she suffered from headaches, severe pain because of peritonitis, and continual vomiting. During these last days, as throughout her illness, she spoke with confidence of her Saviour and laid hold of the promises of Scripture. The words, 'He maketh all things work together for good', were very precious to her, and she would constantly repeat the words, 'Jesus is precious.' Almost with her last breath she whispered to her husband, 'Beautiful! Jesus the Lord. Beautiful!'[25] The end came at 11.45 a.m. on 29 December 1885. A service was held in the Sailors' Rest and her remains taken to Shanghai, where Griffith John's old friend William Muirhead conducted the service.[26]

According to Griffith John, his wife's death was in harmony with her life.[27] What characterised her in life and death was her passionate love for the Lord Jesus Christ. That love she had made known to others, and although she was a person of refined culture and exceptional intellect, it was her joy to serve in Hankow. She exerted a lasting influence upon a great number of sailors, many of whom wrote to her after they had left Hankow. She was much loved by the women of the church, and until the end attended to her class in the Girls' School and her class in the hospital. It was only in her last days that she had reluctantly stopped working with the Bible woman. For a long time both of them had visited the women faithfully, and Mrs John would preach to them as they gathered together in a home or on the street. In his bereavement Griffith John knew once again that faith is strengthened when tested. The example of his wife inspired him, and the belief that she was still alive. Referring to that conviction in a letter to Sparham a week after the funeral, the widower wrote: 'I am trying to think of this aspect more and more, and it makes me glad.'[28] What made everything meaningful were the providence and love of God: 'He doeth all things well, and I know that He has done even this in love.'[29]

Another cause of concern to Griffith John was the Chinese habit of taking opium. Ever since 1856 he had to face the problem of this evil. In the church context he and other church leaders had made it clear that the habit had to be broken before membership could be considered. Once the hospital was set up it was possible to have medical as well as spiritual help for those caught in its grip. From 1884, however, another aspect of the problem emerged: it was realised that some Chinese were taking opium *after* becoming members in the church. They were sent to the hospital to be helped, and told that if they did not stop they would be excommunicated. 'I am glad to be able to say that, with two or three exceptions, all have been reclaimed.'[30] In spite of this encouragement the missionary was perplexed by the opium-smoker. Once a person had contracted the habit it was, humanly speaking, impossible to cure him completely. One promising member of the church had to be excommunicated. 'To find that *he* had become an opium-smoker was in itself a great sorrow to me. But to find what a wreck of his former self he had become through this vice made me feel unspeakably sad.'[31]

Opium-smoking was a problem irrespective of Christian principles, but when practised by professing Christians it was bewildering. Griffith John reveals his heart in commenting on the matter:[32]

> I hardly know what to say about converted opium-smokers; . . . but I must confess, after many years of earnest and prayerful efforts to save this class, that my experience has been sad and disappointing. It is not so very difficult to so cure the smoker as to send him out of the hospital healed and reformed. The difficulty begins when he leaves the hospital and gets back into the midst of his old surroundings. The temptations are too strong for him, the craving returns with renewed force, and the poor slave is once more bound fast hand and foot.

The Christian missionary was proclaiming the saving power of the gospel, but was being forced to look on the opium-smoker as an 'unredeemable wretch'. It is possible that some of them had made a false profession initially, but Griffith John believed that others had made a credible one. He was encouraged, however, because a few had been converted and were continuing as faithful members of the church. An outstanding example was Fung.[33] He had heard Griffith John preaching from James 4:8, and when the preacher pointed out that God could see the stained hands, Fung believed that he was speaking to him. The conviction led to a lasting conversion.

The Chinese acknowledged the habit as being evil, although not enough was done to get rid of it. The attitude of foreigners angered Griffith John and missionaries in general. Opium-smoking was a curse on the life of China, and Griffith John deplored the attitude of those who suggested that the opposition to it was an 'Exeter Hall craze'[34] (Exeter Hall, London, where important missionary meetings were held). In Britain it was regarded by many as innocent, because the Government and many individuals were gaining financially from the opium trade. In China the actions and words of the British Government were taken as expressions of Christian morality. This was bound to hinder Christian work in the country. So far as the missionaries were concerned, opium-smoking was an 'unmitigated evil'.[35]

The years from 1884 to 1886 were a period of fluctuating

experiences for Griffith John. There had been real setbacks and
real advances. Apart from the demands at Hankow, he had to
supervise the work in other parts of Hupeh and think of ways
of extending to Szechwan. He renewed his efforts in these
directions in 1887. Hanyang was situated about six or seven
miles from Hankow, but this did not prevent a number of persons from attending Kia Kiai chapel, where they made a significant contribution to the life of the church.[36] They were anxious
to have a chapel of their own in Hanyang and, although poor,
they had bought a piece of land for that purpose. Help was
received from Hankow and Wuchang which made it possible
to build the chapel. On the day of the opening in 1887 a number of converts were baptised.[37] With the establishment of this
church the relationship between the Christians in Hanyang,
Hankow and Wuchang was strengthened. There was now a
fellowship of churches.

When, in 1888, Griffith John was considering how to proceed with respect to Szechwan, he recalled his journey with
Alexander Wylie in 1868. They had then travelled hundreds of
miles without seeing a single Protestant missionary, and
realised that it would take a long time to establish a work in
that province. During the last twenty years a number of missionary stations had been established, the CIM being especially active in the province. Not only did the LMS have a few stations there, but 'We can boast also of not a few converts in
those distant regions, and they are multiplying every day.'[38] It
was still difficult, however, to make real progress. The geo-
graphical problems were enormous. Szechwan was a vast
province with a population greater than that of the whole of
Japan. Steamers could go up the Yangtze as far as Ichang in
four or five days, but from there on to Chungking, roughly the
same distance, it took almost a month. The dangers of the
rapids were just the same as in 1868. Griffith John was looking
forward to the fruit of Archibald Little's work, who was
preparing to place a steam boat on the upper Yangtze.

On John's recommendation the LMS had arranged for Mr
and Mrs Taylor to go to Chungking, but Mrs Taylor's ill health
prevented them. Wilson and his wife, Griffith John's fellow
workers, were prepared to go, but they were prevented by
riots in parts of the province. By 1887 Szechwan was peaceful,

and the Wilsons left for Chungking on 1 November 1888,[39] accompanied by Wang-king-foo, who had been recommended to the work by Griffith John.[40] Wang had been a small huckster hawking his wares in Hankow, where he had met with the missionary in 1876. His first request for baptism was delayed, but when it actually took place it led on to a consistent and active Christian life. He spent some time in the service of the American Bible Society, which gave him added experience before going to Szechwan. No one would be attracted to him physically, but when inspired by the gospel his face could shine. His life was short and full, for he died at the early age of thirty-six. Griffith John himself would have liked to go to Szechwan, but the other demands upon him made it impossible. It is surprising that he even considered the possibility. His mind was at peace because he knew that the Wilsons were experienced workers and he thought highly of them. The Welshman felt very pleased with the expedition and was glad that he had a hand in it. 'In some respects I look upon Szechwan mission as a child of the Hankow mission, and as my own child in a special sense.'[41]

The call of the churches north of Hankow was still strong. They had to be visited as often as possible. In 1889 Griffith John and C. G. Sparham journeyed together for a hundred miles.[42] They started from Liu village, covering an average of thirty miles a day. At the end of the first day they arrived at Whitesand, where they stayed in a most unpleasant inn. Most inns in China were cold, dark and filthy places where gambling was carried on all night, and where all kinds of insects and animals would disturb the guests. This was the strategy John had devised for such visits:[43]

My plan in travelling overland is to secure two benches and a door, or two square tables, at every inn, and have my own bedding laid upon the top. In this way I manage to get beyond the leaps and bites of these little tormentors. In these inns the lodger is almost sure to have two or more pigs for chums. Just as we were going to ascend our lofty beds the pigs were brought in, and one by one they made their beds in front of our bedroom door. After a little squealing and grunting on their part, we all settled down for the night,

and both they and ourselves were soon drowned in deep
slumber.

Evan Bryant's experience was even more unusual. He came
across cave dwellings. Whole villages were found hidden on
the hills or in solitary places, comprising houses, barns, beggars' dens, lodging houses and chief inns, all underground.
Bryant and his helpers were given one room in which they had
to eat, sleep and wash. They only slept for three hours and
then moved on after having a breakfast of bread and butter
and chocolate. Similar reports were received from other countries, with Christian workers referring to the 'dirty coffee
houses' of Turkey and the 'stinking inns' of Mongolia.[44]

As John and Sparham continued on their way from Whitesand it began to rain, and they found shelter in a small hut
occupied by two women.[45] The discussion revolved around the
theme of eternal life, and one of the ladies told the missionaries that she was prepared for death, pointing to the coffin and
funeral clothes in her bedroom. John made use, as he often did,
of the story of the woman of Samaria in John's Gospel, chapter
4, emphasising that eternal life is a gift to be received from
God, that it is of grace, not of merit.[46] Soon after leaving it
began to rain again, and this time they found shelter in the
Barley Town inn which was even worse than the one in
Whitesand. Not only were the conditions bad, but the empty
house next door had also been occupied by a company of beggars. It was six o'clock before they settled to sleep, and Griffith
John would gladly have exchanged the place for the poorest
stable he had seen in Wales.

The travellers wanted to reach Yingshan in the hope of hearing something about Lo, one of the converts. They met his
father, who informed them that Lo was expected home any
moment.[47] When he did arrive he brought Liutsai, another convert, with him. Lo wanted to congratulate Griffith John on the
invitation he had received to be Prime Minister of England. He
was slightly confused—the Welshman had been invited to be
chairman of the Congregational Union.[48] Lo and his friend persuaded the missionaries to visit Liu village which was fifteen
miles away. During their visit there Griffith John administered
the first Protestant baptism in that district. There were further

encouragements when they called at Yingshan on the return journey. On a Sunday John baptised Lo's father and mother and, with Sparham, preached and distributed tracts. 'At the close of this Sabbath day we felt that we had taken possession of Yingshan in the name of the Lord.'[49] Griffith John felt close to the Lo family, the husband and wife, their son and the wife's sister who was a vegetarian. As he sometimes confessed, he could find it difficult really to love a Chinaman: 'It is not easy to find a Chinese that you can *love*, but I can truly say that I *love* Mr Lo, his father, his mother and his aunt.'[50] The travellers had another bad experience as they journeyed back to Hankow, once again in one of the inns. They were disturbed all night by the gamblers, who seemed to be as fresh at six o'clock in the morning as they were the previous evening.

They had heard even in Hupeh that Griffith John had been invited to be the chairman of the Congregational Union. John himself was thrilled that he had been nominated, thrilled both personally and because a missionary had been acknowledged. He had no doubt as to his response: '*I cannot leave China just now*, and I don't feel equal to the task of occupying the Chair of the Congregational Union.'[51]

Workers: need, training and support

As the work progressed the need for missionaries increased, and the growing burdens of the work demanded more detailed consideration of how to prepare them for the work after arriving in China. Attention was given to this matter during 1883, and the following year a new prospectus for missionaries was introduced. It was much more thorough than the one prepared in 1874. 'The Standards of Examination' were drawn up for three years:[52]

FIRST YEAR

1. *Translations*

   a) *Christian Literature*

   The candidate shall be able to read and translate any portion of
   i. The Gospel of St John, 1st Ep. of Peter and the Ep. to the Galatians.
   ii. *The Catechism of Christian Doctrine*
   iii.*The Mission Hymn Book*, Hymns 1-50.

b) *Native Literature*
   i. The *Sacred Edict* chapter 1 with commentary.
   ii. The *Book of Rewards and Punishments* pp.1-10 with commentary.

c) Edkins' *Progressive Lessons* Exercises 1-36.

2. *Writing*
To write from dictation any portion of Edkins' *Progressive Lessons*, exx. 1-12 making tones and aspirants.

3. *Speaking*

SECOND YEAR

1. *Translations*

   a) *Christian Literature*
      i. St Matthew's Gospel, the Acts and 1st Ep. to the Corinthians.
      ii. The Christian Trimetrical Classics.
      iii.The whole of the *Mission Hymn Book*.

   b) *Native Literature*
      i. The *Sacred Edict* chs i-viii.
      ii. The Confucian *Analects*, with commentary.

2. *Writing*
To write from dictation any portion of the Sermon on the Mount, making tones and aspirants.

3. *Speaking*
To deliver a sermon to the converts on Sunday.

THIRD YEAR

1. *Translations*
      i. (a) The Epps to the Romans and Hebrews.
         (b) Burns' *Pilgrim's Progress* in Mandarin.

3. *Writing*
To write from dictation a portion of Edkins' *Progressive Lessons*, Exx. 1-12 making tones and aspirants.

The main emphases are quite evident. First of all, the attention given to the biblical doctrines in John's Gospel, Romans and

Hebrews; secondly, the care taken with the native language and literature, and, lastly, the practical application in the context of preaching. A note was added at the end: 'The Peking version of the New Test. shall be used in the Examination, till a change be desired by the Committee.'[53] This was the version prepared by a 'band of giants' to give China a translation in northern Mandarin. It was one of three versions aimed at the people in general, the other two being Dr Medhurst's Mandarin version of the New Testament and Schereschewsky's version of the Old Testament.[54]

The language study was demanding, but Griffith John was sure that intelligence and commitment could overcome all obstacles. He was expecting more workers from Britain, but he was more interested in quality than in quantity. At home in Britain much excitement had been created by the testimony of the 'Cambridge Seven'.[55] They had stirred up in many a zealous response to the demands of mission overseas, while at the same time the LMS Society was in financial difficulties. Griffith John welcomed any advance in Christian work in China, including that of the CIM, but did not think that the LMS should be unduly discouraged, and that for at least two reasons: first of all, because of the God to whom they could turn, and also because of the commitment of the workers belonging to the LMS.

Concerning the 'Seven' he felt that the capital made out of 'their name and fame strikes me as something that Paul would have looked upon with great contempt'.[56] The Welshman had met three of the seven, and would not hesitate to say that in point of ability and education not a few in the LMS would be superior to them. C. T. Studd had spent some days with him, and John believed him to be 'a most lovable man, and thoroughly consecrated'.[57] He was not, however, of great mental capacity or profound erudition. The LMS missionary was sorry that he had not met Stanley Smith who, according to reports received, was 'the finest thinker among them'.[58] The consideration of social standing was not of primary importance. 'All we want are able men and consecrated men come they from any class they may.'[59]

Griffith John had another opportunity to make reference to Hudson Taylor's men when discussing financial support for

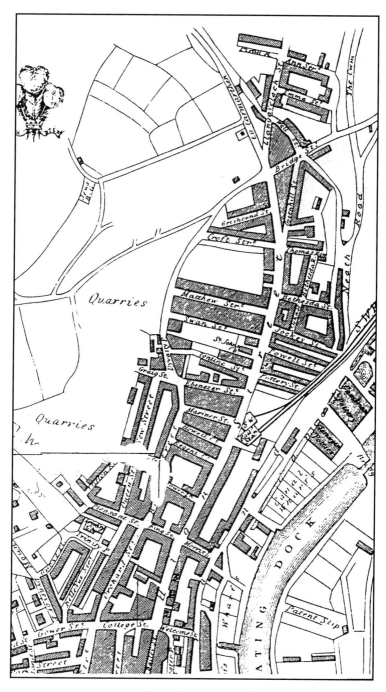

1. Plan of Swansea, 1851

2. Margaret John

3. Jeannette John

4. Griffith John in 1906

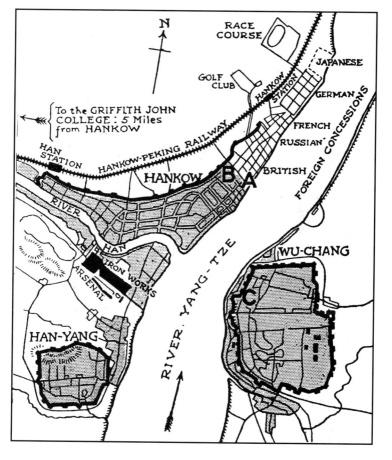

5. Plan of Hankow, 1904

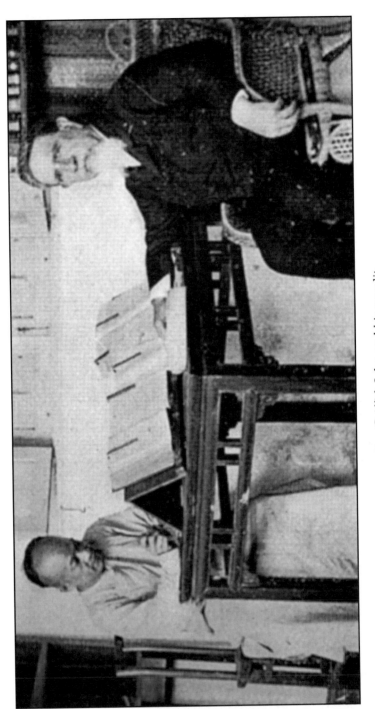

6. Griffith John and his pundit

7. Hankow chapel

8. The printing shop

9. The tract depot

10. Mission stations

11. John, Sparham and Peng

12. Conference of evangelists

13. Greig, John (seated) and Sparham with trophies from Hunan

14. Griffith John and Hudson Taylor

15.   Family group

REVEREND GRIFFITH JOHN D.D.

16.   Tombstone in the Congregational cemetery, Sketty, Swansea

missionaries.[60] The matter demanded his attention because so many at home were thinking superficially of mission work overseas. It was regarded as a virtue if a missionary could do as much work as possible for as little financial support as possible. After all, it was argued, the missionary is called of God and should be satisfied with a small salary. Sweeping statements were also made about missionaries. It was suggested that many were bread-and-butter workers, and many had mistaken their calling. According to Griffith John, only a few would fit into either category. The majority were dedicated, underpaid and overworked.[61]

Because of financial problems the LMS had suggested two levels of payment, involving a decrease in wages and expenses. In responding, Griffith John reminded the Directors that some of the married missionaries were finding it difficult to make ends meet; yet many of them were contributing personally to the work in Hankow and other areas. If the Directors' suggestion was accepted this would not be possible, and some missionaries would have to sacrifice even more. If such an appeal was being made to overseas workers, it should be made to all the Society's workers. Griffith John had heard of deputation workers who were being paid second-class fares when they should not really receive them. Such a practice was 'immoral'. The Directors were appealing for 'cheap men', which was a most dangerous path to take:[62]

I believe the whole thing will turn out a failure the moment it is tried practically. If you could bring all your missionaries down to the low salary it might work; but the attempt to replenish your missions with *cheap* missionaries, and put them to work side by side with financially more highly favoured, will prove, I venture to predict, a great mistake. Herein the Inland Mission is consistent and wise. All the missionaries *on the field* from Hudson Taylor himself down to the weakest of the brethren, are on the same level *financially*. If any other rule than this had been adopted the mission would have gone to pieces long ago. I have very little sympathy with this 'cheap missions' cry.

While admiring the CIM, and glad to regard Hudson Taylor as

'a dear friend of mine', Griffith John once again reminded the Directors of the excellent work the LMS missionaries were doing in China. In terms of accessions the Society in Hankow could boast as many as the Inland Mission in the whole of China. He did not want to create a spirit of rivalry but did want the Directors to keep in mind the reality of the situation in China.[63]

Before responding to the Directors in this way Griffith John had a plan in mind regarding self-supporting missionaries.[64] It was a joint scheme, as he was supported by Arnold Foster, a self-supporting missionary who was also an agent for the LMS and a member of the Hankow Committee.[65] Griffith John summarised the idea:[66]

My idea is to establish a mission that shall be organically connected with the LMS but independent of the LMS so far as pecuniary support is concerned. I can see no other way by which we can multiply our agents in this and adjoining provinces.

The Directors expressed general approval in February 1889, but John and Foster were still waiting for a definite answer in December 1890.[67] Nothing came of the proposals.

Literary activity

Griffith John was taken up with the preaching of the gospel, but he did not lose sight of other means to evangelise and educate the people. He himself said, 'In order to obtain the best possible results, you require three things—the scriptures, the tract and the living voice.'[8] His own living voice was heard almost until his death. The tract was important for him from the very moment he arrived in Shanghai, and he had to study carefully the different versions of the Scriptures. While continuing with his preaching, Griffith John gave more attention to his literary activities during the period 1882 to 1890.

After returning from England in April 1882, Griffith John immediately made time for writing tracts, and six of them were ready by October of that year.[69] The Hankow Committee acknowledged the significance of John's literary work, and on 27 July 1882 gave its hearty approval to it by agreeing 'That the sum of Tls 60 be added to the estimate for 1883 to defray the salary of a Chinese writer for Mr John'.[70] More tracts, from Griffith John and others, called for greater effort to distribute them. The Tract Society was developed into The Central China Religious Tract Society (1884), with Griffith John as chairman and John Archibald as secretary. According to the report for 1883, a total of 340,000 tracts had been distributed and, in a list for 1886, over thirty of the tracts had been written by Griffith John. Forty colporteurs were employed, and such was the activity that the tracts soon reached the rest of China, Korea and Japan.[71]

As a tract writer Griffith John knew how to appeal to the Chinese in different ways. The scholar was reached by such a tract as *The Gate of Virtue and Wisdom*, and the author was thrilled that it had reached the students who were sitting the MA examinations after three years study.[72] Other missionaries reported that it had been used in Chekiang, and they had ordered 10,000 copies.[73] Although many of the tracts had a strong apologetic aspect, the main aim was evangelistic, as is evident from such titles as *On Regeneration, The Atonement* and *The True Saviour of the World*. Others had a religious and moral emphasis: for example, *A Cure for the Opium Habit, Leading the People in the Right Way* and *The Parent*.[74] The tract was a handy means of reaching the people. If left with an individual or in a home, it would often be picked up and read after the colporteur had gone on his way. The missionaries could not afford to do this with a whole Bible or Testament. Griffith John knew that he and others had been criticised for tract and Scripture distribution on the ground that there was so much waste, but he defended the method, arguing that many had to be distributed in order to reach the few. The Chinese would not show interest in the gospel openly, but would quite possibly read of the good news in the secrecy of the home. There was, he believed, a biblical basis for this method in the parable of the sower. The seed was sown on the hard ground, the wayside and the thorns, as well as on the good ground.[75]

As a student of the Chinese language and the Christian Scriptures, Griffith John knew well how important it was to have a good translation of the Bible. The pioneering work done by Robert Morrison and William Marshman opened up

the way for the Delegates' Version (1847-53). This was prepared by eight British and four American scholars, and then
presented to selected delegates, six of the eight from Britain
belonging to the LMS.[76] The version was welcomed by an individual like Dr Muirhead and by the British and Foreign Bible
Society. It had its critics, and one of the most outspoken was
Griffith John. According to him the common people could not
understand the translation, and there was need for another
one.[77] Since 1877 there had been an interest in an Easy Wen-li
translation, and Schereschewsky had discussed it with the
Welshman before he left for his second furlough.[78] When he
returned some of his friends urged Griffith John to take up the
work, and he had encouragement also from the National Bible
Society of Scotland. He started on Mark's Gospel, which he
completed quickly. The report from Scotland for 1883 listed a
number of events, and then added that there was one other
matter that should be mentioned:[79]

> It is that the Society should undertake the publication of a
> Wen-li New Testament, revised by the Rev Griffith John,
> aided by various missionaries, with a view to the presenta-
> tion of the Scriptures in the book language of China, but in a
> style more simple and familiar than that of the Delegates'
> Version. The Gospel according to Mark has already been
> published.

Griffith John continued to work at a rapid pace. In twelve
months' time the Gospels and the Book of Acts were ready and
the letter to the Romans completed for the press.[80]

The translator was always anxious to emphasise that he was
working independently of others, and described his method as
follows:[81]

> Right before me was my Greek Testament, and around me
> the best commentaries I could find in the libraries of my
> brethren in this region, as well as in my own library. I trans-
> lated every verse from the Greek Testament consulting the
> English version and the commentaries as I went along.
> There are some passages in the Gospels and many in the
> Epistles, on which I have bestowed days and weeks of
> thought and reading.

Griffith John's grandson remembered going to his grand-father's room at six o'clock in the morning to find him busy at work. In the hot summer weather he would be found on the sofa on the veranda with the English Bible, Greek New Testament and Hebrew Old Testament.[82] He kept up his language study throughout his ministry, and he must have had access to some good books, with such men as Alexander Wylie and David Hill working in Hankow.

Griffith John's energy did not wane. By the beginning of July 1885 he could say, 'I should finish my translation of the N.T. within ten days if all is well.'[83] All was well, and the work was finished only a little later, which was a cause of great rejoicing for the National Bible Society of Scotland: 'The most important event in the history of the China Agency for the year, if not of the Society itself, is the completion and issue of the Wen-li Testament, revised by the Rev. Griffith John.'[84] He realised that translation is an ongoing activity and knew that revision work would be needed. In addition to revising the New Testament, the Old Testament demanded his attention, and Griffith John started immediately on the translation of the Psalms. He also wanted to make the Wen-li translation the basis of a Mandarin version.

Griffith John was working for the National Bible Society of Scotland, but he had a desire to serve the British and Foreign Bible Society, to which John Archibald was quite sympathetic. When Samuel Dyer heard of the possibility he immediately sent word to the Directors in London and the proposal was 'favourably entertained'. Dyer suggested that Griffith John should unite with J. Edkins and Bishop Moule to discuss a plan of work; alternatively, it was argued, he should join with Dr Burdon and Dr Blodget (but Blodget was already engaged in translation independently of the others).[85] All these discussions were taking up a great deal of time, and Griffith John was still expecting word from London. The BFBS was being very cautious, but the delay was taken as a refusal and was deeply regretted by Samuel Dyer and Griffith John.[86] The former was grieved at the thought of having to break the news to Griffith John. John's reaction was to start on the Mandarin version himself. Just before the end of 1887 he could say, 'I am taking study work more quietly this week having finished my Mandarin version of the four Gospels.'[87]

The revision of the Wen-li and the Mandarin translation proceeded steadily. The BFBS had a change of heart and, after discussions with the Scottish Society, they both agreed to ask Griffith John 'to undertake the preparation of a new Mandarin Colloquial Version for China'.[88] A joint request was drawn up and a clear plan of procedure, in the hope that Griffith John would respond positively. He was to be responsible for the first draft of the translation, which would be sent to six representatives of the two societies. A sub-committee, chaired by Griffith John, would look in detail at all corrections before publishing, a work which would be supervised by the chairman. It would be the responsibility of the sub-committee to revise the first edition.[89] The Welshman's answer could be summarised in one word, 'Impossible'.[90] In explaining his position he expressed his thanks for the honour of being invited to act as translator, but he was nearly sixty years of age and the project would take a long time. There were practical problems, and he did not like to undertake any task without some assurance that it could be completed. Added to these conditions was the fact that he was busy with the Wen-li revision. Consequently, 'Impossible' was the only possible answer.

After five years of commitment the Wen-li text was ready, 'In a condition that may be regarded as fixed for many years to come'.[91] Griffith John was given much help by David Hill, William Muirhead and E. B. Simmons, who acted as advisers, and nearly thirty missionaries sent in their suggestions to the translator. When the advisers disagreed on a particular reading, Griffith John would make the final decision. Progress was also made with the Mandarin version, which was finished by 1889, and he gave the copyright to the National Bible Society of Scotland, for which he received a gift of £105.[92]

Others were in the field, revising and translating, including John Chalmers, J. Edkins and William Muirhead. An aspect of Chalmers' work was to compare the Delegates' Version, Burdon and Blodget's Version and that of Griffith John—'an awfully *difficult* and delicate work'.[93] Chalmers believed that the Delegates' Version was better than the others because of 'its greater ease'. Three chapters of Chalmers' Epistle to the Romans were sent by Muirhead to Griffith John, and his response was sent to the translator, who referred to it in a letter to K. Kenmure: 'John comes down on me with a sledge hammer, writing to Shanghai and to me. But I am not hurt at all.'[94] In spite of the criticism he was still optimistic that Griffith John would work with him quietly and objectively. This was a dream that was not realised.

Another matter which demanded the attention of the missionaries was that of a Union Version for China, and eventually they had to decide on three versions that would be acceptable throughout China. After a long period of discussion and disagreement a significant step forward was taken at the Shanghai Missionary Conference in 1890: 'The result has been to develop a unity hitherto unattained among us in regard to these questions.'[95] It was agreed to have a Bible in three literary forms, High Wen-li (classical), Wen-li (simple but chaste), and Mandarin. Griffith John was not present, but he was invited to sit on one or more of the committees. For six days he experienced anguish of soul, and then decided to send his answer to David Hill and J. C. Gibson. He had sympathy with the venture, but after careful consideration he had to refuse the invitation to be part of it:[96]

> The task, however, is a gigantic one, and will involve an enormous expenditure of time and labour on the part of the translators. I am speaking now of the work itself, apart from the scheme. Even if the scheme were the most simple and workable possible, the work would tax all the time and absorb all the energies of each translator for ten or fifteen years. But the scheme is a very complicated one, and is likely to give rise to many inconveniences of a nature peculiar to itself, and thus lengthen out the time and increase the labour to no small extent.

Griffith John was willing, however, for the committees to make use of his translations.

In spite of what seemed to be a final answer, many friends urged Griffith John to reconsider. For a moment he hesitated —'I might help them with the New Testament at least'[97]—but even when C. Mateer and J. W. Stevenson wrote to him he would not change his mind. He sent two letters to explain his position again, one to Mateer and one to Stevenson,[98] mentioning the reasons he had already given and adding four other points: the text that was to be the basis of the work, principles of translation, lack of a common Chinese basis, and disagreement between himself and Burdon. These points were not elaborated, but the issues involved would be well known to Mateer and Stevenson. Had Griffith John accepted the invitation, he would have worked with George S. Owen on the Mandarin panel and been associated once more with Evan Bryant, his former co-worker, who was an adviser on a number of matters.

A number of tensions appeared during this busy period of translation work. It was becoming more and more acceptable to translate the Bible as a group rather than as individuals. In China, the Rev. G. F. Fitch pointed to the many who had worked on the LXX and the Delegates' Version; but Bishop Moule argued that Luther's work clearly demonstrated that a good translation could be produced by one person.[99] It was not long before Griffith John joined in the argument. Boldly he declared, 'I believe in my own version.'[100] It is true that he had presented the Wen-li version to a number of missionaries for comment, but he would no longer follow that procedure. If a committee was suggested to look at his work, then he himself would choose its members. This was contrary to Evan Bryant's opinion, who did not think that a version by one man would ever become a common version, that is, acceptable to all Protestant missionaries.[101]

The work of a panel or a committee came to be generally accepted as preferable to the work of one man, and it is now a *sine qua non* of a dependable Bible translation.[102] There are a number of reasons for adopting this method. It is very easy for one man to be biased, but members of a panel can correct each other. A number of people can share notes in a fruitful way and learn from one another. A number of pairs of eyes can detect mistakes more easily than one person and, together, panel members will have a variety of styles in translating, yet these can be related in such a way that they are not conflicting.

Not only did Griffith John insist on working alone, but he also argued that the basic principles laid down for any translation, whether by an individual or a group, should be absolutely clear. Lack of understanding and agreement was one criticism he had of the proposals made at the Shanghai conference. One clause stated: 'That the text that underlies the Revised English Version of the Old and New Testaments be made the basis, with the privilege of any deviation in accordance with the Authorised Version'.[103] Bishop Moule offered three criticisms with which Griffith John agreed: the Bishop did not believe that enough competent scholars could be found; there was a strong adherence to the *textus receptus*, and it would create animosity amongst scholars and missionaries. In agreeing with the Bishop, Griffith John acknowledged that it would be possible, perhaps, to use the text of the Revised Version for the New Testament.[104]

With the same confidence with which he discussed the text, Griffith John published his principles of translation:[105]

1. Aim at making the version an exact image of the original.
2. Use the words, and only those words, which shall clearly express all the meaning of the original.
3. In so far as it is possible, use those words which best correspond with those of the original.
4. Where a translation *ad verbum* would result in an obscuration or a perversion of the author's meaning, abandon a *literal* version and translate *ad sensum*.
5. In doubtful passages a version *ad sensum* is to be preferred to a *literal* translation.
6. Where particular words are wanting in Chinese, have recourse to circumlocution, if by doing so the sense can be made clear.
7. In all cases consult the genius of the language in which the version is made, and let its characteristic qualities rule as far as faithfulness to the truth and exactness of interpretation will permit.

No one could change Griffith John's mind, although there was strong opposition to some of the points, especially numbers 5 and 7.

Underlying these points was his conviction about the method of translating. Dr Chalmers, having changed his mind, became 'the champion of bald uncompromising literalism'; and George S. Owen, speaking of China at the time, exclaimed:

'Unfortunately literalism is in the air here just now.'[106] Like George Owen, Griffith John was critical of such an approach. Both of them would prefer to be in the tradition of the Lollard John Purvey, who had argued for clarity, claiming that a word-by-word translation was bound to cloud the meaning. Griffith John believed this:[107]

> To translate is to carry ideas and thoughts from one language into another; and a true version is one in which the ideas and thoughts are translated in harmony with the genius and laws of the other language, and with the fullness, force and beauty possible to it as a medium. It is hardly necessary to observe that a perfect translation into any language is impossible.

His views were in harmony with the two Bible Societies, Girdlestone of the British and Foreign stating that the aim of translation is 'to give the sense of Scripture', and the Scottish Society saying of Griffith John's Wen-li translation, 'The aim is to produce a version thoroughly idiomatic, and intelligible to the mass of readers in China.'[108] Bishop Moule shared Griffith John's convictions and made that known in the discussion on the northern Mandarin version: 'well read by a reader who knows it, the Peking is quite intelligible to an average city hearer read as it stands, except where the nature of the passage makes exposition indispensable'.[109]

Griffith John confirmed his arguments with examples of what he considered to be wrong or misleading translations. Bridgeman, translating word by word, had failed to be idiomatic where the native language demanded it. In English his translation of Matthew 26:52 would be 'Return the sword to its old place', which could also mean 'native country'; and John 8:15, 'Ye judge men after meat', prompted John to say that this was 'nonsense to the Chinese mind'.[110] The Welshman also argued that unnecessary words should be omitted. This was his response to those who had criticised him for leaving out words like 'therefore' and 'but'. To include them every time they occurred 'would make its pages grotesque and repulsive in the Chinaman's eyes, and in very many instances a puzzle to the intellect'.[111] It is significant that Griffith John is appealing not only to the intellect but also to the eye, which would be important to the Chinese. The translator was also accused of 'redundancy', and it was pointed out that one chapter of the Wen-li translation contained one hundred and fifty more characters than the equivalent Delegates' section.[112]

Griffith John was advocating a view which he, and others, had to fight for, but the view has now gained the ascendancy: 'A translation which transfers the meaning and dynamics of the original text is to be regarded as a faithful translation.'[113] Generally accepted, although strongly opposed in some quarters, is what Eugene A. Nida has called a 'dynamic equivalent'.[114]

As the scholars translated the Scriptures it was impossible to avoid theological problems. In China, as in many other countries, the meaning and usage of the term for 'baptism' led many into deep waters, although Griffith John was not directly involved in this controversy. Neither was he directly involved in the argument concerning the best names for the persons of the Trinity, especially that for God the Father. The Bible Societies in Britain decided to use *Shang Ti*, while the American Presbyterians used *Shen*; the former was a name for one of China's national gods, whereas the latter could mean 'God' or 'Divinity'. John believed, however, that 'faithfulness to the truth' was all-important for the translator.[115] He was dealing with the Christian Scriptures, in which the revelation of God was found. It was like other books, and yet very different from them. Consequently, care should be taken with the text, both in relation to revelation and also in relation to preaching. The Bible was the preacher's handbook, and no translator should lead him astray, for he had to proclaim God's saving message to a needy people.

'The missionary needs be a man of strong faith, ardent hope and burning love. The joy of the Lord should shine forth in his countenance, ring in his voice, and quicken his footsteps. He should be the brightest and happiest of men. Nevertheless, if he is not penetrated with a deep sense of the solemnity of his ministry, his preaching and teaching will be of little use.'

A Voice from China, 115-16.

'The Church must go down on her knees, and down there in the dust abide, till the work is done.'

China, Her Claim and Call, 62.

6
Hankow:
riot and fruit
1890–1900

The year 1891 was significant for Griffith John personally and for the Mission. His daughter Mary married C. G. Sparham, and husband and wife settled with her father.[1] He extended his study and rearranged the house for the sake of the married couple. This was also for his own good: 'My old study tried my eyes greatly, and did no small damage to my eyesight. I have put a new window into it for Sparham, so he will be much better off. My study, with necessary alterations made to the home has cost me Tls 450.'[2] Their home was one of four houses in the LMS compound. Griffith John and the Sparhams lived in a semi-detached house, next door to Dr and Mrs Gillison; the unmarried ladies occupied the detached house, and the Bonseys the bungalow. During 1891 the experienced missionary gave attention to two areas in particular: medical work and the better training of national workers.

Healing and rioting
A small hospital had been opened in 1866 under the care of Dr Reid and Margaret John, Griffith John's first wife, who acted as nurse and matron. The new building was dedicated to her memory as the 'Margaret John Memorial Hospital'. As usual, John himself was more than ready to contribute financially, giving most of the money needed for the venture. It was designed by Arthur Bonsey: 'It contains one large ward with ten beds, a small private ward, an isolation ward, an operating room, a sitting room for the patients, and bedroom and parlour for the Chinese matron.'[3] Dr Gillison took charge of the medical work, while Mrs Bonsey had general oversight of the hospital.

With the progress there was renewed tension. Once again

there was friction as to how the hospital should be supported financially. Foster and Gillison advocated the 'Faith System', which meant that they would not ask the people of Hankow for support. Griffith John, C. G. Sparham and Terrell, on the other hand, were quite happy to do so and saw nothing wrong in going to the people. Indeed, they felt strongly about the matter; they were convinced that the money was there, but the people had to be asked before they would give it.[4] Writing to the Directors, Griffith John reminded them of the past, when he, Dr Reid, Thomas Bryson, Dr Mackenzie, and even Dr Gillison, had unceasingly gone round seeking subscriptions for the work. In a long letter to the Directors explaining his position, John gave his main reasons for adopting the collecting method:[5]

1. I was extremely anxious at the commencement of my missionary work in Central China to have a Hospital connected with it; but I saw no chance of the Directors taking up the idea unless I could show them that the Community would take an interest in the Institution, and do something substantial towards its support.
2. I have been anxious all through my missionary career to save the Society as much as possible.
3. I know that in thus doing I was acting in accordance with the policy of the Society, and the wishes of the Board. The policy of the Society is clearly laid down in the Book of General Regulations, page 10, no. 30.
4. I have always felt it to be nothing but right and fair that the Foreigners who make their money in China should be asked to contribute towards an Institution which has for one of its chief aims the physical weal of the Chinese.

Even if the reasons would not satisfy the Directors, he was writing with the 'full approbation' of his conscience. John informed them that he would continue to adopt the same plan, appealing at the same time for a grant to the hospital. Lady workers were appointed and, as Thompson points out, the opening of the hospital helped to break down prejudice, as a lady doctor could deal with Chinese women in a way a male doctor could not. This marked the first appointment by LMS of a lady medical missionary in connection with the mission in Central China.[6]

Although Griffith John had the better training of national workers at heart, it was difficult for him to draw up a plan and put it into operation. That was his desire: 'Our minds are working towards this point, and no doubt will reach it sooner or later.'[7] Until a training centre was opened, the next best thing was to arrange a conference for national preachers and deacons. Apart from the speakers, seventeen men attended for the fourteen days of instruction, discussion and prayer. Foster lectured on Pastoral Theology, G. Sparham on Geography and Mission in the South Sea Islands, Gillison on Physiology, and Griffith John devoted twelve hours altogether to the study of twelve chapters of the Epistle to the Hebrews. Besides the lectures there were sessions on experiments in chemistry and a consideration of social issues for Chinese Christians—idol worship, theatregoing, opium-smoking and the binding of feet.[8] The impact on John's own mind and the zealous responses of the national workers assured the missionary that he would have to make a permanent arrangement to train potential leaders.

The following year, 1892, Griffith John grasped the opportunity to further an aspect of medical work. He had met with Liu-Tin-tsung, a leper, in 1878, and in 1879 accepted him as a candidate for baptism. When Liu and two other lepers visited the missionary in February 1892, he was convinced that he should do something to alleviate the suffering of the lepers. Dr Walton arrived in 1893, and the two men made preparations to open a hospital at Hsiaokan, encouraged by a gift of £200 for building purposes from the Mission to Lepers, with a promise of £50 p.a. for costs. The Home was opened on 7 April 1895.[9] A little later, when the Belgian railway was opened, Griffith John took his grandson to see the hospital, travelling at a rate of twenty miles an hour, which was quite a contrast to going there by foot or sedan chair. The mission consisted of two residences, a chapel, a small hospital and an elementary school. 'The main pride of the mission on the medical side, however, was the Leper Hospital, located, of course, in an isolated position outside the city wall.'[10] Under the supervision of Dr Fowler, an artesian well had been sunk to provide water for the hospital. It was believed that some of the lepers had been cured, but it was a sad experience for the youngster to witness the sight of suffering lepers. Looking at 'the poor, rotten faces and hands' was a gruesome experience; indeed it was too much for him and he fainted at what he saw. The visit filled him with admiration for Dr Fowler, but the young lad felt so proud that his grandfather had started it all.[11]

The war between China and Japan hindered all aspects of the work. In 1894 Griffith John reluctantly refused the invitation to be chairman of the Congregational Union of England and Wales. He was taken by surprise by the events of the war, and by the end of the year had realised that his decision had to be final.[12] Not only was it impossible for him to leave at that moment, but the optimist was also looking forward to the end of the war when, he believed, there would be new opportunities for the missionary societies. He could not bear to think of being absent from China when peace was established. He acknowledged the weak position of China because of the conservatism of Peking, the personal ambition of the leaders, continual attacks from the West—and now an attack from a country that had developed rapidly: 'A new maritime nation had appeared almost overnight.'[13] Japan demonstrated her power during the war that was declared on 1 August 1894, the army gaining a decisive victory at Pyongyang, and the navy at Haiyang Dao. Early in 1895 the Chinese fleet was utterly routed at Weihaiwei. 'So the Chinese admiral and other commanding officers committed suicide to save themselves from decapitation and their families from death and confiscation of their estates.'[14] Peace was secured on 17 April 1895, the terms proving most humiliating for China: complete independence was given to Korea, and China had to concede territory in Manchuria and Taiwan and pay indemnity amounting to £40 million sterling.

With the signing of the peace treaty many of Griffith John's fears were removed, but there were still fears as to the reaction in the country. He had realised that Japan was strong enough to conquer China, but he was not sure what the attitude of the Chinese leaders would be to outsiders. Almost immediately some of the officials in certain provinces began to fan an antiforeign spirit. This was very evident in Szechwan, where riots broke out, starting in Chengtu the provincial capital. The property of the Canadian, American Episcopal and China Inland

Mission was destroyed completely. 'Nothing could be more swift and unexpected.'[15] Even bricks, timber and foundation stones were taken away. The policy was apparently to destroy but not to kill, because the lives of the eighteen adults and eleven children there were spared. Ten to twelve other stations in the area were attacked, but the LMS centre at Chungking was spared although the missionaries themselves lived in fear. It seemed that they would have to leave the station, and Mr and Mrs Claxton and Mrs Owen of LMS made the necessary arrangements, hiring a boat in readiness for their escape. There was no need to take that step, however, as the danger passed away; but when the annual examination was held there, another scare arose, for as long as the government representatives and scholars were present there was real uncertainty as to what could happen.

The missionaries at Kucheng were not so fortunate:[16]

When the missionaries at Ku-cheng went to rest on the evening of the 31 ult. they could have had no idea of the existence of imminent danger. Whilst sleeping in their beds, about 1.30 a.m., eighty armed men broke in suddenly upon them, and one man and eight women were barbarously butchered, and several others were badly cut and wounded. One child died of his wounds the next day. The whole thing was over in half an hour. My impression is that it will be found out that official influence was at the bottom of this terrible outrage also. It is absurd to suppose that it is the work of vegetarians merely.

Griffith John felt strongly that the officials should be punished, especially Liu Ping Chang, the Viceroy, and that there should be indemnity for losses.

The outrage created fear outside of Szechwan. In Hankow it was heightened by talk concerning Liu Yung-fuh, leader of the Black Flags, who had overcome the Japanese in Formosa, destroying many of their warships. It was rumoured that he was on his way to China to drive out the foreigners and restore the country's glorious past. Griffith John was confident that Hankow was safe: 'The Gunboat is here and the officials are, I think, on the alert.'[17] He was concerned at the number of refugee missionaries passing through the city to the coast. It grieved him that they had been forced to leave their work, but the accounts they were able to give of the behaviour of the national believers rejoiced his heart. They had pledged to meet together, study the Scriptures and pray, but they would not sing because that would attract the attention of the officials.[18] They showed much courage, and this was a real source of encouragement to Griffith John and his colleagues in Hankow. The sad events of recent months challenged the Welshman to attempt even greater things. He felt that the expulsion of the missionaries from Szechwan was like a trumpet call to advance.

Another cause of concern for Griffith John was the attitude of the British officials in Peking. He believed that they were rather naive: 'Our Ministers in Peking seem to be to be playing with the Szechwan case.'[19] Something should be done immediately, or life in the interior would become impossible. A month later he was more optimistic. Agreements had been made between the local officials and the French consul with respect to compensation for losses. Commissioners had been appointed to investigate the Kucheng affair, and already a hundred arrests had been made, twenty-seven had been tried and twenty-three convicted. Evidence had been received that would convict thirty-one more.[20] Once again the missionary was quite adamant as to the main influence behind the trouble. The Vegetarians had been quite prominent (a misleading term according to Griffith John because they formed a political party determined to get rid of the existing dynasty); but the real influence was exercised by the officials, not the people. It was a source of comfort that the Viceroy was awake and doing everything possible to keep things quiet. 'This being the case, I feel pretty sure that we shall have no serious trouble here.'[21]

Advancing and convalescing

Early in May Griffith John baptised eleven people in Hankow,[22] and in May 1894 baptised Yang Pau-king, a Confucian scholar who had embraced the Christian faith as a result of reading some of Griffith John's tracts.[23] He must have been pleased to see one of the scholarly class being accepted into the church, as this did not happen often. Griffith John's first meeting with

Yang evidenced the missionary's ability to argue a point and his fondness for using the question and answer method. He would never take his opponent lightly and always made sure of having the relevant information at his fingertips. He showed a vast amount of patience in dealing with people, and could persevere with them for a very long time.

The Tienmen area still interested Griffith John. He sent Huing, a national preacher, to the area, but he was rudely ignored by Ch'en Yiien-tai, who was a bitter enemy of missionaries and left the preacher in the charge of a magistrate who treated him most kindly.[24] He reported on the situation in a number of areas; twenty to thirty persons were candidates for baptism in one place, while there was encouraging news from Kingshan. Griffith John and Arthur Bonsey visited that place in 1894,[25] and their first surprise was to find their old enemy Ch'en present in a meeting. In one town the workers were invited to a magnificent feast. They were carried in two chairs and accompanied by a military escort. Between twenty and thirty dishes had been prepared, and despite the possible strain on the stomach Griffith John, in accordance with Chinese etiquette, managed to sample each of them. The greatest surprise was still to come, and that was the number of candidates for baptism: '4 at Pah-tze-n, 23 at King-shan, 14 in Chang village, 10 in Tien-men and 66 at Man-kia-po'—all on the Saturday and Sunday before returning to Hankow.[26] In all his forty years of experience Griffith John had never baptised so many in one week.

Even in a letter dealing with the anti-foreign campaign, Griffith John could devote a section to 'a bit of news that will cheer your heart', referring to the advance in Kinshan during 1894-5:[27]

Last year I gave you some account of a remarkable work that had sprang up in the district of King-shan. I told you that I had baptised there on one Sunday 41 adults and 19 children, 60 in all. Mr Huing, one of our native assistants at Hankow, has just returned from a visit to King-shan. He tells us that all the converts baptised last year remain strong and firm in the faith. There are more than 190 now awaiting for baptism, of whom about a 100 are deemed *quite* satisfactory.

The Christians have bought a large house for Chapel purposes, and paid for it themselves. About 40 villages have
become more or less Christian, and the work looks as if it
might spread all over that part of the country.

There had been a remarkable work in this area, and looking
back over a period of thirteen months 159 baptisms had been
recorded, of whom 108 were adults. Apart from this, many
applicants had to be left waiting, as it was only possible to deal
with a particular number during a fairly short visit, and a wide
area had to be covered. These advances confirmed Griffith
John's belief in itinerant preaching, especially when supported
by national workers. Once again during his visits to these
areas he was impressed by the friendliness of the people.[28]

The advances also encouraged Griffith John to return to
those areas again, and he did so twice in 1896. He was able to
report solid advance in terms of baptisms:[29]

	Adults	Children	In all
Tien Men	16	7	23
King Shan	77	21	98
	93	28	121

Those were the figures for the first visit, and when he returned
in December of that year he reported the baptism of 202 persons, 147 of them being adults.[30] During this visit Griffith John
commented again on the crucial part played by national
agency. In dealing with the inquirers John would divide them
into three classes: first of all, those with sincere motives; secondly, those with mixed motives; and, lastly, those with bad
motives. Of the three classes, the most difficult was the middle
one. Many missionaries believed that such inquirers should be
refused admission immediately, but Griffith John was more
optimistic about them. He believed they should be taken by
the hand and led on, patiently, to higher things.[31]

Griffith John welcomed these encouragements, not only as
signs of progress but also as a cushion to the many blows he
was receiving during this time. In 1895 Mary and her husband
left for England, but the emotional farewell was sweetened by
the LMS centenary celebrations of that year. In the same year

William Owen's wife and Walton died, and the following year
David Hill, the Wesleyan missionary. Since 1893 Griffith John
himself had been troubled with ill health, but his weakness
made the eternal dimension meaningful to him. He realised
that he belonged to heaven as well as to earth: 'earth is growing poorer, and heaven richer'.[32]

During 1896 the experienced missionary was very aware of
his frailty, and had to rest at Kuling, a place he had been mainly
responsible for opening up. One grandson had been ill during
the hot summer of 1894, and another died at the age of four
months. Griffith John, Sparham and others were convinced
that they had to find a sanatorium, away from Hankow, where
children and mothers could go, and male missionaries if need
be. During the grandson's illness, he and his mother had spent
some time with friends in the shadow of some mountains fifteen miles east of Kiukiang.[33] It was such a pleasant place that
Griffith John and a handful of men decided to explore the area.
They set out guided by a woodcutter and charcoal-maker.
When they reached the top of one of the mountains, four beautiful valleys opened up before them, four thousand feet above
sea level, cool, invigorating, fertile, and watered by mountain
streams. When they made enquiries concerning ownership,
'No one owned it, no one lived there, and officials seemed to
be ignorant of its existence.'[34] This was Kuling, an
Anglicisation of the Chinese Kiu Niu Ling, the Old Ox Range.

In the lesser valley, which became known as Hankow Gorge,
Griffith John built a bungalow of white-grey Kuling stone.
Besides the usual dwelling place there were servants' quarters
and John's two studies, one square and one octagonal, so as to
offer a wide view of the mountains. It was named 'Valley of
the Stream' (*Cwm-nant*), reminding him of a relative's home on
the Gower Coast in Wales. More Europeans bought lots there,
and after prolonged discussions with the government the valley was legally registered and the Kuling Estate was formed,
with Griffith John as chairman of the trustees.[35] The place
became a haven for many Europeans, and Griffith John himself
was glad to go there in 1896 and again in 1897. Although very
ill, he regarded both periods as holidays and tried to do as
much work as possible. As was the case in so many ventures,
this one was made possible because Griffith John was able to

depend to such an extent upon private means. He had opened up a place not only for Christian families but for those who were to shape the future of China. The valley became the summer capital of Chiang Kai-shek, and when the Communists took over they occupied it as one of their resorts.[36] Little did Griffith John know in 1896 that he was contributing in this way to the country's future.

Hunan

Recollecting his visits to Hunan, Griffith John comments on the last decade of the nineteenth century: 'The anti-foreign sentiment grew in intensity during the next decade, and the anti-foreign Press became more and more active and violent.'[37] Propagandist literature flooded the country at times, as in 1890 to 1891. This perplexed Christopher Gardner, the British Consul in Hankow. According to Gardner, just to accept compensation for damage was not an efficient way of dealing with serious attacks; something more radical had to be done. Before he could act, the necessary information had to be collected, and he found help in time of need:[38]

> Appropriately enough it was a missionary who gave the impetus and direction to Gardner's fight to suppress the propaganda literature. This commanding personage was Rev Griffith John, a patriarchal figure of mountainous energy who from his headquarters in Hankow directed the work of the London Missionary Society. The missionary and the consul came to constitute an alliance dedicated to forwarding what Gardner liked to call the work of 'Christendom'.

Griffith John's main contribution was hunting out information regarding the source of such literature, and he was quite successful in his attempt. The main instigator, he reported, was Chou Han, and he had specific details included in a letter sent by Chou to the Governor of Hupeh. The investigator also discovered that the centre of activity was a pawnshop in Changsha, the capital of Hunan. Both John and Gardner were anxious to act swiftly, but the Foreign Office in London called for caution and delayed action. This led to strained relationships between the two advocates for action and the authorities in London. The pawnshop was closed, but Chou's influence was not curbed immediately. Gardner was removed to Seoul, Korea, where once again he had to spend a most unsettling period. Griffith John consistently argued that the leaders of such a revolt should be brought to trial and punished. Justice should be honoured, and in consequence mission work could advance peacefully in that area.[39]

The Welsh missionary could be involved in the affairs of Hunan from his centre in Hupeh, but he was always waiting for an opportunity to visit that province again. When he returned from Kuling after his first stay he was still weak, and at the end of the first fortnight he confessed that he had spent most of the time on his back. It was not long, however, before he was ready to knock at that seemingly locked door of Hunan. Having visited briefly in 1880 and 1883, he knew something of the vastness of the area and the strong anti-foreign spirit which was continually expressed there. It was densely populated with twenty-one million people, and was rich in coal, timber and granite. The mountain range at Nanyo had seventy-two peaks, ten caves, thirty-eight springs and twenty streams: 'Thus Hunan is a little kingdom in itself, and a very rich one too.' The people had more character than the people of Hupeh: 'Hupeh men are made of bean curd, but the Hunan men are made of iron.' Men from this province had excelled during the Taiping rebellion; it had produced many prominent leaders, and many officials would retire and come to live within the province: 'All this tended to make the Hun-anese proud, exclusive, and anti-foreign to a degree that is extraordinary even in China.'[40]

His response reveals Griffith John's defiant spirit, and his faith in the national workers. Weakened physically, and know-ing that opposition was to be expected, he ventured to Hunan with Sparham in 1897. The visit was bound up with the labours of the national Christian leaders in that province. One of the outstanding workers was Peng Lau-Seng. In his pre-conversion days he was anti-Christian and anti-foreign, but immediately after his conversion he began to work among the Hunanese in Hankow, preaching passionately and relating his conversion experience.[41] In 1895 he was sent as a colporteur to Hunan, and in 1896 John Archibald succeeded in securing a

house for a Bible Depot in Hengchow. One of the principal
gentry at that place had invited Griffith John to visit him, and
the missionary responded positively, knowing that this would
be an opportunity to visit the converts. The party of three,
Griffith John, Sparham and Peng, set out on 22 March 1897,
travelling by river and reaching Hengchow, 460 miles from
Hankow, in fifteen days—'one of the fastest runs on record'.[42]
They broke their journey at Changsha, as they wished to make
inquiries concerning Dr Wolfe, an eminent German traveller.
They soon realised that his presence had made it impossible
for them to be taken into the city: he had insisted on being
taken into the city at a quarter to four in the morning and, not
surprisingly, had been ordered to leave at a quarter to six, just
two hours later. His visit had the same effect on the officials in
Hengchow.

Before leaving for Hengchow the party heard from Teng, the
publisher of Chou Han, the influential enemy of the Christians, that the leader had severed his connection with the anti-
foreign group at Changsha, had renounced spiritism and was
reading Christian literature. Griffith John was disappointed
that the old enemy was not present at the capital, as a discussion with him could have proved fruitful.[43] The company needed
some encouragement, for their dream of entering Hengchow
was shattered once they came in sight of the place. Awaiting
them was a large crowd of ruffians armed with stones and
mud. When they came within reach, the cursing and the pelting began, forcing the boat across the river to the side where
the Bible Depot was situated and the gunboats were stationed.[44]
They sent their card to the naval officer, but he ignored it and
left the area in the morning. The pelting was renewed and the
missionary boat had to shelter at the side of a gunboat despite
the captain's initial objection. When the district magistrate
appeared he explained that the conduct of Dr Wolfe had
turned the people against foreigners. Griffith John emphasised
that it was his desire to visit the converts, and the magistrate
agreed to discuss the matter with the gentry. While he was
away, the naval officer returned and came aboard the boat, and
immediately the pelting began again, stones falling like hail
and smashing the glass roof. To complicate matters further, the
colporteur came to the boat with the news that the Depot had

been raided and everything stolen. This serious incident had occurred in the presence of the magistrate, but he completely ignored it.[45]

In spite of the turmoil, the converts did manage to visit Griffith John and his friends on the boat. They were especially glad to see Wang-Lien-King, a young man who had been baptised at Hankow. At the time, he was in the service of an important Hunan official and was given the choice of renouncing his faith or continuing in his situation. Wang could not deny his Saviour, and he returned to Hengchow and started working as a self-supporting evangelist. He gathered together a small group of converts and shepherded them carefully and lovingly. Many of the converts discussed baptism with the missionaries—that is, the male converts; it was considered too dangerous for the female converts to make an appearance. They had weighed seriously the possible consequences of baptism, but pressed Griffith John to administer the sacrament, which he did to thirteen candidates:[46]

It was to us joy unspeakable to admit these thirteen into our communion. We have many Hunan men in the Church, baptised at Hankow and elsewhere; but these thirteen were, as far as I know, the first baptisms ever witnessed in Hunan itself. That day, the 6 April 1897, the forty second anniversary of my ordination in Swansea, I shall never forget, and that evening I can never forget. It was a glorious ending to a very stirring day. If there ever has been a Bethel in the world, surely our boat was a Bethel that evening.

After the service they sat down to a meal prepared by the Hunanese Christians. On 8 April the missionaries started on their return journey, reaching Hankow on 16 April after travelling nine hundred miles.

Apart from visiting Hunan, Griffith John made use of the pen to plead the cause of the province. There were two needs, men and money.[47] He prepared his appeal from his sick bed, having spent eight days on his back. It was sent to periodicals and churches in Britain, with a Welsh translation for the people of Wales. The missionary made it clear that weak, nervous men would be unsuitable: 'We want strong fellows for Hunan.'[48] It would be better for them to come out as bachelors, and remain as such for two or three years, after which period it would be possible, perhaps, to send women to that province. John was planning mainly for the Siang Valley, not for the immediate future only, but for the distant future as well. The Viceroy, Chang Chih Tung, had communicated with the Governor of Hunan encouraging him to open up the province to foreign trade. Already the merchants and gentry of both Hupeh and Hunan were planning a railway between Hankow and Changsha, the capital of Hunan. It would probably be four years before the work was completed, but with the eye of faith Griffith John could see mission stations linked by rail, only two or three days' journey away from Hankow. There was encouraging news with respect to the river too, as Yochow at the mouth of the Tungting was to be opened to foreign trade.[49] Improvements in travel were to quicken the process not only of introducing Western trade into China but, more important, the spread of the gospel of the Lord Jesus Christ.

As he thought of the possibilities Griffith John's heart burned within him. It was time to strike while the iron was hot. The Directors were far away in London, but he was determined to convince them of the importance of the work in Hunan. He based his appeal on behalf of Hunan on five main reasons:[50]

1. We in this mission have for many years been praying, working and waiting for the opening of Hunan.

2. It has been a part of our programme from the beginning to establish a strong mission in Hunan as soon as possible.

3. We have already carried out the programme as far as it has been possible. Our native colporteurs have been working there for years, and last year a permanent work was started at Heng-chow, and a native evangelist put in charge of it.

4. The work at Heng-chow has been carried on *openly* ever since the opening of the station, and without the least interference on the part of either the magistrate or the people. The last news from Heng-chow is to the effect that

Mr Peng had just left for Heng-shan, with the view of seeing the magistrate, and putting the work in that city on a
safe foundation.

5. I believe that the gates of Hunan are about to be thrown
open, and that it will be possible for foreign missionaries,
in the *immediate* future, to reside there in safety. Of this I
have no doubt whatever.

In his approach Griffith John insisted on reviewing what had
been achieved. However small that might have been, it was an
encouragement to venture further and attempt greater things.
His aim could be high, but he was convinced that in this situation a measure of success, at least, was possible.

By the end of 1898 he was able to report: 'We are now rejoicing in the fact that the two men for Hunan have been found,
and that the funds needful to start the mission have been sub-
scribed.'[51] The advocate for Hunan was most pleased that one
of them was Albert Greig, who was formerly an agent for the
National Bible Society of Scotland, an experienced missionary
with a good command of the language. Griffith John hoped to
go to Hunan early in 1899 to help Greig settle down, so that he
might supervise the work in Siang Valley. John believed that
there were cities ready for occupation, including Yochow,
Saingyin, Changsha, Siangtan, Hengchow and Hengshan.

As usual Griffith John was impatient. He was even craving
for action when he had to spend some time in Kuling, where he
was supposed to rest. During his stay a conference of missionaries was held there, and although he appreciated the company
of his old friend Hudson Taylor, his comment was 'Talk! Talk!
Endless talk!' What he needed was 'rest and a bit of steady
work',[52] and he believed that after the rest there would be more
steady work for him in Hunan. The promise to visit that
province had to be honoured. Griffith John, Albert Greig and
C. G. Sparham left Hankow on 15 February 1899.[53] The British
Consul General, Sir Pelham Warner, had appealed to the
Viceroy of Hupeh and Hunan for protection for the missionaries. Consequently, they enjoyed peace as they visited, although
they met with rowdy elements. The Christians' welcome was
warm and generous; the visitors were deeply moved by this,

and even more so by the 'multitude of candidates for baptism':[54]

> The admission of so large a number of Hunanese to church
> fellowship added a deep interest to the journey. There were
> baptised in all 192 persons—adults 173, not adults 19. We
> might have baptised hundreds more, for there were many
> hundreds of candidates; but it seemed to us that we could
> not be too careful in regard of this matter at this initial stage
> of the work in Hunan. These 173 adult believers were admit-
> ted only after a very careful examination, and may be regard-
> ed as the very pick of the candidates who came before us.

Whatever the success numerically, Griffith John was always
careful in accepting candidates for baptism, and he continued
to depend heavily on nationals, trusting Peng and Wang especially with a great deal of the work in Hunan. During this visit
in the spring of 1899 six evangelists and four colporteurs were
set apart, the sphere of labour for each of them being clearly
defined. During the same visit Griffith John ventured to introduce another feature of Welsh Nonconformity to the Chinese
scene, in addition to the society, Bible class and Sunday school
which had been introduced already. In Hiaukan the Welshman
now introduced the *Gymanfa* (a preaching festival).[55] The converts erected a stage in the open air and rented benches on reasonable terms. At both morning and afternoon services there
were six to seven hundred people present, about three hundred of them being Christians. In the morning Griffith John
preached; in the afternoon the preachers were the assistants,
with McFarland and John delivering brief addresses of five to
ten minutes. In both services the Scriptures were read, prayers
were offered, and there was 'plenty of singing'. The missionaries acknowledged that this was 'new and strange', but the
event was well received. It was a combination of the old
preaching festival and the more recent *Cymanfa Ganu* (hymn-
singing festival).

In order to confirm the work in any area, it was a tremendous advantage to buy a house; but that could be very difficult
indeed. They succeeded in doing so at Siangtan, purchasing a
huge building for a very reasonable price, the reason for such a
bargain being that a concubine of the owner had committed

suicide there. No one else would dare to live in the place, but the missionaries were thrilled to have it, Griffith John commenting that 'Ghosts in China have often rendered us valuable service.'[56]

The change that was taking place in Hunan is evident from the welcome Griffith John and Greig received on arriving at Yochow in the autumn of 1899. This was the Welsh missionary's fifth visit to Hunan, and they could not believe that it was the same place. 'An official came off to take us on shore, and we were carried to our inn in two sedan-chairs, both chairs and bearers having been provided by the district magistrate himself.'[57] They called on all the officials and were kindly received, even by the district magistrate who had treated John and Sparham so rudely in 1887. He invited them to his private room for tea in the foreign style, that is, with milk and sugar, which the missionaries gladly accepted, but they refused the champagne and the cigars.[58] During their stay the Christian workers bought houses and made plans for building a chapel, vestry and dispensary.[59] They left knowing that the work was in the safe hands of Peng, the superintendent, and firmly believing that greater things were to happen in Hunan. Griffith John said, 'It was opening, but not open.'[60]

The pioneer worker gave a bird's-eye view of the work in Hunan at the end of 1899.[61] Societies working there other than the LMS were the American Presbyterian Mission, the China Inland Mission, the Alliance Mission and the Cumberland Mission. The LMS concentrated on the Siang Valley, with its seven central missions, fifteen branches, twenty-three places of worship, and property in seven walled cities. Of the twenty-three chapels, six were provided by the Society and seventeen by the converts themselves. There were two foreign missionaries and seven paid national evangelists.[62] Griffith John must have experienced great pleasure in reviewing the work in Hunan, but he was still waiting for the day when the province would be completely open. He believed that this was bound to come.

Schools and Boxers
'The years following the Sino-Japanese War are the most tragic and the most fertile in the history of modern China.'[63] As

Chesneaux observes, this period was one of turmoil on account of strife within and attacks from without; yet at the same time the events of the period opened up the way for radical changes early in the twentieth century. Immediately after the War a number of individuals and secret societies grasped the opportunity to implement their ideas. Kang You-wei, backed by a large number of scholars, tried to send a memorial to the court advocating reform in education, banking and industry, and arguing that the Peace of Shimonoseki should not be ratified. This memorial, and others, were circulated to secret societies that had been formed to promote reform.[64] Of further help was the press, especially the new journals that were appearing; one of them, within a few months of the first issue, reached a circulation figure of 10,000. Another reformer, Yan Fu, had received part of his education in England. Unlike Kang You-wei who had tried to reinterpret Confucianism, Yan Fu repudiated the whole system.[65] He wanted to introduce Western philosophy, a kind of social Darwinianism under the influence of Thomas Huxley and Spencer. Both the Chinese reformers were for change and progress.

The Emperor supported reform, and from June to September 1898 ('The Hundred Days') a flood of edicts was issued from the palace ordering reformation of the examination system and the law courts, acceptance of Western arms and drill, and the setting up of colleges and schools in all cities. The University of Peking was established, with the veteran missionary W. A. P. Martin as head of the faculty.[66] The reform that was advocated was inspired by nationalistic aspirations which, on the one hand, developed into a Communist programme and, on the other, were aligned with Christian principles.

A person like Wu Yu-Chang represents one extreme. He was a strong supporter of the 'One-Hundred-Day Reform' advocated by the Emperor, and he summarised the aims as follows:

- the establishment of modern schools;
- abolition of the examination system;
- granting of freedom of speech;
- development of industry and commerce;

- the abolition of redundant government offices and re-organisation of the armed forces.[67]

The other extreme is represented by Sun Yat-sen, who could say with pride, 'I am a Christian; God sent me to fight evil for my people.'[68] It was during this period that he developed his doctrine, and although he had to leave China, he returned to share in the leadership of the Revolution of 1911. He had received part of his education from Protestant missionaries. Other reformers were influenced by Young Allen and Timothy Richard, whose secretary for a time was Liang Ch'i-ch'ao, 'one of the most brilliant of the younger reformers'.[69] If all, or most, of these reforms had been implemented, it would have been too much for the country to cope with them. They were not introduced, however, for a number of reasons: the conservative element was so strong; there were so many divisions in the country; many in leading positions were jealously guarding their interests, and the Empress was afraid that her position was in danger. She took power into her own hands and had the reformers arrested, although Kang You-wei and Liang managed to leave the country.

Protestant missionaries made every possible effort to take advantage of these attempts at reform. Allen and Richard took an active part in the reform movement and, together with men like Hudson Taylor and Griffith John, endeavoured to establish better relationships between themselves and the government, appealing especially for religious liberty which would benefit not only the Christian workers but the whole of China. Regarding concessions to missionaries there could be differences of opinion. When the French accepted an edict of toleration for Roman Catholic missionaries, it was envisaged that the same privileges would be extended to British missionaries. Roman Catholic missionaries were given the right, during certain serious cases of disagreement, to appeal to the Consul or local official. Arnold Foster believed that this was a 'play of Rome for political purposes', but it was Griffith John's opinion that 'Protestants could not afford to place themselves below the Catholics in the eyes of the Chinese'.[70] John gave his support to H. B. Morse, the commissioner at Hankow, in seeking to establish good relations with the gentry in Hupeh and

Hunan, where bitter opposition to foreigners was changing to an attitude of friendliness.[71] He was confident that this process would continue until the province was completely open. He could not accept all the reformers' methods, nor was he happy with all their aims, but change had to come. He was aware too that the situation could change quickly, so great wisdom was needed in knowing how to proceed with missionary work. The reformers could be too extreme in their revolutionary methods, and the conservatives too harsh in repressing them. It was in such a situation that the missionary had to respond. All reformers, despite some differences, especially in method, welcomed Western influences but were strongly opposed to outside domination, and at the time Japan, Russia, Germany and Britain were making efforts to have a slice of the melon.

A most important area for reform was that of education. The Protestant schools were crucial for developments in this field:[72]

Protestant schools were practically the only institutions in China where training in Western learning could be acquired. With the reform movement, then, the better ones speedily became popular. Missionaries, sensing the need, strengthened those already in existence and opened new ones.

Griffith John was one of the men who wanted to strengthen the work of the schools, with particular attention to Hankow. When discussing the work in Hunan with the Directors during 1897-8, he presented to them a plan of education which, he thought, should be established in that city and in the district.[73] In the past he had acknowledged the importance of education, but the more important work of evangelism demanded most of his time. That work was bearing fruit, and there was real need to provide the converts with the best education possible. Now was the time to act, as attitudes were changing in China, a significant example being the development in the Annual Examination at Nanchang, where the Old Testament was included as a textbook, thus creating a point of contact with the better educated classes.

The missionary had changed his mind on one important aspect of education: in the past he had insisted on teaching the Chinese through the medium of their own language, but he now believed that the medium should be that of the English language:[74]

> There was a time when I was strongly opposed to the intro-
> duction of this element into the schools. But the times have
> altered, and my views have undergone a complete change.
> There is in China at the present time a great demand for
> English, and the demand will have to be met. The Chinese
> will have English, no matter what the missionaries say.

The adoption of English, John argued, would bring hundreds of men of high social standing under the influence of mission-aries. It was time for the LMS to be more progressive, or it would not be possible to compete with other societies who were willing to be more flexible.

The plan envisaged by Griffith John and the District Com-mittee at Hankow was to have primary schools (one for boys and one for girls), a high school for both sexes, and a divinity school which would also have a medical department. The for-mal opening of the High School took place in April 1899, John and his helpers being committed to the aim of having 500 pupils.[75] Of particular interest to Griffith John was the Divinity School, and it was a thrill for him to witness its opening on 1 November 1899 with nine students, one of them being Peng Pang Ts'ien, the junior national preacher at the Kia Kiai chapel in Hankow. The report for the first year gives a glimpse into the kind of institution that had been established:[76]

New Testament and Pastoral Theology	Dr John
Old Testament Exegesis	Mr Foster
Church History	Mr Bonsey
Systematic Theology	Mr Sparham

Arithmetic, Geography and national studies also formed part of the course. The students gave great satisfaction to their teachers in terms of study and Christian character. Griffith John was full of hope now that theological training could be developed and confirmed on a permanent basis.

These significant developments soon met with serious set-backs. In May 1900 Griffith John went on his sixth journey into

Hunan, visiting Yochow, Changsha and Siangtan. Although everything was quiet in Hankow, 'The storm was gathering, and its mutterings were distinctly heard in the north.'[77] The Boxers were mustering their forces. They took up arms, as they could see that the path of reform was being blocked by the conservatives. Though the youthful and zealous Emperor supported radical changes, he could not match the cunning of the Empress, and reform was retarded when she had him imprisoned after appearing before her 'as a rabbit mesmerised by a snake'.[78]

The Boxer revolutionaries wanted to drive out all foreigners. They saw them as a threat to the well-being of China and were not slow to draw attention to the opium trade and the fact that the drug had been brought in by foreigners. It was reported that the Boxers practised the occult, which gave them the confidence that they were protected by the spirits against the enemy, and also gained them sympathy from the people, who readily accepted such a belief.[79] To complicate matters further, there was a bad harvest in 1899, leading to riots in many places: 'The Boxer movement found the people ripe for lawlessness, under stress of circumstances which were sufficiently appalling.'[80] They were mainly active in the north-east, but there were repercussions throughout the country. Christians in Shansi (CIM especially) were tortured, butchered and burned, though a number managed to escape, many of them making their way to Hankow.[81] Their arrival in that city took the Christians, including Griffith John, by surprise. He had abandoned all hope for them and looked on the fleeing Christians as the dead raised to life again. They for their part believed that they had found 'the nearest thing to heaven', compared to the riot and hatred they had experienced.[82]

Some of the Christian refugees remained at Hankow, while others made their way to Shanghai. Griffith John estimated that there must have been a hundred and fifty missionaries in the city, with about a hundred more expected soon.[83] The converts in the city were upset and would come to him for help: 'During these three months converts used to come in batches, and fill my study from morning down into the depths of the night. They came for comfort, guidance and help in many ways.'[84] It was natural for them to be afraid, and yet Griffith John knew that this was not a matter for cowardice; natural fear was to be overcome by faith. He himself regarded it as a privilege to be with them, and would not have missed the experience for gold.[85]

In the light of the threat to China and her own uncertain position, even the Empress changed her mind. She felt forced to do so immediately after the attack on the Taku forts by foreign troops of six nationalities.[86] Because of the serious situation in Peking, the foreign powers believed that they had to take this step, which enabled them to reach the city. The invading army committed atrocities as vile as those committed by the Boxers, atrocities which could never be justified. The Empress was frightened. 'In spite of moderate counsels of her old friend Jung Li and the wishes of the Emperor, she gave every encouragement to the Boxers, and on June 24th an imperial decree ordered the killing of foreigners throughout the Empire.'[87]

Griffith John admired the determination of Chang Chih-tung and Liu, the Viceroys of the Yangtze valley, to stamp out rebellion.[88] This gave him confidence that all would be well in Hankow. However, necessary precautions had to be taken. The British Consul at Hankow, Sir Everard Frazer, ordered the evacuation of British women and children. Mary Sparham and her young boy left for Shanghai and then crossed to Japan, but they did not have to stay very long and were able to return to Hankow in October.[89] The Griffith John household did have a fright one evening. The house was situated on the edge of the British concession, and immediately opposite was the Chinese city, with no barrier in between. Shouts were heard from the city, 'Beat them! Kill them!' The Chinese servant Lao Liu, known as 'Old Sixth' (probably because he was the sixth mouth to be fed in the family) went to investigate. He returned smiling broadly and reported that 'Some evil men led by the Boxers were stirring up the people to murder the foreigners. But Chang Chih Tung's men came and made them quiet. All their heads are now off.'[90] The servant was glad of a happy ending.

There were serious disturbances in Hunan. The chapel in Hengchow was razed to the ground and Peng was in danger of losing his life:[91]

Peng has had to fly saving no more than he stood up in, he was able to get his wife and mother away, he had to hide for two days almost starving and then succeeded in getting a boat. He is on his way to Hankow, and we hope soon to see him.

In a matter of weeks most of the LMS chapels in Hunan were destroyed,[92] and it was reported that four priests and thirty Roman Catholics had been murdered in Hengchow.[93]

When the rebellion was finally crushed, one thorny problem to be solved was that of indemnity. The foreign powers made claims, and the missionaries had to decide on their attitude in this matter. Were they to accept compensation for loss of life and property? Generally, missionaries were agreed that they would not accept indemnity for the loss of life, but were happy to accept it for damage to property.[94] This was the view of Griffith John, A. Bonsey, C. G. Sparham and Timothy Richard, but Hudson Taylor and Arnold Foster disagreed. John felt strongly about the matter: 'Not to ask for it would be one of the greatest blunders you could perpetrate.'[95] On 16 July, that is, during the rebellion, three of the gentry were in Griffith John's study to discuss possible payments, having been sent by the Tienmen magistrate.[96] They seemed surprised at the small amount suggested by the missionaries. A little later Griffith John, Arthur Bonsey, Henry Robertson and Edward Wills travelled to Tienmen to settle the indemnity, achieved their aim and returned with the deed of property. Arrangements were usually made with the representatives of the home government, who would draw on the central fund formed by the powers involved in the struggle of 1900, although sometimes the arrangement was made with local officials. Britain received £11.25 million of the total £67.5 million.[97]

Although most missionaries could justify accepting indemnity, it did complicate relationships between them and the government; it also created a mercenary spirit in many Chinese Christians and, according to Hudson Taylor, it was the denial of the meekness and humility of Christ.[98] It could give the Chinese the impression that the missionaries were joining in with the great powers to teach China a lesson, and the compensation could be regarded as 'blood money'.[99] Stephen Neill's comment is pertinent: 'Few missionaries followed the example, but the later history suggests that the greater wisdom was granted to Hudson Taylor.'[100]

It took some months to complete all the indemnity arrangements, but early in 1901 Griffith John was able to report, 'You will be glad to hear that all our claims have been settled for Hupeh and Hunan.'[101] He made a point of expressing his thanks to Chang for his invaluable contribution during the disturbances, doing so in two ways: during the early stages of the trouble he sent a letter to the *North China Daily News*,[102] and when it was over he visited Chang personally in order to thank him. His grandson remembers that visit because his grandfather went 'with even more than usual emphasis on his personal appearance'.[103]

Griffith John was not surprised at all at the short duration of the Boxer rising. 'This is a summer-time trouble. In three months we shall all be back at our posts.'[104] Trials and tribulations would strengthen the church:[105]

I do not take a desponding view of the future, but the reverse. There are glorious days for mission in China right before us. I am surprised to hear that people are talking about giving up the work in China; they must be mad, surely. Our prospects today in China are vastly brighter than they were six months ago. I was beginning to despond at that time; I do not despond now. My heart is full of hope, full of eager expectation. The demand for missionaries will be greater than ever; the demand for the Bible and other Christian books will be greater than ever; the demand for Western education will be greater than ever. The Chinese will be better prepared for the truth of the Gospel and truth of every kind than it has ever been in all the past.

He believed that the period was significant, and that it would mould the future of China. Yet at the same time, although optimistic about China's future as a country, he realised that his emphasis as a missionary should be on reform within the church. What was happening inside the church had to be related to what was happening outside, but the building up of the church should have its impetus in a spiritual source, and the lead must be taken by its own leaders.

'My life work has been the establishment of the Central China Mission. Translating, book making and tract making, have been my pastime.'

Griffith John to Directors, 12 February 1891.

'Had I fifty years more to spare, I would willingly and gladly give them all to the glorious work of making known to the Chinese the love of God in Jesus Christ.'

Griffith John, letter 7 April 1905.

7

From Hankow
to Swansea
1900–1912

When the country was more settled after the Boxer rising, Griffith John renewed his efforts to enter Hunan. He had been encouraged by news of the possibility of financial help from the Arthington Trust.[1] Quickened in spirit by such news, and anxious to see the persecuted Christians, the missionary set out with C. G. Sparham, Albert Greig, Ernest C. Peake and R. Wilson in April 1901.

Hunan is open

Vivid memories of the past flooded his mind, especially the opposition in Changsha. It was there in 1899 that they had obtained a house, but the magistrates would not grant the necessary stamp to make the purchase official. They wondered what kind of reception they would have on this visit. They travelled by steamboat from Hankow to Changsha, and were taken to Siangtan in the Governor's private steam launch. In Hengchow they moved around freely among the people, although it was sad to see the site of the chapel which had been destroyed during July 1900. Out of the twenty to thirty places of worship in the prefecture, all but one had been demolished.[2] The missionaries enjoyed fellowship with the persecuted Christians and marvelled at their spirit of grace and humility. Although they had suffered terribly there was no sign of bitterness or revenge. Their faith had stood the test like gold refined in fire. At Hengchow twenty-eight persons were baptised in one morning, and nine in the afternoon.[3] Griffith John mentioned one remarkable lady at Hengchow: Mrs Wu had opened her house as a meeting place and, through the meetings held there, was able to influence about a hundred persons, nine or ten of whom were baptised on that day.

During the uprising she lost everything but kept her faith.[4]

The trouble of 1900 had changed the attitude even of the officials at Changsha. The missionaries preached openly in the city, but the greatest source of joy was having the Changsha Deed with them, which had been sent from the officials by Peng, allowing the missionaries to occupy the house they had been striving to possess for two years. Griffith John was over-joyed: 'The sight of this document, I need hardly say, made my heart glad. No foreigner had ever held property in Changsha till then.'[5] His dream had been realised. 'The one great fact impressed upon our minds on this journey was this: *Hunan is open*. I have longed for many years to be able to pen that sentence of three words, but could not do so till this visit.'[6]

It was from this journey, probably, that the missionaries returned laden with presents—ceremonial umbrellas, silken scrolls and 'honorific pai', that is, tablets of praise on long poles. Griffith John's grandson recalls the occasion:[7]

> My recollection of this was a procession coming up our curved, concrete garden path, incorporating the umbrellas and 'pais' carried by Chinese Christians, who had gone down to the river Front to meet him, my Grandfather riding in a sedan chair; with a Chinese drum for me, and for me also a goat, its front legs splayed outward in protest, being hauled along by a Chinese coolie, who was pulling forwards on the end of a stout cord which was looped around its horns.

The drum, scrolls and 'pais' remained in the family, but the goat had to be put down, because its bleating made LMS meetings, which were held in Griffith John's study, impossible.

Before the end of 1901 Griffith John and Greig were back again in Hunan, staying for five weeks.[8] Speaking of Heng-chow and two other prefectures John reported that there were five thousand people waiting for baptism. There was 'a beautiful congregation of Christians' in Hengchow, and between twenty and thirty more in the prefecture. In Changsha there was a congregation of between twenty and thirty, where Griffith John had the privilege of baptising six candidates. The great need there was for a new building, and the missionary already had Tls 1,000 in hand for it.[9] So often Griffith John would appeal by example before appealing by word to others. He encouraged others by what he himself did. The work was extending its boundaries, reaching Canton in the south and the Kwangsi Province in the west. The local Christians were being endowed with a portion of the spirit of Griffith John himself.

The real difficulty was the work in Yochow.[10] It was barren land, and it was decided to move the LMS headquarters to Hengchow. Here, in Hengshan and Siangtan, rebuilt chapels were opened by the missionaries. It was at Hengchow that Griffith John celebrated his seventieth birthday, when a feast was held in his honour. The ageing missionary was able to be present, but he was not well enough to eat anything. In spite of this discomfort, 'It was a happy time.'[11] He was more confident than ever about the work in Hunan: 'I never realised more vividly than I did on this journey that the Kingdom of God was in Hunan.'[12]

His hopes being raised, nothing could keep Griffith John from Hunan. He knew that the work was in the capable hands of Peng, Greig and Peake, but he was anxious to see them and rejoice in the emerging harvest after a long period of sowing.[13] A chapel had been built in Changsha, and John and Sparham arranged to be there for the opening, which took place on 1 June 1902, an occasion which gave John tremendous joy because, after all, the place was 'that *mysterious* Changsha, that bitterly *hostile* Changsha'.[14] The city was the most important centre in Hunan, and regarded as one of the most beautiful in the whole of the Empire. Working from such a centre Griffith John knew that he would be able to follow his usual plan, that is, start in the populous places, spread out slowly, establish stations and, as soon as possible, form them into churches.

Griffith John was back again in Hunan in May 1903, this time to confirm the organisation of the churches.[15] He had drawn up rules and regulations for them, and wanted to make sure that they were implemented. Good order was necessary, both for the churches themselves and for future advancement. In Siangtan twenty-seven or twenty-eight were baptised, and six in Changsha, where, also, a military official gave John $200 to build a chapel in Sianghiang, his native city.[16] The eleventh, and last, visit to Hunan was made in 1904, which means that

Griffith John had persevered for twenty-four years. Not for a moment did he give up hope that the gospel would be rooted in that area, and that Christian churches would be established there. The missionaries in Hankow were expecting a deputation from London, and were anxious for the visitors to see as much of the work as possible, including that in Hunan. The two-man deputation, made up of George Cousins and William Bolton, was able to see what had been accomplished by a small band of workers under Griffith John's inspiring leadership.

The two men from London were joined by Griffith John for the journey north of Hankow, to Tsaoshih, Hiaukan and Hwangpi. They left by train at 7.30 a.m. on 2 March and reached Hiaukan at about 11 a.m., where they preached on that afternoon and twice the following day. On the evening of the second day there was a particular welcome for the deputation, when Cousins and Bolton were presented with umbrellas and memorials. The military official insisted on providing chairs and coolies for the next part of the journey, for which they were joined by Dr Fowler. After staying overnight with Mr Burnip in the Wesleyan house, the company arrived at Tsaoshih, where Griffith John was delighted to see the second house which had been built, and the new hospital.

Griffith John preached on the Saturday, and for the Sunday services the chapel was crammed with between five and six hundred people. 'At the close of the service 73 persons were baptised—Men, 55, women, 11, children, 7. Afternoon, I preached, Evening, Bolton, then singing of favourite hymns.' Most of Monday was spent in meeting with the Christian workers, who shared their experiences as evangelists and pastors, the great majority of them being Griffith John's spiritual children. In the evening John preached and baptised nine men. Then the company returned to Hiaukan, where Sparham was waiting for them. The first engagement the following morning was to visit the magistrate, who had invited them to a feast, but the next engagement gave them greater satisfaction, for it was the opening of the Leper Home after renovation by Dr Fowler. This occasion must have thrilled Griffith John's heart, as he had been one of the pioneers of this work. To crown the day's proceedings, the aged missionary had the privilege of baptising thirteen lepers. When the company left for Hwangpi it was dark, but the national Christians lit their torches to create a path for the travellers, who sang hymns as they journeyed forward. The Christians of Hwangpi welcomed them gladly, and an even warmer welcome greeted their arrival back in Hankow on 16 March. They reached the city to the sound of 'Guide me, O Thou Great Jehovah'.[17]

Griffith John and the deputation arrived in Hankow on 16 March, and made preparations immediately to leave for Hunan the following day. John was glad of the opportunity to show the visitors the signs of progress in the work of the gospel in Hunan. What was true of Hengchow was typical of what had happened in Hunan generally: it had a chapel, houses and a hospital bought by the LMS, and also a chapel, houses and hospital given to the LMS.[18] In many areas the churches were making steady progress.

John and Sparham continued to supervise the witness in Hunan, but divided the province into three, with Wilson in charge in the North, Burnip in the Central area, and Greig, Peake and Wilson in charge of the Southern area.[19] Griffith John was amazed at what was happening: 'The growth of the work in that province is, I think, unparalleled in the history of the Society, and there is nothing like it in China in connection with any Society.'[20] No wonder he was indignant when he heard of a suggestion that the missionaries should retire from Hunan and concentrate on Hupeh! 'It is hardly thinkable that any man in his senses could take such a view of the situation, and much less is it thinkable that he should fight for the position for a whole day.'[21] (He is probably referring here to the District Committee, because it was there that all matters of policy were discussed.)

Griffith John was jealous for the work in Hunan and did everything possible to nurture it. At the same time, he was not blind to the fact that other societies were working in the province. It would be so easy to build an empire to glorify the LMS, and jealousies could creep in and create division. Consequently the LMS wisely decided to concentrate on the particular areas of Changsha, Siangtan and Hengchow. This sphere was defined during Griffith John's eleventh and last visit to Hunan.[22] The three head stations had branches in thirteen counties, covering an area of thirteen thousand square miles, with a population of four million. Other societies established stations in Hunan with enthusiasm, and Griffith John welcomed this, regarding it as a 'wonderful development' pointing clearly to the great things God had accomplished.[23] Like Caleb of old, he had asked for a mountain and he had received it.

Education and health

After the troubles of 1900 renewed efforts had to be made in Hupeh as well as Hunan. The chapel erected in Hankow in 1891 had been enlarged in 1899 but had not been officially opened. The opening took place on the first Sunday of the new century and provided the Christians with a comfortable place of worship.[24] The large congregation loved hymn-singing and had a choir with a Chinese organist, but nothing was done at the expense of preaching. Those attending would 'listen with rapt attention to the preaching of Griffith John or one of his colleagues'.[25] The worshipping and teaching aspects were rel ated in the work in the schools, college and hospital. The work was developed as a whole—an outlook that found expression in the fact that students from the Theological, Normal and Medical schools, pupils of the High School, and hospital patients and staff, would meet in the chapel for morning worship.

The Kia Kiai school had forty boys in 1902, none paying less than Tl 500 which, Griffith John felt, was 'very satisfactory', while the school at Hanyang had about seventy boys, a most encouraging number.[26] The theological class had twelve students with whom John was much pleased. He was not completely satisfied, however, and redoubled his efforts to enlarge the Theological College. This, he knew, would demand a great deal of money, but money was soon forthcoming:[27]

Subscriptions from outside for College land and buildings
Our viceroy, Chang Chih-tung, sent us $300, our Governor, Iuan Fang, sent us $200, our Provincial Treasurer sent us $200, the Hankow Taotai sent us $200, the Hunan Government sent us Tls 500, the equivalent of $689.66.

Support from outside was still strong, and Chang's friendship was proving to be lasting. Two 'dear friends' also helped him, but the bulk of the cost was met by Griffith John himself.[28]

Such a response enabled the building to go ahead, and before the end of 1903 the missionary was able to say, 'The new Divinity College and surrounding ground are getting the finishing touches put to them.'[29] Looking at the completed work in November of the same year, he thought that all the buildings were 'exceedingly nice'.[30] He was glad to present the College as a gift to the Mission. The building was pleasant and commodious:[31]

> The College is a handsome two-storey, red brick building, with verandah on four sides, and occupies an area of 84ft by 65ft. It contains lecture hall, capable of seating 200, library, class rooms and dormitories, affording accommodation for sixty students. At the other end of the same compound is the High School, with upwards of a hundred students.

It was dedicated on 18 April 1904, while the London deputation consisting of George Cousins and William Bolton was in Hankow. They took part in the afternoon service, together with Griffith John who presided, and C. G. Sparham and others. Greetings were received from representatives of the American Church Mission, the Wesleyans and the American Baptists. The students and preachers had already met in the morning to express their thanks for the College.[32] Only one thing was lacking, and that was a proper College chapel, but in a few years' time that too was provided.[33]

Hand in hand with the College work went that of the hospital. Griffith John had consistently emphasised the essential relationship between the evangelistic and medical aspects of missionary work. There was now a new opportunity to reiterate that conviction and to realise a marked development in both areas. Considerable improvements were made during that year (1904). New quarters were set up to meet the needs of sick men and women, outpatients and medical students. Linked to the women's hospital was the outpatients' department, double-storeyed, with a narrow passage leading to a courtyard and other buildings. There was a hospital for men, a dispensary, guest room and medical students' quarters. The patients were required to bring their own bedding and clothes. During their stay in hospital they would not only receive medical treatment, but would also be taught from the Scriptures. Even the walls were covered with scenes from the Bible.[34]

The Mission was making good progress, but Griffith John was finding it more and more difficult to cope with all the demands of the work. He had experienced periods of suffering in 1892 and 1896-7, but from 1902 he began to feel his frailty keenly.[35] During that year he suffered from dysentery which left him very weak, and even the stay in Kuling did not have the usual healing influence on mind and body: 'The change has done me good, but I am getting old, and I shall not leave this year with as much energy as in former years.'[36] The following year he was quite unwell with influenza, and this made him fearful of the heat of the summer.[37] He mourned his condition, yet it was not self-pity.[38] When some of his colleagues expressed their concern, John told them they were being over-anxious 'about the old man'.[39] The old man, however, was brought low in 1905 with the sudden onset of the cold weather, making him feel at times as if he were going to collapse.[40]

Other clouds were gathering in the already troubled sky. The young Robertson, whom John held in high esteem, died of typhoid,[41] and the death of Hudson Taylor was a severe blow as they had been 'warm hearted friends right through'.[42] The day before his death the two friends had met in Hankow, and before Taylor left for Hunan they sang a hymn together as on previous occasions. There was some sweetness in the bitter cup, not only because of their friendship, but also in the fact that Hudson Taylor died in Changsha after addressing the churches there.[43] They both regarded the triumph in Changsha as a jewel in their crown of success.

There were encouragements as well. The news of revival in Wales thrilled Griffith John's heart. He was 'deeply interested' in it and prayed that it would flow to England and China: 'I am longing to see some great manifestation of God in China.'[44] In one of his letters to the Directors he enclosed a message for Evan Roberts, anxious to impress on his mind the need of China and the whole heathen world.[45] When he heard that the revival had reached India, John was further inspired to pray for such a movement of the Spirit of God in China.[46] The burden of 1875 was still on his heart.

Another source of joy was his translation work. He committed himself anew to the task in 1902, and in September of that year was glad to report, 'The Pentateuch is finished and carefully revised.'[47] Writing from Kuling in 1904, he informed Sparham that 1 Kings would be finished 'tomorrow' in spite of difficulties with 'Solomon's temple', which he regarded as a 'puzzle'. However, the translator was confident about the nature of his translation: 'I think, however, that my translation gives a clear sense, and that is more than the others have succeeded in doing.'[48] By 1905 there was both confidence and doubt in his report: 'The Old Testament is done now to the end of Proverbs. There is, however, a big piece left undone, and I often wonder if I shall ever finish the work.'[49]

Griffith John could never completely forget the fluctuating condition of his health and his inability to accomplish all that he desired, but for a short time in 1905 all the problems faded away. It was the year of Jubilee. Griffith John had been fifty years in China and it was time to celebrate. By the beginning of October 1905, 'Letters are pouring in on me from all quarters.'[50] Many of them came from Wales, and the tired missionary must have appreciated the LMS's gift of a travelling bedstead.[51] The Congregational Churches of Wales responded to the occasion by taking up the two appeals made by Griffith John, one in April 1905 and the other in September 1906.[52] At the suggestion of Sidney Clarke, who was a deacon with the Rev. Wynne Evans in Chester, it was decided to collect a hundred thousand sixpences. Clarke himself promoted the scheme, selling his home and business, contributing two thousand sixpences and visiting Griffith John in China.[53] It was natural for Ebenezer, Swansea, to respond enthusiastically, and Griffith John's cousin, of the same name, hoped that 'they will come out top'.[54] He obviously believed that a little church pride was in order! In just over a year the same cousin informed him that Ebenezer had collected £43-1-0, which meant 1,722 sixpences.[55] The LMS was also glad of the response, because the Directors were endeavouring to raise £12,000 for the work in Hankow and all the money needed for the College chapel had not been received. A remarkable example was set by Mrs Seth Smith who aimed at collecting £600

and, in February 1907, was only £40 short of this target.[56] Most
of the money had come from within the family, including £50
from H. O. Wills who, with his brother, had grown rich during
the industrial progress of the Victorian period. Many churches
and good causes benefited from this family's generosity.[57]

In Hankow itself three meetings were held to celebrate
Griffith John's fifty years in China.[58] On Sunday 24 September,
the first meeting was held in the chapel in Hankow. Long
before the service was due to start the courtyard was full of
people. 'Inside, the chapel was tastefully decorated with scrolls
and embroideries, and crowded to the door by a large congregation.'[59] It was a stiflingly hot afternoon, but that in no way
dampened the enthusiasm of those present. A number spoke in
the two-and-a-half-hour meeting, both representatives from
churches and missionaries, including J. Young Allen who was
visiting Hankow at the time. The following Thursday a reception was held in the 'Rest', giving Griffith John's foreign friends
an opportunity to join with him in celebration. Good wishes
were expressed on their behalf by Arnold Foster, who surveyed
the development of the work during the 50-year period. 'With
three hearty cheers for Dr John the gathering separated.'[60]

A few weeks later the Chinese Christians held their own
special meeting in an enormous pavilion erected for the occasion. It was a joyous event:[61]

> Just over Dr John's head was suspended the Chinese ideo-
> graph for 'love', made of white chrysanthemums; and
> indeed the key-note of the afternoon was 'love'. 'He has
> loved us' came again and again from the lips of the speak-
> ers. It is something to have taught this great lesson, even
> though fifty years be spent in the teaching.
>
> From *thirty-one counties* in Hupeh and Hunan came a
> delegate or a congratulatory letter. Such is the vast extent of
> the Central China Mission's field! It was one of the most
> moving sights of the jubilee celebrations, native or foreign.
>
> Then—most significant fact—just before Dr John deliv-
> ered a telling speech, came deputations of school children,
> boys and girls (remember it was in China), with their floral
> offerings and good wishes to the man who had begun the
> great work that was setting them free.

Griffith John met with all the delegates present. They would walk up to him, bow, and congratulate him on behalf of the national church.[62] Besides his love for the work and the Chinese people, the other characteristic that was mentioned was his perseverance. He had been in China for fifty years, but he was still battling on, ready to face new challenges.

Before the end of that year of celebration Griffith John was unwell once again. This was a cause for concern to his daughter, but she was more optimistic when she wrote to the Directors:[63]

Dec 29 (1905) my Father had a slight stroke, when for some days he lost the use of the right leg. His recovery has been wonderful, and though still feeling very weak and unable to take up his usual routine, he is able to do a great deal of writing in his study each day.

Early in 1906 three doctors examined the ailing Griffith John, and were agreed in their diagnosis. He had suffered from a slight stroke due to his intense application to translation work, his advanced age, and his prolonged period of service in China.[64] Reporting to the Directors, Arnold Foster, on the basis of the doctors' opinion, made it clear that 'both [John and Sparham] *must* leave China *as early as possible*'.[65] John was convinced that Sparham should leave, but he was reluctant to do so himself, and it was not until the end of March that he agreed to accompany the Sparhams to America, where he would spend some time with his sons Griffith and David. Before leaving, he had to refuse the invitation to be chairman of the Congregational Union of England and Wales, once again responding with that word 'Impossible'.[66] The words he spoke before his departure reveal much of his heart. When at the meeting of the District Committee Arnold Foster expressed sympathy with him and wished him well, Griffith John was only able to respond briefly, but his reply included the words, 'God gave me to China.' The official farewell took place on the second Sunday of April. Foster presided; T'ang, the veteran hospital evangelist, prayed; Liu expressed the good wishes of the church, and Sparham gave a 'stirring address'. When Griffith John responded, he did so almost in a whisper:[67]

May the Spirit FILL your hearts. This is our great need; the
FILLING OF THE HOLY SPIRIT. Read 1 Thess 5:12-22, Quench not
the Spirit, then I shall have no fear for you on my return.
May God have you in His keeping.

His body was weak, but his conviction concerning the Holy
Spirit was still strong. His mind was not clear, but he was
still optimistic, and thinking of returning to China. The
future was uncertain, but he was still sure of God's providence.

America

On his arrival in America, Griffith John was delighted to see
his two sons again after a separation of twenty-five years. He
stayed most of the time with Griffith, an engineer, at 11
Delevan Terrace, Yonkers, moving occasionally to stay with
David, who was a doctor, at 182 Nepperhan Avenue. Griffith
John had never seen the grandchildren, but he soon settled
down with them and was delighted with their company. In
Delevan Terrace, Margaret was 'charming', Bessie 'silent as
ever'; in Nepperhan Avenue, Arthur was a 'fine little fellow',
and Wallace, whom he liked at first, was 'moody',[68] for which
condition the grandfather thought he had the remedy: 'I
believe a good thrashing now and again would do him a vast
amount of good.'[69]

It was not all joy, however, because early in December 1906
Griffith John was quite unwell, and David had to be called in.
The elderly missionary felt he was losing his grip in his right
hand, but he did manage, with difficulty, to write a number of
letters before the end of the year.[70] Although better by the
beginning of the new year, David tried to persuade him not to
write long letters and articles. 'I am coming to the conclusion
that he is right', he conceded.[71]

Although he did cut down on his activities, Griffith John
was still busy. He was anxious to see the 'Biography' through
the press, on which he was working when taken ill in December. 'I have just finished the Biography', he wrote, and in
the same letter referred to Wardlaw Thompson: 'Mr Thompson
has done his part of the work extremely well.'[72] It seems from
this that Griffith John was himself responsible for the content,

but that Thompson had done the actual writing. It was John also who decided on the photographs to be included. It is a pity that neither of them was as selective as he might have been; greater care about this would have made this important work more readable.

Griffith John would spend some time every day reading the newspapers. Some of them arrived regularly, while the Shanghai papers 'come in a heap'. On one occasion the *North China Herald* and three *Celestial Empires* arrived by the same post. Another source of information concerning China was the *Missionary Review*, and Griffith John would send information to Dr Pierson for inclusion in that paper. His link with A. T. Pierson has a Welsh connection. Pierson sent the Welshman a gift of his *New Acts of the Apostles* and informed him that he was going to Wales to help with the Revival (1904-5). The paper he edited, *Missionary Review of the World*, was influential in many countries, including Wales.[73] *The Tyst* (Welsh Congregational weekly) kept the missionary in touch with his own country, while the *Christian World*, *British Weekly* and *British Congregationalist* informed him of developments in Britain in general. George Sparham, who had left for England, would send relevant material to his father-in-law, including the *Daily Chronicle* when there were matters of missionary interest, and the *Somerset and Wilts Journal* when it included an article by Gillison.[74] Not only did Griffith John read widely, but he would also contribute to the papers of the period, including the *Christian World* and the *British Congregationalist*.[75] He was ready too to help a missionary endeavour like the Young People's Missionary Movement, writing the introduction to its handbook in 1907.[76]

Letters, newspapers, periodicals and sermons fed the flame of Griffith John's concern for China. Though living in Yonkers he still thought of that country as his home, and the desire to return was strong. He was quite restless in America and would write regularly to the Directors concerning China. He did not hesitate to advise them on Hupeh and Hunan. Mr McFarland needed a colleague in Hunan and all the stations there were undermanned. In Hankow one man should devote all his time to the Normal School, and one man, at least, should give all his time to the Theological College. He had heard that there was a recommendation to abandon the work in Changsha and Siangtan, news which 'has almost taken my breath away'.[77] This was unbelievable in the light of the work which had been accomplished, accomplished sacrificially by himself, with the faithful financial support of Mrs Craven and her father, who had contributed £100 to the work in Hunan.[78]

In the realm of education Griffith John was anxious to keep the Normal School as an LMS institution. Suggestions were being made that Christian teachers should concentrate on entering Government schools. While not entirely opposed to this move, Griffith John was convinced that 'the first and chief need' was for men in *mission* schools.[79] He welcomed the desire for education which was becoming more general in China, but saw danger in it because the aim was to make China a great military power: 'You go on making the Chinese strong, without attempting to make them good, and the yellow peril, so much talked about, and so much dreaded by some, may become more than a dream.'[80] The missionary schools should grasp the opportunity and take full advantage of the craving for education; this could turn out not only for the good of the children in the schools but for the good of the whole country. It was not just mission schools that were needed, but 'distinctively Christian schools'. In the opinion of the Chinese people these schools were better in terms of teachers and moral standards[81]— in marked contrast to the Government schools which were Confucian in spirit and aim. In promoting this aspect of education, Griffith John continued to emphasise that the LMS was still an evangelistic agency, and that it should never lose sight of that fact.[82]

Griffith John felt that there was real need to revive the work of the Central China Religious Tract Society (CCRTS), but did not believe that would happen without the presence of himself and Archibald: 'We shall see what can be done towards reviving it when we get back.'[83] The workers themselves did not escape criticism. He was very critical of Stewart, and Miss Cousins should have given greater notice of her marriage if she had the good of the Mission at heart, which, obviously, she did not have, according to John, who was of the opinion that 'The born missionaries I fear are extremely few.'[84] As far as Bonsey was concerned, 'Bonsey of course is too busy to write to anyone!!'[85] Archibald, however, Griffith John liked very much, and he was looking forward to working with Bitton after returning to China.[86]

By this time there were many uncertainties in Griffith John's life: his own health, future plans concerning a visit to England, and what would happen even if he returned to China. One thing remained the same, without a shadow of doubt, and that was the gospel he had to preach. Although there were bound to be some changes in different periods, the basic gospel could not change; it had been given for all times. Consequently, Griffith John was grieved when R. J. Campbell made known his radical views concerning the Christian faith, and during his stay in America the Welshman gave much attention to them.[87] He made known his feelings when he heard the Rev. Campbell Morgan of Westminster Chapel, London, preaching in the Presbyterian Church, Fifth Avenue, on 11 August 1907, on Christ's dealings with the Pharisees. The preacher dealt with some accounts of the Saviour meeting with different people as recorded in the Gospel of Luke. He brought out the oneness of Christ with humanity, yet showing at the same time that he was beyond all men. The wonder of Christ's Person was vividly portrayed, and this gave the Welshman much pleasure. When they met in the vestry Griffith John thanked the preacher, saying, 'Thank God, as long as Christ is preached in that way I will not fear the future.'[88] It is interesting to note Campbell Morgan's response to meeting Griffith John. The Englishman felt he had known the Welshman for a long time because of his reputation, and felt almost a reverent fear in the presence of the highly esteemed missionary.

Griffith John was glad of the reassurance he had received from one of the staunch champions of the gospel of salvation by grace alone, but doubts still lurked in his mind as to the influence of the new ideas. The main culprit was R. J. Campbell, but he was influencing others:[89]

I am pained to see how the great facts of the gospel, the facts on which we have been building in China, are openly called in question these days in your pulpits. And what is given as a substitute? Conjections, bog, quick-sand. What would be the use of taking that stuff to China? Translate it into Chinese and it vanishes into thin air.

Campbellism would not do for China. 'It would never convert China.'[90] It was the 'real gospel' that should be sent to
that country, that gospel which the churches had proclaimed
from generation to generation, and that gospel which was
saving the Chinese. It gladdened Griffith John's heart to
know that 'Rogers and Campbell Morgan were speaking
out',[91] but he was disgusted that R. J. Campbell had allowed
that 'anti-Christ', Bernard Shaw, into the City Temple pulpit.[92] As for Campbell, Shaw's only strength was his personality: his theology was as weak as water.[93] If Jesus Christ was
not the Son of God there was no gospel to be preached.
Griffith John had some grounds for optimism from a letter
he received from the secretary of the LMS, and the fact that a
middle-of-the-road man, R. F. Horton, had come out against
Campbell.[94]

The desire to preach the unchanging Christ to the Chinese
was still strong, and the desire to go back to that country was
still alive in Griffith John's heart. At the beginning of 1907 he
had said, 'I am confident that I shall be in China by this time
next year.'[95] William Carey's motto was still meaningful to him:
'Expect great things from God; attempt great things for God.'[96]
He *had* to go back to China and decided to leave before the end
of 1907.

Hankow and Swansea
The Sparhams and Griffith John boarded the *Celtic* on 5
November and had a good journey in spite of some fog and
half a day of gale, arriving in Hankow on 18 December. The
'old man' stood the journey well, but as his son-in-law commented, 'The marks of increased age are upon him.'[97] Welcome
meetings had been arranged for the company: Sparham
preached in the morning, and the chapel was crammed for the
afternoon meeting. Griffith John went to see the Jubilee buildings, which 'exceed my most sanguine expectation', and
preached in English and Chinese during the last Sunday in
December.[98] The text of the English sermon was 'Jesus Christ,
the same yesterday, today, yea, and for ever'. The preacher
urged those present to preach Christ, and keep close to him, so
that he would be faithfully represented before the people of

China. Some of the missionaries were ill, but the returning missionary resolved to help them: 'I am longing to help them, and hope to be able to do so in a day or two.'[99] He set himself a well-defined programme of work, undertaking translation work in the morning, College and general work in the afternoon, and avoiding all strenuous work in the evening.[100]

The welcome he received thrilled Griffith John's heart, but there was a shadow of gloom as he assessed the situation. He came to the conclusion that 'The genius of the mission is not what it was.'[101] He deplored the cutting down of the number of men, the way they were moved around from place to place, and the lack of efficiency in administration. To complicate matters, A. J. Bonsey had been asked to become a member of the Municipal Council, a possibility which alarmed Griffith John because of Bonsey's ill health and the time demanded by such a commitment. The veteran missionary was glad that the Medical School and the High School were progressing satisfactorily, but not so the Normal and Divinity schools, while the evangelistic work was at a low ebb. Thanks to Mrs Jones, the wife of Lewis Jones, the women's section was showing marked progress, in contrast to the men's work.[102]

At seventy years of age it must have been frustrating for Griffith John to witness the changes, knowing that he did not have the energy to respond. He tried to convince himself that it was not so: 'I can face work to any extent', but 'I cannot face worry and depression.'[103] There is a suggestion of desperation in his response that, if things did not change, he would have to reconsider his relationship with the Society. His colleagues were also concerned, as letters written by Arnold Foster, Arthur Bonsey and R. Wilson make clear. Wilson, for example, was sure that 'The difficulty will be to keep Dr John from undertaking too much.'[104]

A few days after Wilson had written to the Directors, Griffith John, in the best of spirits, with Mary Sparham, her son Brynmor, and Nelson Bitton, paid a visit to Siokan, a place very close to his heart. He had visited it so many times, and on this occasion was so proud to point out the house where all the pioneering work had started. Early on Saturday night he was unwell, but he managed to preach on Sunday morning. Dr Fowler had to travel back with the company to Hankow, and he made sure that Griffith John was comfortable. On his return he had to keep to his bed and was unnaturally quiet.[105]

Illness was creating problems at Hankow. Not only was Griffith John a sick man, but Arthur Bonsey had collapsed, and there were fears about Bernard Upward's nervous condition. Arnold Foster was now of the opinion that 'Dr John is not in a condition to form a sound judgement as to the real needs of the work, but he still has his former intensity of feeling as to what must *not* be done.'[106] Foster felt that this placed him and others in an awkward position, as they had to be so careful not to upset the veteran missionary. When he did recover a little he again attended the District Committee meetings, which were held in his study. Some of the matters discussed must have pleased him. It was decided to name the High School, when reopened, the 'Griffith John College', and thanks were sent to Mrs Seth Smith and Mrs Melville Wills for the generous gift of the College Chapel and organ in memory of Rev. R. Wilson, one of John's early colleagues.[107] Other members of the family were also feeling the strain: George Sparham had to take on more and more responsibility in the Mission, and did his best to help Mary to care for her father, because 'He is passing through one of the heaviest trials of his life.'[108] George Sparham would write as many letters as possible for his father-in-law, but some of them he insisted on writing himself, and he was determined to get better. The main problem was the pain in his head, but as Sparham said, 'The old *will* to do is as strong as ever.'[109] Even in this weak condition Griffith John still lectured to the five theological students for an hour or two, two or three times a week. He had already taken them through two of the Gospels. It was essential, however, for him to have more rest, and once again he had to go to Kuling for a few months. During that period the dull pain in the head remained, but his general health was fairly good.[110] Not only were Mary and George concerned for him, but he was also concerned for them and wondered very often how long they were going to last under such strain.

After returning to Hankow, his condition would change from day to day, but he still managed to take his class occasionally.[111] One day he would be feeling tired; the next he would stay in bed; the third day he would attend to his class but return tired, depressed and complaining of a headache. After recovering a little he would express a desire to do something, resolving that once the headache cleared he would start on his translation work again. One upset occasioned painful lameness for a short time, and although this passed it signified that his health was deteriorating. Bonsey felt it was impossible to reason with him: 'If only he could have kept to his translation work! But he cannot do any translation work and ought not to attempt the administrative.'[112] He would not give in. Early in 1909 he was attending District Committee meetings, and in April was a member of a sub-committee to consider a second master's house at Han Kia Tang. That same month Griffith John must have been cheered, as the clock which had been suggested for his Jubilee was on its way to the College Tower. Even this token of appreciation could not keep him from Kuling that year, although he was free from severe pain. A welcome visitor at Kuling during this stay was the Rev. F. B. Meyer, who held meetings there which were a combination of the Keswick Convention and the Shanghai Conference.[113] It is not clear whether Griffith John was present at these meetings, but there is no doubt that he would have liked to be present, as the message was that of holiness, which he, like his friend Hudson Taylor, had pursued all his life.

From the time he returned from America until October 1909, Griffith John had participated in the affairs of the Mission, indeed much more than he should have done. On 6 October 1909 he suffered his fourth stroke, 'the worst that he has had', affecting his speech and his mind.[114] His mind started to wander from place to place; sometimes he was back in South Wales in his father's house, or at his grave longing for him to come out. Even in this condition his pulse was as strong as that of a middle-aged man.[115] The Sparhams had to engage a sailor from Shanghai, originally from Cornwall, to help them in the home. Such help was vital, for it was the beginning of a distressing and upsetting time for the family. Day turned into night, and night into day, creating pressure on George Sparham that could have led to a breakdown. During the early months of 1910 Griffith John was getting feebler, but he did go to Kuling again, driven by a Chinese chauffeur in a motor car and taken to the hills by chair.[116]

During the last months of 1910 and the beginning of 1911,

the usual reports concerning Griffith John's health were 'fairly strong', 'restless' and 'weaker'.[117] Not only was there concern about the missionary's health, but the political situation was causing alarm, as the Revolution Party was asserting itself, especially in Wuchang. Griffith John managed to go to Kuling for a brief period, where he was very quiet and made no use of the veranda specially built for him.[118] The party returned in September, and between then and 10 October events moved quickly, Although the takeover by the revolutionaries appeared sudden, careful plans had been made beforehand, which was the main reason why so little blood was shed during this period. The people generally were surprised, and so was Sun Yat-sen. He was away at the time, but he returned before the end of the year to lead the Party. At long last the Manchu dynasty had fallen. It was the end of a long decline lasting throughout the nineteenth century. Many attempts had been made to overthrow it, but at last it had been crushed.[119]

Because of the trouble Griffith John was taken to Butterfield's Steamer for his safety, but he had to leave hurriedly and found refuge in the CIM centre.[120] An emergency meeting held on 14 October gave authority for Griffith John to be taken to Shanghai, and on to England if necessary. By this time there was growing fear that imperialist forces would attack the revolutionaries before the safety of the foreigners was assured.[121] The pioneer missionary was taken safely to the Victoria Nursing Home in Shanghai, and almost immediately arrangements were made to send him to England. His passage was booked on the SS *Atsuta Maru*, and he left on 17 November 1911.[122] George Sparham describes the scene immediately before leaving Shanghai:[123]

Dr John is as you know suffering from senile dementia, he is now usually quiet and the delusions that so troubled him at an early stage of the trouble have now almost if not entirely ceased. He is however in a very pitiable condition, and is as helpless as a baby of a few months. He cannot feed himself or attend to himself in any way whatever. The situation is the more difficult in that he is so heavy and also strong.

Medical reports had been received from two doctors explaining

Griffith John's medical condition, and also meeting the legal requirement to make George Sparham a 'committee of Dr John's estate'.[124]

The pioneer of Central China, the buoyant young man who had defied all the opposition in the Empire, was now carried from that country as a helpless baby. He had arrived when the Taiping rebels were fighting for the realisation of their concept of a great China: he was leaving when the Revolutionary Party had gained the ascendancy. He had always believed that such a day would come, and now he had witnessed it, yet was unable to appreciate what was happening. He had always believed that the Christian message and the Christian mission-ary would contribute substantially to the formation of the new China. The giant who had been slumbering was now fully awake, and the awakening was to give the Christian church a greater opportunity for advance. This is what Griffith John had hoped and prayed for, but it would be interesting to know what he would have thought of the China of Sun Yat-sen.

Weak and confused, Griffith John was taken to a nursing home in Clapton, North London. It must have been a heart-breaking experience for his grandson to visit him in that place: 'His frame, never big, was meagre and shrunken. His eyes saw but without comprehension. His firm, short step had become a pitiful, tottering shuffle.'[125] His grandfather would only repeat what the grandson said to him, words such as *'Duw a'ch bendithio'* (God bless you) and *'Da boch chi'* (Goodbye).[126]

The end came on 26 July 1912, and his body was taken to Swansea for burial in the cemetery of the Congregational Church in Sketty. It was laid to rest alongside the body of the Rev. Thomas Rees, former minister of Ebenezer, Swansea, and a friend of Griffith John. The funeral cortège, including Guto Sparham and A. J. Bonsey and Wardlaw Thompson (both of the LMS), was welcomed at High Street Station by a party including the Mayor of Swansea, Hopkyn Rees (LMS) and Penar Griffiths. Vast crowds thronged the streets, and Ebenezer was full for the funeral service. As the coffin was brought in Llewelyn Bevan ARCO played the 'Dead March' from *Saul*. The speakers were the Rev. William James (Minister of Ebenezer), Wardlaw Thompson, A. J. Bonsey and the Rev Silyn Evans (Aberdare), editor of the *Tyst*, who related the story of Elijah being taken up by a chariot in a whirlwind and applied it to the taking of Griffith John.[127] When Hudson Taylor died in Changsha, this account of Elijah's death was likewise quoted by someone close to him.[128]

Griffith John would have rejoiced to be in such company, because he shared their secret of triumph over death. He would have rejoiced also in the response of a friend of the family with whom Guto Sparham stayed. Returning from the funeral, her comment was: 'It was not a funeral. It was a revival.'[129] He had given his life to preach the Christ who had gained a decisive victory over death, and he had always looked to God the Holy Spirit to revive his work in him personally and in the church generally. In his funeral service hundreds of people were given the opportunity to share in that victory, and to experience the quickening work of the Spirit of God.

A brief service was held at the graveside, when William Owen (China) and D. Picton Jones (Africa), both of the LMS, took part. The story of the long life was summarised in the words inscribed on the coffin:[130]

Griffith John D.D.
Chinese Missionary
Born 1831. Died 1912
'A true and faithful soldier of Jesus Christ'

The vast majority present had never seen him, but all of them were of one heart as they paid tribute to this great man of God.

The photograph of Griffith John, found in so many chapel vestries, continually reminded the people of Wales of the one who symbolised all that was heroic in a missionary. For many of them he belonged to that realm which is above criticism. Centenary celebrations were held in a number of places in 1931, including Swansea and Liverpool,[131] and his memory lingered in the minds of the minority even in 1963. In November of that year a Memorial Garden was opened at Brynmelin, Swansea, near Griffith John's home.[132] It was a grey, cold day, but about two hundred people gathered together for the occasion. The Mayor of Swansea performed the opening ceremony, and the Rev. Griffith John Sparham unveiled the plaque. A young people's meeting and a pageant presented by the churches of Gowerton were held in Ebenezer, the day ending with a missionary rally conducted by the Rev. Glyn Richards. Speakers at this included Rev. Myfanwy Wood and Rev. Maxwell Janes (both of the LMS), and there was a response from G. J. Sparham. The choice of a garden was very appropriate, as Griffith John's life was fragrant with grace and pointed to the beauty of the Lord Jesus Christ.

'God and His love; Christ and His Cross, the Gospel as God's *one* remedy for China and the whole world, were realities to him. His trust in God was implicit.'

Part of Griffith John's tribute to Hudson Taylor.
The words could be applied to the Welshman himself.
A. J. Broomhall, *Hudson Taylor*, Book Seven, 512

'*Life* it is that has come suddenly into our midst, not death.'

Words spoken by one of the company
present at Hudson Taylor's death.
A. J. Broomhall, *Hudson Taylor*, Book Seven, 510.

'It was not a funeral. It was a revival.'

Words spoken by a friend of the family
immediately after Griffith John's funeral service.

'Preach, Preach, Preach.'

Griffith John's consistent exhortation
to missionaries.

8
Griffith John:
character, creed and contribution

Griffith John was a striking figure physically: he was short of stature and broad-shouldered with a large head. He was strong both physically and spiritually, and at all times an individualist. Evan Bryant, fellow countryman and fellow worker, remembered vividly his first meeting with him:[1]

> His costume was the reverse of clerical. A Scotch cap on his head, a black tie round his neck, a long light brown jacket, and a stout stick in his hand. He walked with short, fast, firm steps, as one who had something pressing to do, and meant to do it.

Nearer to the end of the century a grandson referred to his grandfather's quick, short step, adding that he was usually dressed in black, the only difference from his former attire being that he now wore a Shakespeare collar and a black clerical bow-tie.[2] He was so unlike his friend Arnold Foster, who was tall, good-looking, and a person who, during his student days at least, would enjoy a glass of sherry and smoke a cigar.[3] Such luxuries did not appeal to the Welsh Nonconformist taste of the person who had been brought up in Ebenezer, Swansea, and at the College in Brecon. Even the 'moderates' in Ebenezer would be unhappy with the sherry.

The quick step and the stout stick point to Griffith John's determination. Once he was convinced of a particular path, it was difficult, if not impossible, to dissuade him from taking it. He had an iron will. His determination and strong constitution enabled him to endure suffering and fatigue. His courage, both

191

physical and moral, was exemplary. It was this courage that was revealed during his journey with Alexander Wylie in 1868, and that enabled him to face the two hundred in Wei village, to visit Taiping rebel territory and defy local officials. On a number of occasions he knew what it was to lose blood, and to be overcome by sickness and heat; but he would still persevere.

His determination stemmed from human resolution and superhuman faith. Griffith John believed strongly in the gospel and in its power to change the lives of men and women. He had faith not only in the gospel of God, but in the providence of God as well. The missionary believed that whatever he was doing was meaningful. Nothing was an accident. He was not working in the context of a closed universe, but in a world which belonged to God, and into which God had come in the Person of Christ, in whom the Father was revealed. God's purpose was not always clear, but he could be trusted at all times. He was working out his purposes in the present for the future good of China and, also, for eternity. This latter dimension marked out the missionary from those who only worked for the political and commercial welfare of the Chinese. According to Griffith John, the three main religions of China— Confucianism, Taoism and Buddhism—had no satisfactory answer to the eternal state after death. It was the Lord Jesus Christ alone who had brought real life and immortality to light.

Consequently, the missionary was enthusiastic, and could enthuse others as well, whether fellow missionaries or national leaders. One who met him described him as 'the magnetic little Welshman',[4] and added that it was dangerous to talk to him if you wanted to avoid your responsibility concerning overseas mission. He could stick to a person, as well as to his work, like a leech. It is significant that when he first left for China he pinpointed what he believed to be a person's strength. Quoting Sir T. L. Buxton's words in his Journal, 'The longer I live, the more I am certain that the great difference between men, between the feeble and the powerful, the great and the insignificant, is energy—invincible determination', the Welshman added, 'Which I fully believe and upon which I am determined to act'.[5] This is a noble sentiment, but one that brings with it the attendant danger of misusing power. Griffith John believed he had gained the victory over this temptation when he left Wales for China. He could have been one of the most popular preachers of the day in his home country, and that would have given him profound personal satisfaction. That desire, however, had to be crucified, and his energy channelled to the service of China. His responsibility, he felt, was to consecrate his energy, and whatever greatness and power might follow would be to the glory of his God.

Strengths can also be weaknesses. Griffith John was enthusiastic, but at times this could make him stubborn. A good example of this is his translation work. Many in China turned away from him because he was bent on doing his own thing. He was possibly unwise in not going to Shanghai in 1890, where he could have worked with other missionaries. Yet, on the other hand, one might argue that his stubbornness was justified, in that he completed his work on the New Testament and made considerable advance on the Old Testament, whereas the panels appointed at Shanghai took much longer than the Welshman to complete their respective tasks. His optimism also clouded his judgement at times—regarding the Taiping rebels, for example—and he could be simplistic in his analysis of the nature of the opposition in China. According to Griffith John, the officials were to be blamed for the hostility to foreigners in general and missionaries in particular, while the people were, on the whole, friendly. In many situations this was the case, but there is also evidence that the *people* in China could adopt an anti-foreign attitude: 'Overt popular hostility to missionaries and converts, moreover, was much in evidence throughout China in the latter decades of the nineteenth century, and this hostility was far from being the product solely of incitement by "superiors".'[6]

Griffith John's stubbornness, however, did not weaken his sympathy with all kinds of people. He had a warm heart, and though he confessed to finding it difficult to love the Chinese, the unanimous testimony during the celebrations of 1905 was, 'He has loved us.'[7] This love also sanctified human affections. Griffith John loved his home and his family, and it must have been heart-breaking for him to leave all his children in Britain except for Mary. This is an agonising problem for the overseas worker, but Griffith John knew that if there was a divine call, then human sacrifices had to be made. Even so, the possible emotional harm to such children can be very real. Mary was with her father, and this was a tremendous joy to him. In the home there would be family prayers, grace at meals, and on Sunday evenings time even to relax, which must have been precious to the industrious missionary. He would lie on the sofa singing from the Welsh hymn-book to Mary's accompaniment, 'Llanfair' being one of their favourite tunes. He could relax and he could be cheerful, but he was a fundamentally serious person.[8] Thomas Bryson used to say of him, 'Levity is as far from him as from a Chinese sage',[9] and his grandson could speak of a 'Puritanical and stern side to his nature'.[10] No cards or alcohol were allowed in the home, not because they were evil in and of themselves, but because they could lead to gambling and excessive drinking. When the young lad went with a friend to the Russian Church and spent two hours holding a taper candle, his grandfather was disgusted because that was 'idolatry'. A ballet dance in a Christmas play was 'overcast with all possible vice'.[11]

A time of celebration like the coronation of Edward VII brings out the conflicting attitudes in Griffith John. Arrangements were made at Kuling to mark the occasion with a bonfire, but news was received that Edward had appendicitis. The missionary and his friends decided to continue with the bonfire as it was an opportunity for them to enjoy themselves, but it is possible that they were also glad of an excuse to glorify the monarchy of England. In the opinion of his grandson, his grandfather was no 'jingo-patriot', but 'He was glad in an intelligent way of the achievements of Britain.'[12] It is true that he was not influenced to the same extent as were some other missionaries by the pomp and glory of the British Empire; his devotion to the Chinese people would hold him back from such an extravagant attitude. Yet there is something sad in the way he could at times refer to himself as an 'Englishman', and even use that term to create fear in the Chinese people. He became more pro-British during the last decade of the century. The Manchu dynasty was being weakened; English was given more prominence in education, and the partition of China was becoming a possibility. There were so many foreign powers with interests in China that it would be wrong, according to Griffith John, for England to stand aside. If the Yangtze Valley fell to English hands, it would be 'a cause of great rejoicing'.[13]

The energetic, enthusiastic and stubborn Griffith John set high standards for himself, and he expected others to do likewise. He was totally committed to the work in China himself, and was very critical of any slackness in other missionaries. There are hints of criticisms in his letters to the Directors, but he is much more open in the letters to his son-in-law, mentioning many by name and even ridiculing their shortcomings. As usual, he was quite specific in his demands: 'We want men with the three G's at least—grace, gumption and grit'.[14] *Grace* was essential; and yet the Welshman agreed with the point made by Jonathan Lees—that if a man lacks grace he can receive it for the asking, but he would despair of a missionary without common sense, which he could not receive anywhere. He deplored what he regarded as a fact, that not many missionaries with all three qualities were to be found in China.

Griffith John discusses in more detail the characteristics required in a missionary—and they are all to be found in the man from Ebenezer, Swansea. On the basis of the account in 2 Kings, chapter 6, especially verses 15 and 16, Griffith John maintains that *faith* is essential for any Christian work. It is not theoretical, traditional, historical or creedal, but a practical resting of the soul on God. It is trusting God when means are available, and trusting God when they are not available. Moses was a man of faith at Rephidim and at the Red Sea. Usually God supplies the means for the work, as he did in raising up William Carey to usher in a new period in the history of mission work overseas. In the tradition of Carey, Griffith John argued that the duty of all missionary societies was 'to perfect their agencies and bring them up to the requirements of the times and age'.[15] In the account in Kings, faith brought 'spiritual vision'. Elisha prayed that God might open the eyes of the young lad. John confirmed his argument by quoting two texts: 'Blessed are the pure in heart: for they shall see God' (Matthew 5:8), and 'The secret of the LORD is with them that fear him; and he will show them his covenant' (Psalm 25:14). God will direct the path of the man of faith.[16]

Another secret in the life of Elisha was his 'sense of the

Divine care and protection'. Once again, Griffith John deals
with the doctrine of *providence*. Elisha knew that the chariots of
fire were around him, keeping not only the prophet safe but
the young lad as well. Such an assurance will enable the missionary to face all kinds of suffering and temptation. A glorious example was the behaviour of the martyrs during 1900.
They were safe in life and they were safe in death. It was only
the Saviour who had to go through the experience of being forsaken by God, and that was in order that God might be with
us. He has promised never to forsake his people.[17]

Prayer, the third characteristic of the life of the missionary, is
the 'Secret of Power'. Elisha was a man of prayer, and in developing this theme Griffith John relates the account to the parable in Luke 18 concerning importunity in prayer. The man of
prayer must have faith in the existence of God and a conviction concerning the personality of God. Believers should not be
misled by the widow's importunity into thinking that persis-
tence in prayer will change the mind of God. When praying,
the believer has to submit himself to the will of God, as Christ
taught the disciples, 'Thy will be done':[18]

> It means the bringing of my will into active sympathy with
> the will of God, so that I shall find it impossible not to will
> what God wills, and seek what God seeks. It means to trust
> the Divine will at all times and in all circumstances, deem-
> ing that higher will the best.

The believer does not change the mind of God but is changed
by God.

If there is such submission, it is possible to have the right
attitude to the problems of prayer.[19] According to the scientist,
the laws of nature are fixed and cannot change; consequently it
is meaningless to pray for rain, sunshine and harvest. The
metaphysical difficulty is that, since God is infinite, how can
he be influenced in any way by mere mortal creatures? In the
experiential realm, one of the main problems is that of un-
answered prayer. Before addressing these problems, Griffith
John lays down two premises. Man is a religious being, and
the Lord Jesus Christ, who knows God perfectly, tells us to
pray. As far as the scientific difficulty is concerned, the believer

would say that he believes in a personal God who rules over nature. If man, who has to obey the laws of nature, can control them for his own purpose, surely God can do so.[20] In any case the attitude of the scientist changes from period to period. Griffith John quotes from an article in the *Spectator* which made the point that 'There is a certain subversion of our ideas as to what is and what is not possible.'[21] In considering the metaphysical difficulty, the point is made again that the believer does not change God's mind but must be willing to be changed by God. He must not be used for our selfish enjoyment. In the context of experience, two examples are given: that of Paul, and that of Christ and Lazarus. Paul asked for the thorn in the flesh to be removed. God said 'No' by not removing it, and said 'Yes' by giving Paul more grace to accept the 'No'. Christ delayed the answer to Mary and Martha, but he was sure of what he was doing.

Behind the characteristics of the missionary's life are the missionary's motives. He can have good, healthy reasons for going overseas, politically, socially and even religiously. They can be 'sweet and inspiring', but there must be that 'supreme motive': 'The emphasis must be placed on THE RELATION OF THE MISSIONARY ENTERPRISE TO JESUS CHRIST'.[22] Griffith John had, in a childlike way, trusted the Lord Jesus Christ when he was eight years old, and in 1875 he had become a 'glorious reality' to him. With Paul, he was amazed that this person had loved him: 'He loved *me*, and gave Himself for *me*.'[23] The missionary responds to Christ's love. Christ also commands and sends. Like the early leaders at the end of the eighteenth century, Griffith John gives much attention to the commission of Christ in Matthew 28. It is love that brings forth obedience,[24] and that must be in a context of being called personally by God. The need is not the call.

Griffith John did not like the tendency in his day to thrust men and women into missionary work. So often the argument was presented, 'Unless you can give a reason why you should stay at home, it is your duty to go abroad.'[25] On that basis many would go out to different fields, but a good number would return as failures. The same Christ is realising his dominion over the whole of the world. When men and women are brought to accept the Christian faith and act upon it, they are preparing for the day when Christ will openly demonstrate his lordship. Christ had died; Christ rose again—'And that is not all, He will come again and take us to Himself.'[26] The work of Christ and the labours of his followers have a cosmic significance. This eschatological motive is found in Griffith John, although it is not always central in his thinking.

The presence of the risen Christ is made a reality through the ministry of the Holy Spirit. He is omnipotent and will overcome all difficulties, not only externally but internally as well. Even in his weakness the missionary should not despair. The Holy Spirit can even break the power of sin: 'He cleanses the heart and fills it with love—love to God, and love to man.'[27] He is also the Spirit of revival, and can visit the people with exceptional power as on the day of Pentecost.

Of all the tasks which the missionary has to consider, preaching is the most important.[28] Although he was aware of the fact that the method was new for the Chinese, Griffith John insisted on it at all times because he believed that it was ordained of God. The content and the method were foolishness to the people of China, but God's way had to be honoured. Thomas Bryson was told by Griffith John himself that not a day would pass without him preaching formally to a congregation or informally to a group of people.[29] The burden of the message was the love of God made known in the atoning death of Christ. This was the gospel, the good news from God.

Griffith John's preaching, both in English and Chinese, was eloquent, passionate and powerful, and he felt deep sympathy with those to whom he preached. For him, preaching was not a performance in front of an audience, but the means of establishing a relationship between himself and the hearers, and between all of them and God. The impact of his preaching could be profound. It is true that a lasting work of grace will not of necessity follow many tears, but they are significant in the Chinese context. The Chinaman would not easily weep in public, but on many occasions those listening to Griffith John could not but weep. When preaching he would stand on the platform, Bible in hand, with a summary of the sermon: 'Sometimes he forgets his book and notes, and in the fire of his earnestness he speaks with vehemence, pacing to and fro on the platform.'[30] He had 'a tongue of fire'. The same author paid tribute to Griffith John in a

Conference in 1911: 'Would that the greatest missionary preacher who ever came to China, had been in his former strength and able to join in it, rather than, as he was in his old age and affliction, unconscious even of the work that went on around him.'[31] Others drew attention to the response of the congregation. Hopkyn Rees saw that 'The congregation was swaying as the wind sways the ripening and golden grain.'[32] Griffith John's grandson described the effect as 'electric': 'He would hold them as in a vice. Until he had finished no one stirred. I did not witness the following incident, but my father told me of it; how he had seen a congregation of Chinese rise in their pews and move forward toward the pulpit, apparently quite unconsciously, as he preached to them.'[33]

Griffith John and Alexander Wylie were one with the CIM in emphasising itinerant preaching. The Welshman made Hankow a centre from which he could travel. The restless soul was at peace in doing such work: 'One often feels at the end of a hundred or two hundred miles tour, having spent a fortnight or three weeks in preaching from town to town and village to village, that he could dare anything and endure anything.'[34] The national preachers were also encouraged to take part in this work, and it was a joy to Griffith John when, in 1867, five converts offered their services gratuitously. His attitude is in keeping with his ecclesiology, as his desire was to turn the stations into churches as soon as possible. He wanted the Chinese believers to be missionary-minded and church-centred.

Theologically, Griffith John did not have a rigid system. He had been brought up as a Calvinistic Congregationalist, but felt that there was a need for flexibility in working out his doctrine. He believed in heaven and hell, but was sure that the older Welsh preachers had presented the suffering of hell in a physical, crude manner. His approach was to emphasise that no one was worthy to go to heaven, but that Christ could take them there. Rather than dwell on the eternal consequences of sin, which he accepted, the preacher would proclaim Christ's power to save from the power of sin. Positively, Griffith John rejoiced in the hope of being with Christ. In what does heaven consist? 'In being with Christ, and in sharing with Christ in His eternal glory. I want nothing more.'[35] On the other hand, he did not give due attention to the eternal consequences of sin and could be deliberately vague in dealing with hell. The doctrine of the atonement was at the heart of Griffith John's belief. It was on the cross that the love of God was revealed, but it is a love revealed to all men, not only to the elect. Christ died for all men. The gospel gives a sense of sin and forgiveness: 'And this He does by revealing God as the sin forgiving God, and the sacrifice of Himself as the ground of Divine forgiveness.'[36] He dwelt on this theme because the Welsh missionary deplored the impression given in many sermons that the Son persuaded the Father to forgive sinners. Rather, the Father's love provided the atonement in order to declare his love, and the Son came willingly in obedience to the Father's will.

The discipline of theology did not take place in a vacuum. Griffith John had to apply it not only to his preaching but to developments in missionary thinking in China and the main religions of that country. The work of his fellow Welshman, Timothy Richard, was illustrative of a significant change taking place in China (and it was happening in other countries as well). His thinking was in marked contrast with that of Hudson Taylor, although there were some similarities. Both thought that it was proper to dress like Chinese in order to be one with them; both made continual efforts to alleviate the suffering of the people, and both thought in terms of winning the whole country for Christ. Unlike Hudson Taylor, Timothy Richard developed a social emphasis, with which the former was very unhappy, and to Hudson Taylor and the sect of the CIM Timothy Richard and his friends were on a false trail. By the beginning of the twentieth century the gulf between him and the orthodox mission was 'unbridgeable'.[37]

The LMS pioneer took a mediating position. Griffith John was one with Hudson Taylor in his evangelicalism, which emphasised preaching for the salvation of individual men and women. They were also one in their spirituality, in terms of prayer, holy living and assurance of heaven. On the other hand, Griffith John had sympathy with Timothy Richard's social emphasis, but disagreed with him in that he had made it central in his thought and activity. The LMS man, especially towards the end of his stay in China, strongly advocated a thorough system of education, with teaching through the medium of English, while schools and divinity colleges should be closely related to the work of hospitals. Use should be made of Chinese periodicals, and Griffith John contributed to Young Allen's paper, *The Chinese Globe*. (Allen was regarded as radical in his thinking.)

The Welsh Congregationalist believed that the Welsh Baptist had gone too far in his emphasis on the social nature of the gospel. Like Hudson Taylor, John was disturbed because, although he had been converted in the 1859 Revival, Timothy Richard sounded as if he were ridiculing the old-fashioned gospel:

> That instead of presenting Christianity by means of a few devotional books, as something touching the soul alone, preparing it for eternal bliss after death, we presented Christianity as the *Kingdom of God* to be established, not only in the hearts of men, but also in all institutions on earth, for the salvation of man, body and soul, now and hereafter, and that those who did the best to improve this world, were the best fitted for eternal bliss hereafter.

On this foundation Timothy Richard built two walls:

> 1. That instead of preaching to the millions of the poor and needy—preaching was addressed to the *leaders*.
> 2. That instead of preaching all the time to the thoughtless multitudes—most of the time should be devoted to preaching to *devout souls*.[39]

The three main convictions were, therefore, that the kingdom of God should be established not only in the hearts of individuals but in institutions as well; secondly, that the leaders should be approached because, usually, the people followed them; and, lastly, that most of the missionary's time should be spent with devout persons, not with the masses and uninterested individuals. In developing these themes Timothy Richard was influenced by John Nevius, with whom he had worked for a while, and by a sermon of Edward Irving on Matthew 10.[40] Both men argued for an approach to the worthy — those who represented the good ground—and these should be sought out in the government, amongst the scholars and the gentry.

Griffith John was unhappy with such an approach. Although Timothy Richard acknowledged that preaching was a means of presenting the gospel, Griffith John insisted on making it central. It was God's ordained means of reaching the people. His motto was, 'Preach, Preach, Preach'. The message was for all classes, but, unlike Timothy Richards, the Congregationalist argued for working from below not from above (although he could be very effective in dealing with the scholars). His message was the good news of salvation from sin: Timothy Richard's was that of the kingdom of God being realised on earth. The former argued that those who are assured of heaven will be busy in the Saviour's service on earth, while the latter argued that those who are active on earth are better suited for bliss in heaven. Griffith John remained convinced that 'Social regeneration, even national education, could do little until a spiritual regeneration had taken place.'[41]

There is strength in Timothy Richard's reasoning. If those in authority adopt Christian principles it can have a tremendous effect on a whole country. It is possible to realise the ideal of a Christian nation, the kind of state and society the Puritans had in mind. On the other hand, it has its weaknesses. It can lead to nominalism, when the people just follow the leader, or to the arrangement that the religion of the prince is the religion of the people. Timothy Richard's policy could be implemented when Sun Yat-sen was in authority, but not when the Communists took control of the country. From that time, until now, opposition to the Government has been crushed, but the church is still strong. The believers are persevering and overcoming because of their unflinching faith in the gospel. Government and other institutions can be removed overnight, but not the faith in the hearts of men and women, whether rich or poor, scholarly or unlearned. Griffith John would be very much at home with the Chinese Christians of today.

Like other missionaries, Griffith John had to relate his message concerning the unique Saviour to other religions in China. The civilisation of the country was religious, and in many ways had reached high standards.[42] There were three main religions, Confucianism, Taoism and Buddhism, and the Chinese were happy to acknowledge all of them. To make the claim that Christ is unique in a country where three religions were acknowledged made clashes inevitable. Generally, missionaries presented Christ as the final revelation of God, and they also opposed aspects of religious life in China, especially ancestor worship and transmigration of souls. How they approached this clash must be marked out carefully, because sweeping statements are made in this context. Arnold Bennett states that the majority of converts in China agreed 'with the fundamentalist view of Hudson Taylor and Griffith John'.[43] Lionel Caplan, discussing Hinduism in India, but making a general statement, says: 'Despite considerable differences of theology and ritual among the many denominations represented on the mission field, there was a common basis of evangelicalism and a sharing of the view that there could be no meeting point with non-Christian religions, which had to be attacked, destroyed and replaced by Christianity.'[44]

As far back as the Shanghai conference in 1877, it was proclaimed that 'Denunciation of ancestor worship and idolatry by early missionaries had been discarded and discouraged by most, including Hudson Taylor.'[45] Griffith John, dealing with the failures of the religions of China and the finality of the Christian gospel, could say:[46]

Let me not be misunderstood. I do not mean to say that there is no truth in these non-Christian creeds; neither do I mean to say that they have done no good in the past. There is much truth in some of them, and some of them have been productive of much good. None of them are wholly false, and none of them are without some soul of goodness. But I do mean to say that there is much darkness in them all, and that the darkness in some of them is much greater than the light. They are now mere obstacles in the way of all true progress.

The attitude of Griffith John is well expressed by his grandson: 'His approach to the non-Christian Chinese was rational, not dogmatic. His mental activity was always so; his conclusions were orthodox.'[47]

Behind Griffith John's thinking is the concept of general revelation. God is at work everywhere, and whatever is good has
its source in him. He is at work through the Holy Spirit, but
this general work in common grace does not lead to salvation.
It is the Spirit of God which keeps men from becoming
demons: 'If God had not been in China, China would have
been a hell.'[48] The God who has revealed himself in a general
way is the God who has also revealed himself in a particular
way in Christ. In no way would Griffith John compromise on
what he believed to be distinctive in Christianity. He acknowledged that 'The science of comparative religion is a very fasci-
nating study', very helpful, but it had its dangers as it could
draw the missionary away from the Person of the God-man, or
place him in a class with other religious leaders.[49]

Even as early as 1862, Griffith John had considered in some
detail what he thought to be the deficiencies of Chinese religion, especially Confucianism.[50] He dealt with the different
traditions within that religion, and his main criticism was that
Confucius stressed so much of the practical that he ignored the
motive behind the action. Attention was concentrated on the
overt action. When trying to determine what constitutes a
good act, the main line of approach within Confucianism was
to emphasise that the immaterial is good, but that to come into
contact with the material nature of man can lead to sin. Griffith
John argued that the Lord Jesus Christ traced the seat of failure
to the heart, to the very innermost being of man, to his motives
and desires. Man's nature was sinful. All the major missionaries agreed in underlining as the main weakness of
Confucianism 'not recognising the fact of sin as man's chief
failure'.[51] Having such a serious view of man's condition,
Griffith John thought of salvation in terms of salvation from
sin, which was accomplished by the sinless Son of God.

Griffith John could adopt the role of the apologist, sometimes successfully and sometimes less so. After marshalling
very effectively the witness of non-Christians to the greatness
of Christ, he would show how they had failed to grasp the
deity of the Saviour. Then he would proceed to present the testimony and demands of Christ himself.[52] The apologist could
also fall back on the traditional approach, appealing to the
work of William Paley and concentrating on the external evid-

ences for the existence of God, an approach which was not quite so convincing. He even argued that phenomena like the eclipses were a sure proof of the existence of God.[53]

Preaching the only salvation found in the unique Person of Christ was Griffith John's delight, and he could do so effectively. Not only Gilbert Warren, but many others too, regarded the Welshman as the greatest preacher who had come from the West to China. However, Griffith John's contribution as an author must not be neglected. As he himself said of the work of CCRTS and the National Bible Society of Scotland in China: 'Nothing is published by either of these societies without passing through my hands and receiving my imprimatur.'[54] Such was the confidence that both societies had in him. It would be impossible to estimate the good done by the tracts he wrote. Expressions of indebtedness to them were continually received by the missionaries personally, and by the District Committee in Hankow. His radical principles of translation of the Scriptures were held resolutely in the face of conservative opposition from those who advocated a literal, word-by-word rendering. He contributed substantially to the triumph in China of the 'dynamic equivalent' view.

Griffith John's personal influence was considerable, in the English community in Hankow, and with secular as well as religious leaders in Hupeh and Hunan. The CIM and the Wesleyan Mission regarded him highly, and individuals like Thomas Bryson, Hopkyn Rees (both LMS) and Hannah Jones (CIM) were heavily indebted to him—and not least, of course, his son-in-law George Sparham, who was moulded as a missionary in Griffith John's shadow. Sparham followed his father-in-law in the Divinity College, and became one of the leading figures of the LMS mission in China. Hundreds of Christians revered Griffith John as a man of God, and his family remembered him as a faithful husband and tender father. During such a long period of service in China it would be difficult to determine the key to his success, but two characteristics that must be mentioned are his energy and his patience. Both were grounded in faith in God, the one who sustained him and gave him persevering grace. Griffith John worked hard, because he was conscious of the brevity of life, and because he knew God had plenty of time to accomplish his purposes. This is why, in spite of the fact that he rejoiced at seeing visible fruit, he was never governed by the cry for results and statistics:[55]

> The invisible results are, I verily believe, far greater and far more important than the visible. The growth of our work is similar to that of a plant. The root of a plant takes a longer time to grow than the stem; but maturation takes less time than either. The giant oak is wrapped up in that tiny acorn; but to develop it, the acorn must have time to strike its roots, and the sapling must be exposed to the necessary influences. Summer and winter, spring and autumn, the stormy winds and soft breezes have all had a share in, and were all necessary to, the development of the baby-oak into the fair tree you see today. So it is with our work. All great work requires time.

This is a salutary warning to those (and there are many in our day) who are cajoling God to work in a way that would be pleasing to them.

Although he was patient and was not ruled by statistics, Griffith John did see the fruit of his work, and that in a remarkable way. The 'firsts' of the early years of Shanghai and Hankow could be mentioned, the building up of the work in Hupeh, the entry into Hunan, the opening up of Kuling, the journey of 1868, translation and literary work, and the many national workers he nurtured to take the lead in the church, most of them brought to faith under his own preaching. William Bolton refers to this aspect of his work: 'It is rarely given to a man to see what Dr Griffith John has seen, to share in harvesting so much of the fruit of the seed he himself has helped to sow.'[56]

It is also true that he laboured, and that others entered into his labour. He was a pioneer and blazed the trail for others. He was preacher, evangelist, translator, author and adviser. There is more than a grain of truth in the claim that Griffith John was the father of the Christian mission to Central China, and that he was:

> The apostle of Central China, who baptised the first Protestant convert in that vast region; who founded its first

Protestant Christian Church, and who lived to know that sounds of Christian praise were arising week by week from Chinese voices worshipping God, in every city and almost every township of the two great provinces of Hupeh and Hunan.

References

Chapter 1

1. Census Returns, 1841, 1851; NLW, Deposit 132B; the 'Autobiography' included in Wardlaw Thompson, *Griffith John* (London, 1906). A correspondent claimed that Griffith John was not born in Swansea, but on the Gower ('G.H.' in the *Swansea Leader*, 3 August 1912) but the 1851 Census refers specifically to 'Llangyfelach'.
2. Background, Gwyn A. Williams, *The Merthyr Rising* (Croom Helm, 1978), *ibidem*, 'The Merthyr of Dic Penderyn', *Merthyr Politics: The Making of a Welsh Class Tradition*, ed. Glanmor Williams (Cardiff, 1966); David Jones, *Before Rebecca* (Allen Lane, 1973); Jones comments on the activity of the Merthyr colliers, and adds, 'Yet the Breconshire workmen were quiet; the colliers in the neighbourhood of Swansea, already discontented because of the truck system, did not riot', 155. For Richard Lewis (Dic Penderyn), and Lewis Lewis (Lewsyn yr Heliwr), *Dictionary of Welsh Biography* (London, 1959); Lewsyn was condemned to death, was reprieved and transported; Dic was executed in Cardiff.
3. NLW, Deposit 132B; Census Returns, 1841.
4. Norman Lewis Thomas, *The Story of Swansea's Districts* (Neath, 1965), 120, gives 148; G. Penrhyn Jones, 'Cholera in Wales', *Journal National Library of Wales*, X, Summer, 1958, 152.
5. G. Penrhyn Jones, op. cit.
6. Wardlaw Thompson, op. cit., 3.
7. Thomas Rees, John Thomas, *Hanes Eglwysi Annibynol Cymru*, ii (Lerpwl, 1872), 45-55 [*HEAC*]; Glyn Richards, *Braslun o Hanes Ebenezer, Abertawe* (Llanelli, 1954), W. James, *Canmlwyddiant Eglwys Ebenezer, Abertawe* (Abertawe, 1904).
8. The four found in *Dictionary of Welsh Biography*, op. cit.
9. Summary by Ieuan Gwynedd Jones, 'Y Ddinas a'r Pentref', *Cwm Tawe*, ed. Hywel Teifi Edwards (Gomer, 1993), 96-7; Ieuan Gwynedd Jones, ed., *The Religious Census* 1851 (Cardiff, 1976), vol. 1, details for Swansea Subdistrict, 258f.
10. Wardlaw Thompson, op. cit., 5.
11. W. James, 'Jubili y Dr Griffith John', *Y Diwygiwr*, Mai 1905.
12. Wardlaw Thompson, op. cit., 6.
13. ibid., W. James, 'Y Dr Griffith John', *Y Geninen Gwyl Dewi*, Mawrth 1913, Hopkyn Rees, *Byr Hanes Cenadwr Cymreig* (Dolgellau, 1905), 7.
14. *HEAC*, op. cit., 79-80; T. Stephens, ed. *Album Aberhonddu* (Merthyr, 1898), 69-70; John Williams, *Eglwysi Annibynol Abertawe* (Merthyr, 1915), 52-4; Glyn Richards, op. cit., 7, with photograph of Thomas Davies.
15. Wardlaw Thompson, op. cit., 8.
16. ibid., 6.

17. 'Sunday School Report', *Report Commissioners on Education*, 1847, Part 1. Leslie Wynne Evans points out that there was a decrease during the period 1841-46, when considering all the Sunday schools, one possible reason being 'the type of working-class population in the area', *Education in Industrial Wales, 1700-1900* (Cardiff, 1971), 246.

18. Journal of Griffith John, NLW, Glyn Richards Collection [Journal]; Thompson does not include this reference.

19. *Report Commissioners*, op. cit.; *Swansea Guide*, 1823.

20. John Williams, op. cit.; Hopkyn Rees, op. cit., 7-8; W. James, *Y Geninen*, op. cit.

21. Glanmor Williams, ed., *Swansea* (Christopher Davies, 1990), 72.

22. Evan Griffiths (1795-1873), *Dictionary of Welsh Biography*; for High Street, *Swansea Guide*, 1823. In contrast were parts of St John's Parish, 'Developments here put pressure on the northern suburb of Swansea, and the area of High Street above the gate was used for high-density and low-quality housing that acquired considerable notoriety in the nineteenth century', Ralph Griffiths, ed., *The City of Swansea Challenges and Changes* (Alan Sutton, 1990), 10.

23. NLW, Deposit 129B.

24. D. Brinley Roberts, 'Davies y Binder', *Honourable Society of Cymrodorion Transactions*, 1985, and, especially, the situation in Mynyddbach and district, e.g., 211, 212, 214, 221, 222.

25. For a survey of relevant literature, Huw Walters, 'Y Wasg Gofnodol Gymraeg A'r Mudiad Dirwest, 1835-1860', *National Library of Wales Journal*, Winter 1993. For the background, John Thomas, *Y Diwygiad Dirwestol* (Merthyr, 1885), R. W. Lambert, *Drink and Sobriety in Victorian Wales*, c.1820–c.1895 (Cardiff, 1983).

26. John Thomas, *Y Diwygiad Dirwestol*, op. cit., 130-31.

27. NLW, Deposit 131B; cf. case of Isaac Harries, Mynyddbach, D. Brinley Roberts, op. cit., 225-6.

28. John Williams, *Y Ganwyll*, Medi 1893 (Ebenezer Chapel magazine), *HEAC*, op. cit., ii, 75, 78, 80.

29. *HEAC*, ii, 42-3; Stephens, *Album Aberhonddu*, op. cit., 123; *Congregational Year Book*, 1904, 178-9, which gives the information that 'A small section of the permanent members of Ebenezer resented the ardent reform methods of their pastor'—the main reason why he left for Ebley in 1861. The Maine Law is a reference to the first state prohibition law passed by the State of Maine in America (1846). Temperance leaders in Britain wanted the government to follow the example of Maine.

30. Wardlaw Thompson, op. cit., 13.

31. ibid., 8.

32. School of Oriental and African Studies, CWM, 'Printed Questions'. He also taught at a small school according to Jenkyn Morgan and John Toriel Williams, *Annibyniaeth ym Mlaendulais* (Aberdar, 1924), 13.

33. W. James, *Geninen Gwyl Dewi*, op. cit.; NLW, G. Sparham, 'Reminiscences', Glyn Richards Collection; when his son-in-law, G. C. Sparham, was on furlough in 1896, he visited Cwm-nant, guided by a cousin of

Griffith John, of the same name, 'Griffith John and his Work', *Chronicle*, April 1905.

34. Wardlaw Thompson, op. cit., 9.

35. ibid., 11.

36. NLW, Journal, Glyn Richards Collection. 'Ar yr 11eg Awst wedi daearu gweddillion marwol y tad yn ngladdfa gysylltiedig â chapel Ebenezer, sylwodd Mr Jacob ar y gwr ieuanc yn crynu i'r fath raddau, fel yr ofnodd y syrthiasai i'r bedd gan ddwysder ei alar', 'Y Parch Griffith John, China', *Y Diwygiwr*, Ionawr 1882. Translation of above quotation: 'On the 11th August, after burying the mortal remains of the father in the cemetery connected with Ebenezer, Mr Jacob noticed that the young lad was shaking so much that he was afraid that he would fall into the grave, so intense was his mourning.' This is a real insight into the response of the young lad; the author gives 11th August as the burial day, but Griffith John himself gives the 11th as the day of death, at 10 o'clock in the evening. The article in the *Diwygiwr* also gives details of the tuition given by Mr Jacob.

37. Reference to the shop by David Gray, 'Atgofion', *Y Tyst*, 10 Rhagfyr 1931. Later, in 1858, Griffith John sent a gift to Mr Jacob, as an expression of gratitude for the tuition; a sum of £16 was involved, but Jacob says, 'As he is *now* better off than I am I will receive the £5 with a most sincere heartfelt thanks as an expression of his kind gratitude to me', and adds towards the end of the letter, 'My salary has never supported us one month since I have been keeping a house.' E. Jacob to David Griffiths, Swansea, Aug 4/58, NLW, Glyn Richards Collection.

38. Glanmor Williams, ed., *Swansea*, op. cit., 295.

39. Norman Lewis Thomas, op. cit., 123.

40. *Cambrian*, 10, 31 August 1849.

41. Glanmor Williams, ed., *Swansea*, op. cit., 116; Norman Lewis Thomas, op. cit., 122-3.

42. Norman Lewis Thomas, op. cit., 122, 124-5.

43. *HEAC*, op. cit., ii, 41; John Davies, *Y Lloffyn Aeddfed* (Abertawe, 1852), 37; Thomas Rees, *History of Protestant Nonconformity in Wales* (London, 1883), 429-30. Finney's *Lectures* were translated in 1839, and the *Sermons* in 1841.

44. E. T. Davies, *Religion in the Industrial Revolution* (Cardiff, 1965), 59.

45. D. G. Williams, *Y Ddwy Gymanfa Fawr* (Llanelli, 1927), 80.

46. *Religious Census*, 1851, op. cit.

47. Geraint Dyfnallt Owen, *Ysgolion a Cholegau'r Annibynwyr* (Llandysul, 1939), 124.

48. 'Llyfr Cofnodion Coleg Aberhonddu', *Y Tyst*, 17 Rhagfyr 1931.

49. NLW, Journal, Glyn Richards Collection.

50. Wardlaw Thompson, op. cit., 14, 15.

51. Geraint Dyfnallt Owen, op. cit., 124, and educational tradition, 26, 36-7.

52. 'Apel Oddiwrth Dr Griffith John', *Y Dysgedydd*, Tachwedd 1906.

53. Hopkyn Rees, *Byr Hanes*, op. cit., 11. John had received a call from the Congregational Church at Aberaman, *Y Dysgedydd*, Mawrth 1912.

54. CWM, 'Candidates' Papers'; NLW, Journal, Glyn Richards Collection;

Wardlaw Thompson, op. cit., 20-1, 55.

55. 'Candidates' Papers', op. cit.

56. ibid., Wardlaw Thompson, op. cit., 22.

57. CWM, Answers to Printed Questions.

58. NLW, Journal, Glyn Richards Collection.

59. Meller also worked with William Lewis, Khasia, the Calvinistic Methodist missionary. Noel Gibbard, 'Cyfraniad Cymru i Waith y Beibl Gymdeithas Mewn Gwledydd Tramor', Ph.D., Cymru 1992, 103 n. 43.

60. Wardlaw Thompson, op. cit., 32.

61. NLW, Journal, Glyn Richards Collection.

62. 'Abertawe', *Yr Amserau*, 18 Ebrill 1855.

63. 'Urddiad Cenhadwr i China', *Y Dysgedydd*, Mehefin 1855, 'Abertawe', *Yr Amserau*, 18 Ebrill 1855, H. M. Hughes, *Griffith John* (OUP, 1914), photograph of bill of services between pages 26 and 27.

64. 'Cenadwr Eto', *Y Diwygiwr*, Ebrill 1855.

65. *Y Dysgedydd*, Mehefin 1855, op. cit.

66. ibid.

67. Noel Gibbard, Traethawd Ph.D. op. cit., Pennod 5, v; CWM, 24 June, 20 August 1842.

68. 'Atgofion Personol', *Y Tyst*, 10 Rhagfyr 1931.

69. 'Y Genadaeth Chineaidd', *Y Dysgedydd*, Gorffennaf 1855.

70. NLW, Journal, Glyn Richards Collection.

71. Wardlaw Thompson, op. cit., 45.

72. NLW, Journal, 9 June 1855, Glyn Richards Collection.

73. ibid., 6 June 1855.

74. Wardlaw Thompson, op. cit., 46.

75. NLW, Journal.

76. Wardlaw Thompson, op. cit., 46.

77. The journey took 127 days according to Thompson, op. cit., 43; 128 days according to H. M. Hughes, op. cit., 28, and William Robson, *Griffith John* (London, n.d.), 16, gives 120 days.

Chapter 2

1. Kenneth Scott Latourette, *A History of Christian Missions in China* (London, SPCK, 1929), chapter xiv.

2. ibid, 232, Brian Stanley states that the missionary movement was 'unequivocal' in its condemnation of the opium trade, 'Yet, almost without exception, evangelicals accepted the outcome of those wars, believing that God had turned evil of human design to the good of his saving purposes', *The Bible and the Flag* (Leicester, Apollos, 1990), 109.

3. A. J. Broomhall, *Hudson Taylor and China's Open Country* (Hodder & Stoughton and OMF, 1981), Book One [in a series of seven], 122, and map 120. British Settlement was north of the city, 'an area that was sparsely populated; the ground was covered with mulberry trees, cotton, and ancestral graves. Within this area, British nationals could apply to their consul for lots, which they then could acquire from Chinese owners by individual agreements', Betty Peh-Ti Wei, *Shanghai, Crucible of Modern*

China (OUP, 1990 ed.), 37.

4. Jean Chesneaux, Marianne Bastid, Marie-Claire Bergere, *China from the Opium Wars to the Revolution of 1911* (Harvester Press, 1977), 38-9.
5. 'Memoirs of a Colleague', *Chronicle*, 1931; Broomhall, Book One, op. cit., 291-2; Wardlaw Thompson, op. cit., 338.
6. Wardlaw Thompson, op. cit., 47.
7. Isabella Bird, *The Yangtze Valley and Beyond* (Virgo, 1985) [first published 1899], 25.
8. 'Shanghai is a mean-looking and busy city; its crowds of toiling, trotting, bargaining, burden-bearing, shouting, and yelling men are its imposing feature. Few women, and those of the poorer class, are to be seen . . . Even a wheelbarrow—the only conveyance possible—can hardly make its way in many places', ibid.
9. 'Then the sword of Damocles fell. They received notice to be out of the LMS house by October 1. The Griffith Johns were expected', Broomhall, Book One, op. cit., 283.
10. Wardlaw Thompson, op. cit., 48; Noel Gibbard, 'Traethawd Ph.D.', op. cit.
11. Jane R. Edkins, *Chinese Scenes* (London, 1863), 71.
12. Bitton Nelson, *Griffith John* (1913), 33.
13. Wardlaw Thompson, op. cit., 48-9.
14. ibid. 51.
15. William Robson, *Griffith John*, op. cit., 114.
16. CWM, 5 October 1855.
17. NLW, Journal, Glyn Richards Collection. Hudson Taylor was grateful to receive a copy of Wesley's Hymns and a number of periodicals,'But he was most glad of the apparatus and materials for chemical analysis in his study of Chinese materia medica' (August, 1855), Broomhall, op. cit., Book One, 283.
18. Wardlaw Thompson, op. cit., 46; 'China', 'Missionary Magazine', *Evangelical Magazine*, July 1857.
19. Wardlaw Thompson, op. cit., 50. The Directors were 'gratified' by his progress, CWM, China East, Outgoing, Directors to Griffith John, 9 September 1856.
20. NLW, Journal, Glyn Richards Collection.
21. Wardlaw Thompson, op. cit., 53.
22. NLW, Journal, Glyn Richards Collection.
23. Wardlaw Thompson, op. cit., 54.
24. CWM, 6 October 1857; Wardlaw Thompson, op. cit., 67.
25. CWM, 6 October 1857; NLW, Journal, Glyn Richards Collection; Wardlaw Thompson, op. cit., 58.
26. NLW, Journal, 22 September 1857, Glyn Richards Collection.
27. Wardlaw Thompson, op. cit., 74.
28. NLW, Journal, 1 April 1858, Glyn Richards Collection.
29. ibid, for those dates.
30. ibid, 7, 21 October 1858, 10 February 1859.
31. Latourette, *Missions in China*, op. cit., 277-9.
32. ibid., 279.

33. Wardlaw Thompson, op. cit., 79-80.
34. CWM, 6 November 1858; Wardlaw Thompson, op. cit., 85.
35. ibid.
36. Full report, *North China Herald*, 8 July 1859, also, CWM, 8 July 1859, Wardlaw Thompson, op. cit., extracts, 98.
37. *North China Herald*, op. cit.
38. ibid.
39. NLW, Journal, 13 July 1859, Glyn Richards Collection.
40. Broomhall, op. cit., Book Three (1982), 181.
41. CWM, Aug 19/59, Margaret John, ' to her Mother'.
42. Wardlaw Thompson, op. cit., 107. Similar account, different wording, copy of a letter sent by Griffith John to David Griffiths, 3 September 1859, NLW, Glyn Richards Collection.
43. ibid., 108.
44. ibid., 105.
45. NLW, Journal, 22 January 1858, Glyn Richards Collection.
46. ibid., 24 January 1858.
47. ibid., 6 February 1858.
48. CWM, 5 October 1856; Wardlaw Thompson, op. cit., 60.
49. ibid.
50. Wardlaw Thompson, op. cit., 59.
51. J. N. D. Anderson, *The World's Religions* (IVP, 1975) is a good introduction to the theme of Christianity and other religions.
52. Wardlaw Thompson, op. cit. (revised edition, 1908), 285.
53. CWM, 15 June 1858; 'Missionary Magazine', *Evangelical Magazine*, October 1858.
54. CWM, 6 October 1857.
55. ibid.
56. ibid., 15 June 1858.
57. For Alexander Duff and Timothy Richard: Stephen Neill, Gerald Anderson and John Goodwin, eds., *Concise Dictionary of the Christian World Mission* (Lutterworth, 1970).
58. CWM, 15 June, 30 July 1858; Wardlaw Thompson, op. cit., 82-3; 'Missionary Magazine', *Evangelical Magazine*, October 1858.
59. CWM, 30 July 1858. Some missionaries argued against paying Chinese workers in order to make the churches self-supporting from the beginning; others gave freely and the Chinese could take advantage of such liberality: 'The majority of missionaries, however, endeavoured to follow a middle course, putting Chinese agents on salary and aiding Chinese congregations, but attempting gradually to reduce the proportion of foreign contributions', Latourette, *Missions China*, op. cit., 423-4.
60. CWM, 6 October 1857.
61. NLW, Journal, 7 April 1858.
62. ibid., and 25 April 1858.
63. CWM, 15 June 1858.
64. NLW, Journal, 14 April 1858, Glyn Richards Collection. Methods of admission varied: some missionaries asked detailed questions, others

rehearsed them with the candidates, and a few asked trick questions, but this was soon discontinued; examples in Jerome Ch'en, *China and the West* (London, 1979), 103-5.

65. ibid., 2 March 1856, earlier than the date given by Wardlaw Thompson, op. cit., 95. The following is a description of Pastor Hsi's condition before he was delivered from opium smoking: 'He became a complete wreck, and for a whole year and a half never left his couch. During lucid hours between the intoxication of the poison, he was plunged into the depths of misery, remorse and despair. At times he struggled to conquer the craving that was killing him but in vain. Relentless as a vulture, the vice to which he had yielded had him now in its grasp', Mrs Howard Taylor, *Pastor Hsi* (London, 1954 ed.), 17.

66. Isabella Bird, op. cit., 497.

67. Griffith John, *China: Her Claims and Call* (London, 1882), 47; also, Griffith John, 'The trade is immoral, and a foul blot on England's escutcheon', Wardlaw Thompson, op. cit., 287.

68. NLW, Journal, 10, 14 April 1858.

69. ibid., 17 May 1858.

70. ibid., 5 March 1858.

71. CWM, 5 October 1856.

72. Philip A. Kuhn, 'The Taiping Rebellion', *The Cambridge History of China*, vol. 10, Part 1, eds, Denis Twitchett and John K. Fairbank (CUP, 1978); Latourette, *Missions China*, op. cit., ch. XVII; Lindsey Brine, *The Taeping Rebellion* (London, 1862), and for Roberts, 294-9. Wardlaw Thompson, op. cit., ch. V; Chesneaux, et. al., op. cit., Chapter Four; Richard Lovett, *History of the London Missionary Society* (vol. 2, 1899), 514-17.

73. Broomhall, op. cit., Book Two, 131, 294.

74. J. A. G. Roberts, *China Through Western Eyes* (Alan Sutton Press, 1991), 53.

75. *Cambridge History*, op. cit., 296.

76. Chesneaux, et. al., op. cit., 91, 93-4.

77. Broomhall, op. cit., Book Three, 203.

78. Wardlaw Thompson, op. cit., 127.

79. ibid.

80. Roberts appeared in the *North China Herald*; examples found in Journal, Glyn Richards Collection; 'Missionary Magazine', *Evangelical Magazine*, October 1860; Wardlaw Thompson, op. cit., 128f.

81. 'Missionary Magazine', *Evangelical Magazine*, October 1860, letter dated 16 July.

82. CWM, 6 March 1861.

83. ibid., 16 August 1860.

84. ibid. Description of Taiping Sunday, Roberts, op. cit., 55-6.

85. 'Missionary Magazine', *Evangelical Magazine*, November 1860.

86. Broomhall, op. cit., Book Three, 212-13; Wardlaw Thompson, op. cit., 144.

87. Hendrik Z. Kloekers, Netherlands, Chinese Evangelisation Society and joined the BMS.

88. NLW, Journal 6 November 1860.

89. ibid., 9 November 1860.

90. ibid.
91. ibid.
92. ibid., 10 November 1860.
93. ibid.
94. ibid., 14 November
95. ibid., 16 November.
96. ibid., 17, 18 November.
97. ibid., 19 November.
98. ibid.
99. ibid., 20 November.
100. ibid.
101. Edict: Robson, op. cit., 46-7, Wardlaw Thompson, op. cit., 147.
102. NLW, Journal, 26 November 1860.
103. ibid., 27-30 November, 1 December 1860.
104. CWM, 2 February 1861; Robson, op. cit., 49.
105. ibid.; 'Missionary Magazine', *Evangelical Magazine*, July 1861.
106. ibid.
107. NLW, Journal, Glyn Richards Collection.
108. CWM, 22 April 1861.
109. ibid.
110. ibid.
111. NLW, Journal, 19 April 1861, Glyn Richards Collection.
112. CWM, 6 April 1861.
113. Broomhall, op. cit., Book One, 177, 305, 380.
114. A. E. Hughes, *The Invasion of China by the Western World* (London, 2nd ed., 1968), 68; Ralph Covell makes the same sweeping statement in making the point that W. A. P. Martin was an 'exception', *W. A. P. Martin* (Christian University Press, 1978), 88.

Chapter 3

1. Broomhall, op. cit., Book Three, 263.
2. NLW, Journal, Glyn Richards Collection.
3. Letter 13 July 1861, 'Missionary Magazine', *Evangelical Magazine*, November 1861.
4. ibid.
5. Isabella Bird, op. cit., 60.
6. CWM, 1 January 1864.
7. ibid. Nearly forty years later: 'The unpaved roadways are usually foul quagmires owing to the perpetual passage of water carriers; where big dogs of the colour of dirty flannel, with pink patches of hairlessness, wrangle over offal', Isabella Bird, op. cit., 65.
8. Isabella Bird, op. cit., 70, 76 [streets]: 'In them hundreds of people eat, sleep, bargain, gamble, cook, spin, and quarrel, while they are the sculleries, sinks, and sewers of a not inconsiderable portion of the population', 75. Coffin makers and barbers had a brisk trade. Not only had death to be faced, but hair as well. 'Their [barbers] business is an enormous one in China, where hair is regarded as an enemy to be battled

with', ibid., 76.

9. ibid., 73.
10. Letter 13 July 1861, 'Missionary Magazine', *Evangelical Magazine,* November 1861.
11. CWM, 13 July 1861.
12. Wardlaw Thompson, op. cit., 185.
13. Griffith John: 'During the two years I lived in it I lost two children, and had I been compelled to stick to it my missionary career, instead of being a career of more than fifty years, would probably not have been one of twenty'. *Voice From China* (London, 1907), 193.
14. P.S., letter CWM, 18 September 1861.
15. Bitton, *Griffith John,* op. cit., 59.
16. CWM, 1 January 1864.
17. ibid.
18. NLW, Journal, 17 November 1861, 17 December 1865.
19. ibid., 16 March 1862, CWM, 28 December 1864, Wardlaw Thompson, op. cit., 152.
20. CWM, 25 March 1862.
21. ibid., Wilson to Directors, 11 September 1862.
22. NLW, Journal, Glyn Richards Collection; CWM, 1 January 1864; Griffith John, *Voice China,* op. cit., 195-6. Two Mission Houses were also built in 1863 at a total cost of £1096, CWM, China East, Outgoing, 20 April 1863.
23. CWM, 1 January 1864; *Y Ganwyll,* Medi 189; Wardlaw Thompson, op. cit., 216.
24. NLW, Journal, 7 January 1863.
25. ibid.
26. ibid.
27. ibid., CWM, 1 January 1864.
28. CWM, 7 January 1865. Latourette quotes Wheeler, *The Foreigner in China,* that the Christians were accused 'of scooping out the eyes at death to compound silver, of not honoring their ancestors, of making no distinction between rich and poor.' Latourette, *Missions China,* op. cit., 467.
29. ibid., 14 August 1866; NLW, Journal, 3 September 1866.
30. CWM, 14 August 1866:

The Committee of Hankow	1095.00
	20.00
The Chinese	126.09
The Governor of the Province	81.50
Taels	1322.59

31. ibid.
32. CWM, 16 July, 7 August 1866; Wardlaw Thompson, op. cit., 204.
33. CWM, 7 January 1865.
34. Edward Rowlands, 'Blaenffrwyth Canolbarth China', *Y Tyst,* 10 Rhagfyr 1931, Wardlaw Thompson, op. cit., 215-16.
35. CWM, 29 December 1865; Wardlaw Thompson, op. cit., 213-14, Robson, *Griffith John,* op. cit., 155-6.
36. CWM, 29 December 1865.

37. ibid.
38. ibid.
39. ibid.
40. ibid., 8 January 1866.
41. ibid.
42. Wardlaw Thompson, op. cit., 211-12.
43. ibid., 216.
44. Mrs Howard Taylor, speaking of China, 'Men and women who in Western lands would be described as spirit-mediums abound', *Pastor Hsi*, op. cit., 157, and the experience of the Pastor's wife having evil spirits cast out of her, chapter 13.
45. NLW, Journal, 1 January 1862, Glyn Richards Collection.
46. ibid., including copies of letters, 14 August, 15 August 1863; Wardlaw Thompson, op. cit., 193-4, 196.
47. NLW, Journal, 15 July 1867 (Arthur), 20 September 1869 (died 16 June 1870), Glyn Richards Collection.
48. CWM, 1 January 1864.
49. Wardlaw Thompson, op. cit., 197.
50. NLW, Journal, 26 September 1861, Glyn Richards Collection.
51. Wardlaw Thompson, op. cit., 198.
52. NLW, Journal, 17 September 1862, 17 July 1863, Glyn Richards Collection.
53. Wardlaw Thompson, op. cit., 190.
54. Evan Bryant (1839-1918), Noel Gibbard, 'Traethawd Ph.D.', op. cit., 5.
55. CWM, 25 March 1862.
56. ibid.
57. ibid.
58. NLW, Journal, 20 January 1864, Glyn Richards Collection.
59. CWM, 28 December 1864.
60. ibid.
61. ibid.
62. ibid. 'This day received the deeds for a new piece of land in Wu chang fu with the Wu chang fu's seal affixed to it. This is a great triumph', NLW, Journal, Glyn Richards Collection, 16 July 1864.
63. CWM, 28 December 1864.
64. NLW, Journal, 22 Januaury 1867, Glyn Richards Collection; Griffith John, *Voice China*, op. cit., 196-7.
65. Thomas Bryson: Lovett, op. cit., 556-581f.; Annotated Register LMS Missionaries (SOAS).
66. Details in Wardlaw Thompson, op. cit., 245f., 257f.
67. CWM, 16 April 1869.
68. NLW, Journal, 19 April 1867, Glyn Richards Collection.
69. CWM, 30 May 1867.
70. ibid. Wardlaw Thompson, op. cit., 209; NLW, Add MS 384D, Griffith John to Thomas Rees, 6 January 1865.
71. Wardlaw Thompson, op. cit., 218.
72. ibid., 218.

73. 'The Chinese Circular on Foreign Missions', *Chinese Recorder*, November 1871.
74. ibid.
75. 'China', *Monthly Reporter*, September 1869.
76. *Annual Report* (BFBS), 1869, 238. Griffith John himself: 'I believe this is the longest journey that has ever been made by a Protestant missionary in China', CWM, 5 September 1868.
77. Main sources; detailed report of Alexander Wylie, *Journal of the North China Branch of the Royal Asiatic Society*, NS, V, 1868; 'China', *Monthly Reporter*, September, November 1869; summaries: Noel Gibbard, 'Traethawd Ph.D.', op. cit., 5, iii, Robson, *Griffith John*, op. cit., 96-100, Wardlaw Thompson, op. cit., 227-9; reference: Griffith John, CWM, 19 November 1888.
78. Wylie, *Journal Asiatic Society*, op. cit.
79. ibid.
80. ibid.
81. ibid. 'Among the interesting features of Sha-shih are a ninth century seven-storeyed pagoda, with eight faces, each face recessed on each storey, and containing a stone image of Buddha, and a dark and foul staircase, leading to a remarkable view from the top', Isabella Bird, op. cit., 85.
82. *Monthly Reporter*, September 1869.
83. Wylie, *Journal Asiatic Society*, op. cit.
84. *Monthly Reporter*, September 1869.
85. Wylie, *Journal Asiatic Society*, op. cit.
86. ibid. '*The Chinese Gazetteer* notifies one thousand rapids and rocks between Ichang and Chungking, a distance of about 500 miles, and in winter this does not seem an outlandish estimate', Isabella Bird, op. cit., 8.
87. Wylie, op. cit.
88. *Monthly Reporter*, September 1869.
89. ibid. Missionary situation in Wan in 1899: 'At that time though missionaries had been settled at Wan for some years, and had been able to rent this beautiful house (CIM), there was not a Christian in the city. The ladies had only lately arrived as it had been thought not a safe place for them', Isabella Bird, op. cit., 172.
90. *Monthly Reporter*, November.
91. ibid., Wylie, *Journal Asiatic Society*, op. cit.; description of the race, Robson, *Griffith John*, op. cit., 99-100.
92. *Monthly Reporter*, November 1869.
93. ibid.
94. ibid., Wylie, *Journal Asiatic Society*, op. cit.
95. ibid.
96. ibid.
97. Wylie, *Journal Asiatic Society*, op. cit.
98. Wardlaw Thompson, op. cit., 230; Robson, *Griffith John*, op. cit., 100.
99. *Monthly Reporter*, November 1869.
100. ibid.

101. 'No one can have much experience of committee work in connexion with our great societies without feeling that the furlough system tends at times to develop human weakness', Richard Lovett, *James Chalmers* (London, 1902), 120.

102. CWM, Home Correspondence, 7 January 1871.

103. ibid., 7 November

104. 'Pigion o Araeth y Parch Griffith John', *Y Diwygiwr*, Tachwedd, Rhagfyr, 1871.

105. Wardlaw Thompson, op. cit., quoting the *Nonconformist*, 295; 'Undeb Cynulleidfaol Abertawe', *Y Diwygiwr*, Tachwedd 1871. For his stay in Wales, D. A. Griffiths, 'Atgofion Personol', *Y Tyst*, 10 Rhagfyr 1931.

106. CWM, Home Correspondence, 28 March 1871.

107. ibid.

108. J. Harris Jones (1827-85), *DWB*; George Palmer Davies (1826-81), Noel Gibbard, 'Traethawd Ph.D.', op. cit., 6-7.

Chapter 4

1   CWM, 13 May 1873.

2.   ibid.

3.   Wardlaw Thompson, op. cit., 301. Appreciation Arnold Foster, translated by Ap Hefin, 'Mrs Margaret John', *Y Tyst*, 10 Rhagfyr 1931, includes reference to Mrs John buying a slave in order to save her life. It was estimated that 40,000 had been sold during a period of a few years. Edward Shillito quoted a Chinese assistant, 'I never saw love until I saw Mrs Margaret John', 'Griffith John', *Chronicle*, December 1912.

4.   Evan Bryant, CWM, letter 22 November 1872.

5.   CWM, Report 1872.

6.   ibid., 19 February 1876.

7.   ibid., 15 January 1874. 'Every day when the patients are assembled in the waiting room, the Gospel is proclaimed to them by the missionaries', notice of 'Report of the LMS Mission Hospital', *Chinese Recorder*, July-August, 1876.

8.   ibid., 8 February, 26 March, 13 November 1875.

9.   ibid., 8 February 1875.

10.   Latourette, *Missions China*, op. cit., 390.

11.   Robson, *Griffith John*, op. cit., 109-10; a Bible woman was employed, 'Y Maes Cenhadol', *Y Diwygiwr*, Mai 1876.

12.   CWM, 27 August 1877.

13.   William Owen: E. Lewis Evans, *Cymru a'r Gymdeithas Genhadol* (Llandysul, 1945), 150-1; Foster: Amy Foster, *Arnold Foster, Memoir* (LMS, 1921); Mackenzie: Mary Bryson, *John Kenneth Mackenzie* (New York, n.d.).

14.   CWM, 6 December 1879.

15.   ibid., 27 November 1874.

16.   Robson, *Griffith John*, op. cit., 128, 'She seemed to possess the practical nature of Martha with the contemplativeness of Mary', ibid.

17.   ibid., 135; *Y Diwygiwr*, Mai 1876, op. cit.

18.   Steven Barabas, *So Great Salvation* (Marshall, Morgan & Scott, 1952), for

an account and interpretation of Keswick teaching.

19. ibid., 150.

20. Dr and Mrs Howard Taylor, *Hudson Taylor and the China Inland Mission* (London, 1921 ed.), 175, and Ch. XII, entitled, 'The Exchanged Life; Broomhall, op. cit., Book Six, 35-6.

21. Wardlaw Thompson, op. cit., 32. It was during this time (no specific date is given) that Mackenzie reported, 'A meeting for the promotion of holiness among the missionaries here was held at Mr John's. Great blessing received by all present', Mrs Bryson, *Mackenzie*, op. cit., 60.

22. 'Griffith John Apostol Mawr China' (editor), *Y Tyst*, 10 Rhagfyr 1931.

23. *Y Diwygiwr*, Mai 1876, op. cit.

24. ibid.

25. CWM, 25 November 1875.

26. ibid.

27. Griffith John refers to his remarkable conversion, and his emergence as the 'main pillar' of the church at Hiau-Kan, 'A God's Man for the People', *Chronicle*, September 1897; Wardlaw Thompson, op. cit., 351-2. Also, account of the notable convert, Pastor Hsi, Mrs Howard Taylor, op. cit.

28. CWM, 5 February 1876; Wardlaw Thompson, op. cit., 356; during the cold season, 1875-76, Griffith John made seven journeys with Mackenzie, Robson, *Griffith John*, op. cit., 132.

29. Bryson, *Griffith John*, op. cit., 77; J. Wallace Wilson does quote the response of Griffith John, 'This is a proud day for me. I have shed blood for my Master when trying to tell the people of the love of God for them', 'Memoirs of a Colleague', *Chronicle*, 1912. Mackenzie also has a description of the journey, Mrs Bryson, *Mackenzie*, op. cit., 74-81.

30. CWM, 5 February 1876; Bryson, Griffith John, op. cit., 78.

31. Mrs Bryson, Mackenzie, op. cit., 82-3, 88.

32. CWM, 5 February 1876.

33. CWM, 25 November 1878; Wardlaw Thompson, op. cit., 353, 359.

34. ibid.

35. ibid.

36. ibid.

37. ibid.

38. CWM, 23 April 1880; Griffith John, *Voice From China*, op. cit., 221-2; Wardlaw Thompson, op. cit., 341-4.

39. Wardlaw Thompson, op. cit., 340-1, report by Archibald, who paid tribute to Griffith John's energy and leadership, but the Welshman was also ready to acknowledge Archibald's remarkable contribution to pioneering work. Referring to a visit to Hunan, John says, 'This must be regarded as the first real missionary journey in Hunan, and the palm of the pioneer is justly due to Mr Archibald', Unpublished History of the National Bible Society of Scotland (N.B.Soc.Scot.). It is not clear whether this was the journey with Griffith John (end of December 1879–beginning of 1880), or a previous visit by Archibald.

40. ibid., 342.

41. ibid., 343.
42. Griffith John, *Voice From China*, op. cit., 221.
43. ibid., 222.
44. Wardlaw Thompson, op. cit., 346.
45. CWM, 23 April 1880.
46. ibid. In the same letter quoted John Archibald, who had been to the place two years previously. 'I cannot but be struck with the change. The progress made is more than I expected to see in my day. Instead of being hunted from corner to corner, and treated with all sorts of insolences until I was glad to get to my boat again, I this time found a house ready to accommodate me, and lots of Christians waiting to welcome me.'
47. ibid.
48. Latourette, *Missions China*, op. cit., 421-2, says that anti-Christian placards and pamphlets 'seem to have picked out for criticism features which were more characteristic of Roman Catholics than of Protestant practice', and mentions celibacy, treatment of the dead and interference in lawsuits, 467 n. 2.
49. CWM, 28 April 1880.
50. ibid.
51. ibid.
52. 'At the close of the service I baptised an old man of 74, a young man of 29, and a child of 5. This was a memorable service, and I feel sure that it will never be forgotten by the converts of Hiau-Kan', ibid.
53. Wardlaw Thompson, op. cit., 363-4.
54. ibid.
55. Unpublished History of the National Bible Society of Scotland, Society Archives, copy from the secretary.
56. Booklet, SOAS, title and date missing, but includes correspondence between Griffith John and the Rev. John Locke, who was supported by Bishop Boone. Griffith John's main points: 1. Proselytising wrong; 2. Teaching of Locke, e.g., baptismal regeneration; 3. Attitude to missionaries of other denominations; 4. Bishop Boone's father would be unhappy with the approach; 5. Some of those accepted by the Episcopal Church would have been disciplined if they had stayed with the LMS. CWM, LIB O PAM LXXXV, 85, no. 4.
57. Griffith John, *Voice China*, op. cit., 125.
58. ibid.
59. Broomhall, op. cit., Book Six, 107-8; Hudson Taylor, 'I have written asking special prayer for the outpouring of God's Spirit, not only at the Conference but before, that we may all go up filled with the Spirit, and not merely *hoping* for a blessing', Dr and Mrs Howard Taylor, op. cit., 296. Griffith John, 'Our most pressing need in China is a baptism of the Holy Ghost', *China and Her Claims* (London, 1882), 61.
60. *Records of the Protestant Missionary Conference, Shanghai* (Shanghai, 1877); *Chinese Recorder*, 1877, 239f., 489f.; Broomhall, op. cit., Book Six, 108f.; Latourette gives details of numbers: 'Of the 142 present, 74 were men, 52 were women, 72 represented American societies, 49 British societies, 1 a

German society, 4 were unconnected with societies, and 16 were honorary members'. *Missions China*, op. cit., 413 n. 251.

61. 'The Shanghai Missionary Conference', *Wesleyan Methodist Magazine*, October 1877.
62. *Records*, op. cit.; Broomhall, op. cit., Book Six, 110f.; *Wesleyan Methodist Magazine*, op. cit., October, November.
63. Broomhall, op. cit., Book Six, 114.
64. Griffith John took part in these discussions, *Records*, op. cit.; Wardlaw Thompson, op. cit., 322-3. Griffith John and the Rev. Talmage were responsible for the devotional services, and the Welshman sat on a number of committees, 'Division of the field of Labour', 'Literature Committee', 'On Opium' and 'On Preparing a Document' (for the literati), 'The Shanghai Missionary Conference', *Chinese Recorder*, June 1877.
65. Broomhall, op. cit., Book Six, 109.
66. Latourette, *Missions China*, op. cit., 413.
67. CWM, 25 November 1878, 'I believe that I have got on as well with colleagues as any missionary in China; but I assure you that it has cost me something to do so. And then they fail to get on with each other, and I am expected to keep right with them all, and keep matters going.'
68. ibid., 2 July 1878.
69. ibid., 25 November 1878.
70. ibid.; also, 2 July 1878.
71. ibid., 24 June, Mackenzie to Mullens.
72. ibid., 8 May 1879; Annotated Register of LMS Missionaries (SOAS).
73. ibid., 8 November 1880.
74. ibid.
75. ibid., 17 February, 10 March 1879, 30 March 1880.
76. ibid., 18 January, 18 March, 16 April 1881.
77. 'Gwaith Cenadol y Parch Griffith John a'i Gyd-lafurwyr yn Hankow', *Y Diwygiwr*, Mai 1881 (parhad Mehefin, Gorffennaf).
78. CWM, 2 February 1881.
79. ibid.
80. Wardlaw Thompson, op. cit., 373.
81. Llewelyn David Bevan (1842-1918), *DWB*.
82. Wardlaw Thompson, op. cit., 373, 374.
83. CWM, 13 June 1881.
84. 'Nodiadau Misol', *Y Dysgedydd*, Ionawr 1882; full report, *The Nonconformist and Independent*, 13 October 1881, 972-3, 978, at the close of the address, 'loud and prolonged applause'; also included articles by John, 'China and Missions', 28 July 1881, 716-17, 'Foreign Missions and the Churches', 12 January 1882, 24-5.
85. 'Valedictory Services', *Missionary Chronicle*, March 1882; 'Ymadawiad y Parch Griffith John a Mrs John', *Y Dysgedydd*, Mawrth 1882.
86. Noel Gibbard, 'Traethawd Ph.D.', op. cit., 19.
87. CWM, 6 June 1882.

Chapter 5

1. CWM, 1 September 1882.
2. ibid.
3. ibid.
4. ibid.
5. ibid.
6. ibid.
7. ibid., 11, 27 September 1882, 22 March, 25 May 1883.
8. ibid., 31 July, 4 November, 1 December 1882; Wardlaw Thompson, op. cit., 396.
9. Wardlaw Thompson, op. cit., 395.
10. ibid., 394, 395.
11. ibid., 392. Charles George Sparham: born 1860, Brighton, educated Cheshunt. Married Mary John, 1891. Born organiser, church politician; worked to unite Presbyterians and Congregationalists in China. Two sons: Rev Griffith J Sparham and Mr Brynmor Sparham. Died 1931; Mary, his wife, 1950; *Chronicle*, 1931, with photograph, Annotated Register of LMS Missionaries (SOAS). Arthur Bonsey (1858-1942), China 1882; Principal of Griffith John College, 1914. Thomas Gillison (1859-1937), born Baldernock, Sterlingshire; studied medicine in Edinburgh. Annotated Register of LMS Missionaries (SOAS).
12. Wardlaw Thompson, op. cit. 396.
13. CWM, 15 February 1883.
14. ibid.
15. Griffith John, *Voice China*, op. cit., 224; 'Griffith John in Hunan', *Chinese Recorder*, August 1891: the report, dated 23 February 1883, sent to the *Christian World*.
16. CWM, 15 February.
17. 'The Committee was of one mind as to the desirability of closing the bargain at once, and thus securing one of the best sites for our work which Hankow presents. It is the intention of the Chairman to write to three or four friends soliciting further aid, and in this he has the full sympathy and hearty approval of all his colleagues', ibid., 12, 1884. Robson, *Griffith John*, op. cit., 150.
18. CWM, 17 January 1884.
19. ibid., 13 March 1884.
20. Robson, op. cit., 150.
21. ibid.
22. ibid., 151.
23. ibid.
24. CWM, 6 January 1886.
25. ibid.
26. Robson, *Griffith John*, op. cit., 141-2.
27. CWM, 6 January 1886. Mrs Bryson refers to her as 'a lady of exceptional ability and attractiveness', 'Seven years with Griffith John in Central China', *Chronicle*, April 1905.
28. 'In the highest sense she is still living, and living in higher and intenser

life than she could have lived here. I am trying to think of this aspect more and more, and it makes me glad', NLW, John to Sparham, Saturday, Shanghai, January 1886, Glyn Richards Collection.

29. 'But I am calm with God in the midst of the furnace. He doeth all things well, and I know that He has done even this in love. What I cannot *see* now, I shall *see* hereafter', CWM, 6 January 1886.
30. Wardlaw Thompson, op. cit., 405.
31. ibid.
32. ibid., 406.
33. Robson, *Griffith John*, op. cit., 156.
34. Wardlaw Thompson, op. cit., 407.
35. ibid.
36. Robson, op. cit., 155.
37. ibid.
38. CWM, 19 March 1888.
39. ibid.
40. ibid.; 'Wang King-foo', *Chinese Recorder*, October 1892.
41. CWM, 19 November 1888.
42. CWM, 26 December 1888, 7 January 1889; 'A Missionary Journey', *Chronicle*, May 1889; Wardlaw Thompson, op. cit., 410-19.
43. Wardlaw Thompson, op. cit., 411.
44. Noel Gibbard, 'Traethawd Ph.D', op. cit., 231-2.
45. Wardlaw Thompson, op. cit., 412.
46. ibid., 413. 'When parents reach middle age in China, it is a son's first duty to present them with handsome coffins, as a token of filial affection', Mrs Howard Taylor, op. cit., 67.
47. ibid., 415.
48. ibid., 419.
49. ibid., 417, and adds, 'When I think of Ying-shan, what rejoices me most is the thoroughly satisfactory character of the converts we have there. Mr Lo himself is a perfect gem.'
50. ibid., 418.
51. ibid., 421.
52. CWM, 12 January 1884, including Minutes Hankow Committee, 10 January 1884.
53. ibid.
54. Broomhall, *Bible in China*, op. cit., 83-4.
55. John Pollock, *The Cambridge Seven* (IVP, 1955, Marshalls, 1985).
56. 'The way these men have been honoured because of their social position and the capital made by the mission out of their name and fame strikes me as something that Paul would have looked upon with great contempt, and Christ would have condemned as unworthy of himself and his cause', CWM, 16 July 1885.
57. ibid.
58. ibid.
59. ibid.
60. ibid., 12 March 1889.

61. ibid.
62. ibid.
63. Griffith John's desire concerning missionaries: [that] 'They shall live as long as possible, enjoy the best possible health, and carry on their work with the best possible vigour', *Voice From China*, op. cit., 214. Would urge missionaries to be careful regarding their health, and heed the warning from the life of James Chalmers, Mrs Bryson, op. cit.
64. CWM, 3 December 1888, 15, 21 January 1889.
65. ibid., 12 January 1884.
66. ibid., 12 November 1889, and plan included in the *Chronicle*, April 1889.
67. CWM, 26 April 1889.
68. Griffith John, *Voice From China*, op. cit., 155.
69. Wardlaw Thompson, op. cit., 334.
70. CWM, Minutes Hankow Committee, 27 July 1882.
71. SOAS, United Society Christian Literature Collection, including Catalogue for 1884.
72. Robson, *Griffith John*, op. cit., 119-21; Griffith John, *Voice From China*, op. cit., 132.
73. Wardlaw Thompson, op. cit., 335.
74. United Society Christian Literature, Catalogue, op. cit.
75. Noel Gibbard, 'Traethawd Ph.D', op. cit., 373.
76. Background: Marshall Broomhall, op. cit.; W. Canton, *History of the British and Foreign Bible Society*, vol. 5 (London, 1911); Alexander Wylie, 'The Bible in China', *Chinese Recorder*, November, December 1868.
77. Cambridge, University Library, Minutes Editorial Sub-Committee, BFBS, No. 16, 24 October 1884, 2 December 1885.
78. 'The Easy Wen-li New Testament', *Chinese Recorder*, April 1886.
79. *Annual Report* (N. B. Soc. Scotland), 1883, 33. The Society was encouraged by the demand: 'The demand, however, for copies from all parts of China, the testimonies of competent missionaries, and the interest excited by the new version, sufficiently justify the Directors in resolving to undertake the expense of publishing it', *Quarterly Records*, 1884, 30-1; Griffith John: 'From the many letters received by Mr Archibald and myself, it is clear that the work is appreciated as supplying a want which has been long and greatly felt.' 'Hankow-Hian Kian', *Chronicle*, April 1884.
80. *Annual Report* (N.B. Soc. Scot.), 1884, 30-31; CWM, 11 August 1884.
81. *Chinese Recorder*, April 1886, op. cit.
82. NLW, 'Reminiscences', Glyn Richards Collection.
83. CWM, 6 July 1885.
84. *Annual Report* (N.B. Soc. Scot.), 1885, 33. Griffith John realised that he could not satisfy all the critics and all their ideals, but rejoiced in the response from three eminent men who had advised him. 'He trusts that they will go on and finish their work, and that the next edition of it will appear with "the imprimatur of three splendid names", namely, those of Messrs Muirhead, Faber and Archdeacon Moule', *Quarterly Records*, 1886, 37-8. Moule's conclusion: 'All I see of Mr John's version leads me to hope

that it may after all become our—if not Authorised yet however—Common Version of the New Testament; always allowing our excellent Brother *three or four years at least* to perfect its rendering in communication with the brethren.' 'Mr John's New Testament', *Chinese Recorder*, February 1886.

85. Cambridge, Editorial Sub-Committee, No. 17, 24 February 1886–1 September 1887; *Chinese Recorder*, December 1890.

86. ibid., Editorial Correspondence, No. 22, 25 January 1887. Some time had also been taken up to discuss the possibility of producing a tentative edition of the Burdon and Blodget version. The BFBS recorded Griffith John's response to this proposal: 'He intends to stick to his own work of improving his version, and he thinks that Dr Blodget and Bp Burdon will stick to theirs.' Editorial Sub-Committee, No. 17, 1 September 1886.

87. *Chinese Recorder*, December 1890.

88. Cambridge, Editorial Correspondence, No. 23, 12, 16, 20 December 1887.

89. ibid., 16 December; *Memorandum, Resolutions of the Shanghai Conference* (London, 1890), 16; Wardlaw Thompson, op. cit., 442.

90. ibid., No. 23, 18 April 1888. It was clear from January that discussions would not proceed. 'The Wen-li Version has been submitted to the severest criticism, and I am now working on a revision of it, with these criticisms before my eyes. I am quite willing to receive criticisms on the Mandarin Version also, and that from all quarters; and I would promise to bring out a revised edition of it, as I have done of the Wen-li Version, in the light and with the help of all such criticisms; but more than this I *cannot do*', *Memorandum*, op. cit., 36.

91. *Annual Report* (N.B. Soc. Scotland), 1888, 33. Critical review by 'H' arguing against the use of the *textus receptus*, and claiming that there were mistranslations, 'The New Testament in Chinese', *Chinese Recorder*, May 1888.

92. *Annual Report*, op. cit., 1889, 35, 57-8. Scotland was more ready than Wales to honour Griffith John. The Scottish Committee 'felt it almost as a personal honour when the University of Edinburgh marked its regard for his distinguished services as missionary and translator by conferring upon him the degree of Doctor of Divinity.' *Quarterly Records*, 1889, 25.

93. Cambridge, Editorial Correspondence, No. 25, 30 November 1889.

94. ibid., No. 25, 4 March 1890.

95. ibid., No. 26, 6 June 1890, No. 25, 30 November 1889; Broomhall, *Bible in China*, op. cit., 87. Dr Wright of the BFBS was sarcastic concerning Griffith John's non-attendance at Shanghai: 'Sir, I am sorry that your great missionary, Dr Griffith John, is not among us. Mr Archibald has told us that "he has been kept away by modesty". You will all admit that any deficiencies on his part in that respect have been amply supplied by his representative. I trust that Dr G. John, when he learns how unanimous and enthusiastic you are in favour of United Standard Versions, will join cordially with you, and, like Bishop Burdon and Dr Blodget, place not only his version but himself on the missionary altar'. *Memorandum* op. cit., 17, addressing the chairman of the Conference ('representative' could be referring to Sparham). The Directors were sorry that

Griffith John refused to attend the Conference. 'The incident of a little personal controversy raised by Dr Wright's foolish words is, after all, only of temporary interest, and will be forgotten before long. You at any rate can afford to pass by such things without notice. But the work to which you are invited is a work of national and permanent importance.' CWM, China East, Outgoing, 12 September 1890.

96. CWM, 2 June 1890. Bryson expressed 'bitter disappointment', as did David Hill, because 'There is no man who can do so much to help or to hinder the work either in China, or you might say in the whole world as yourself', ibid., 8 July 1890.

97. ibid., 30 November 1890; Mateer had written 20 November, and Stevenson 29 December 1890.

98. ibid., 12/14 January 1891; Wardlaw Thompson, op. cit., 446-53.

99. 'On a New Version of Scripture in Wen-li', *Chinese Recorder*, August 1885; 'Mr John's Version, or Another?', ibid., October 1855.

100. Cambridge, Editorial Correspondence, No. 21, 16 July 1886.

101. ibid., vol. 22, 5 October 1887, Editorial Sub-Committee, 1 September 1887. Bryant was faithful to the policy of the BFBS. Rule: 'That whenever it is practicable to obtain a board of competent persons to translate or revise a version of the Scriptures, it is undesirable to accept for publication the work of a single translator or reviser', *Memorandum*, op. cit., 36; S. Dyer (BFBS) disagreed, supported by Mr Caidwell: 'Mr Caidwell of the China Inland Mission and Mr Dyer are in favour of a new version by Mr John', Editorial Sub-Committee, No. 17, 1 December 1886.

102. Milton C. Fisher (member of panel New International Version), 'Normative Principles for Bible Translating', *The New Testament Student and Bible Translation*, ed. John H. Skilton (Presbyterian & Reformed, 1978), Owen Evans, 'Cyfieithu'r Gair i Iaith y Bobl', *Y Gair a'r Genedl*, gol. E. Stanley John (Abertawe, 1986).

103. 'A Communication from Bishop Moule', *Chinese Recorder,* January 1891.

104. Cambridge, Editorial Correspondence, No. 27, 24 February 1891.

105. 'Leading Rules for Translation', *Chinese Recorder*, October 1885; Wardlaw Thompson, op. cit., part of letter, 437-8.

106. CWM, 10 July, 23 December 1898.

107. 'Leading Rules', op. cit.

108. R. B. Girdlestone, *Suggestions for Translators* (London, 1877), 10; *Annual Report* (N.B. Soc. Scotland), 1884, 30-1; 1889, 57.

109. Cambridge, Editorial Correspondence, No. 21, 4, 11 November 1885, 16 July 1886.

110. ibid., No. 25, 4 January 1890.

111. 'Leading Rules', op. cit.; compare 'a' and 'ac' in Welsh, Gwilym H. Jones, *Newydd a Hen yng Nghymraeg y Beibl* (Undeb y Gymraeg, 1988), 6.

112. Cambridge, Editorial Sub-Committee, No. 16, 18 June 1884.

113. J. Beekman and J. Callow, *Translating the Word of God* (Zondervan, 1975), 21.

114. To some extent every translator has to use a 'dynamic equivalent': discussion, D. A. Carson, *The King James Version Debate* (Baker Books, 1979).

115. 'Leading Rules', op. cit.

Chapter 6

1. CWM, 31 December 1891.
2. ibid., 12 February 1891, and he made the point that he had saved the LMS a great deal of money, while the CIM were paying Tls 300 for a 'wretched Foreign house'. He kept the study very neat, taking care of all details, including a supply of blue, black and red ink, and a clean blotting pad. NLW, 'Recollections', Glyn Richards Collection.
3. *Chronicle*, July 1891.
4. CWM, 9 May 1893.
5. Griffith John, 9 May 1893, and Sparham, 9 May 1893. Foster appealed to George Müller for support of his view, 'Nevertheless, the plan which Mr Foster did actually propose to us today, is a plan which George Müller would never have proposed', 9 May, op. cit.
6. Wardlaw Thompson, op. cit., 462.
7. *Chronicle*, August 1891.
8. Wardlaw Thompson, op. cit., 563-666.
9. CWM, 16 July 1895.
10. 'Reminiscences', NLW, Glyn Richards Collection.
11. ibid.
12. CWM, 11 February 1895.
13. Broomhall, op. cit., 219.
14. ibid., 212-13. Griffith John, after Wei-hai-wei: 'The terrible defeat should bring them to their senses, and I sincerely hope that it will do so, and that this war will come to a speedy end', dated 12 February, at end of letter, 11 February 1895.
15. CWM, 12 August. Referring to Peking, Broomhall says, 'In every month of 1895 the American legation at Peking had occasion to report on the dangerous position in which American missionaries were placed', op. cit., Book Seven, 216.
16. ibid.
17. ibid.
18. ibid., 18 July, 'Almost to a man the converts behaved splendidly in the midst of their trials.'
19. ibid.
20. ibid., 9 September 1895.
21. ibid.
22. ibid., 9 May 1893.
23. 'Y Genadaeth', *Y Dysgedydd*, Hydref 1894.
24. ibid.
25. Wardlaw Thompson, op. cit., Griffith John, *Sowing and Reaping*, Letter 1.
26. *Sowing and Reaping*, op. cit.; 'Y Genadaeth', *Dysgedydd*, Mawrth 1895.
27. CWM, 16 July 1895.
28. *Sowing and Reaping*, op. cit., and account, 'A Most Encouraging Tour', *Chronicle*, February-March, 1896.
29. ibid., Letter 2, 'A Faithful Tour Among Outstations'; *Chronicle*, July 1906.

30. ibid., Letter 3.
31. Wardlaw Thompson, op. cit., 574.
32. ibid., 517. Griffith John was deeply grateful for Mary's care—'I am not sure that I should have been a living man to day but for Mary's loving care of me'—and was honoured by an address, worked on satin: 'It is a magnificent piece of work' and 'ought to move many hearts', CWM, 18 February 1895.
33. 'Recollections', NLW, Glyn Richards Collection.
34. Wardlaw Thompson, op. cit., 519, 'During my forty-two years in China I have had hardly any holiday life. Last year and this have been the only years in which I have taken any holiday whatsoever, and in both years I have been driven away by illness', ibid., 520.
35. ibid., who says in 1906, 'Fully 1200 Europeans now find a resting place there during the heat'; worked in close association with the Wesleyans, CWM 2 March 1896.
36. 'Recollections', NLW, Glyn Richards Collection.
37. *Voice From China*, op. cit., 225. Griffith John was prominent in the expansion of literature during this time, and one author has pointed out how the Hunanese responded angrily to this expansion: 'Thus it seems no coincidence that the great upsurge of anti-Christian literature of the early 1890's in the Yangtze Valley, stemming chiefly from Hunan, came directly on the heels of the great expansion of the literature work of the Central China Religious Tract Society based in Hankow in the late 1880's.' Suzanne Wilson Barnett, John King Fairbank, eds., *Christianity in China* (Studies in American–East Asian Relations, 9, Cambridge, Mass. and London, 1985), 21.
38. Edmund S. Wehrle, *Britain, China and The Antimissionary Riots, 1891–1900* (Minneapolis, 1966), 66.
39. ibid.; Griffith John urged Gardner 'to apprehend Chou, the real cause of the riots'. 'One of the most violent anti christian pamphlets originally published in Hunan is styled "Kwei chia o Kai sze", The Devil Doctriners ought to be killed.' Report to Home Office, 28 September 1891, P.R.O., FO17/1128. It was believed that Chou was the author.
40. *Voice From China*, op. cit., 217, 218, 'The gentry and the scholars of the province had been looking on Hunan as the palladium of the empire, and the ultimate expulsion of the foreigner was a fixed article in their creed', 219. Reports to the Home Office expressed the same opinion: 'The centre of the whole movement is in Hunan. The Hunan men have been the leaders of the movement', and the investigators of the attacks 'daren't touch the leaders—but seize a few of the less guilty subordinates', P.R.O. FO17/1127.
41. Wardlaw Thompson, op. cit., 486-7.
42. CWM, 20 April 1897, Thompson, op. cit., includes most of the letter, 489-92.
43. CWM, 20 April 1897; Griffith John, *Voice From China*, op. cit., 225-8.
44. CWM, 20 April 1897.
45. Griffith John, *Voice from China*, op. cit., 227.

46. ibid., 229, and CWM, 20 April 1897, which does not contain the reference to Swansea.

47. CWM, 23 December 1898.

48. ibid.

49. ibid.; full of optimism, 'When fully manned the Society's Mission in the Siang Valley will be one of its finest in China'; closing he says, 'May God inspire us all with the needful faith, courage and liberality, and Hunan shall be Christs'.'

50. ibid., 20 January 1898.

51. ibid., 23 December 1898.

52. 'Reminiscences', NLW, Glyn Richards Collection.

53. CWM, 3 March 1899; *Voice From China*, op. cit., 230.

54. Wardlaw Thompson, op. cit., 494; *Voice From China*, op. cit., 232.

55. CWM, 3 March 1899.

56. *Voice From China*, op. cit., 232-3. Hudson Taylor, the CIM leader, sent a letter of congratulations and encouragement to Griffith John when he returned from the journey, SOAS, CIM, JHT, 17 June 1899, Box 16.

57. Wardlaw Thompson, op. cit., 496.

58. ibid., 497.

59. CWM, 9 November 1899.

60. *Voice From China*, op. cit., 235, 236. Peng had permission to worship at Hengshan; translation of document, which appeared in the *North China Daily News,* included by Griffith John in *Chronicle*, January 1898, op. cit. When writing the article he had just heard that electricity had been used in the examination hall at Changsha.

61. ibid., 235-6.

62. ibid. There were encouragements in terms of baptisms in Hunan and Hupeh: 1898 – 809, including 660 adults; 1899 – 637, including 574 adults, 'Gwaith Cymdeithas Genadol Llundain yn Hunan ac Hupeh', *Y Cronicl Cenadol,* Mehefin 1900.

63. Chesneaux, et.al., op. cit., 293.

64. ibid., 309; his books were read by Mao Tsetung, ibid., 314.

65. ibid., 315. 'The events of 1895 gave Yan Fu the determination and the opportunity to express his ideas.'

66. ibid., 321-2, Latourette, *Missions China*, op. cit., 492.

67. Wu Yu-Chang, *The Revolution of 1911* (Peking, 1962), 41-2. His response to reform: 'When the edicts proclaiming reforms came one after another I and the other supporters of reform were frantic with joy', 43.

68. Brian Stanley, *Bible and the Flag*, op. cit., 142-3. He says, 'In reality Sun's creed was a mish-mash of ideas culled from progressive social Christianity and a variety of Western secular thinkers such as Darwin, Marx and Henry George', 142.

69. Latourette, *Missions China*, op. cit., 492.

70. Wehrle, *Britain—China*, op. cit., 80.

71. Broomhall, op. cit., Book Seven, 263, 291.

72. Latourette, *Missions China*, op. cit., 493.

73. CWM, 20 January 1898.

74. ibid., and Wardlaw Thompson, op. cit., 521-2.
75. CWM, 11 April 1899.
76. ibid., Annual Report 1900, cf. 9 November 1899, opened with 8 students; Griffith John 'Gwaith Cymdeithas Genhadol Llundain yn Hunan a Hupeh', *Cronicl Cenadol*, Mehefin 1900. Appointments for staff: a. General knowledge of the NT; b. Good knowledge of one of the Gospels; c. Catechism of Christian Doctrine; d. Preaching to the heathen. CWM, Bonsey to Directors, sending Minutes Hankow D.C., 11-17 January 1899.
77. Griffith John, *Voice From China*, op. cit., 23.
78. Broomhall, op. cit., Book Seven, 280.
79. Latourette, *Missions China*, op. cit., 503. He points out that the foreigner used the black art, but he could be resisted by stronger forces: 'The secret initiation and mystic ceremonies were thought to insure the protection of the spirits and to render the recipients invulnerable to sword, spear or bullet.'
80. Archibald E. Glover, *A Thousand Miles of Miracles in China* (London and Glasgow, 1931 ed.), 7.
81. Glover, op. cit., 360-1. Detailed, recent account of the period, Broomhall, op. cit., Book Seven, Part 4.
82. Glover, op. cit., 360.
83. CWM, 10 August 1900.
84. Wardlaw Thompson, op. cit., 527.
85. ibid.
86. [May 1900], 'when the unthinkable took the foreign community by surprise and the Empress Dowager championed the Boxers', Broomhall, op. cit., 318; he relates that, of the eight-nine missionaries in one province, forty-seven were killed with their children.
87. Latourette, *Missions China*, op. cit., 505.
88. Timothy Richard was in close contact with Chang, who became a prominent leader in matters of industry and education. Jerome Ch'en, *China and the West*, op. cit., 108, 117, 153, 254. A good photograph of Chang in the *Chronicle*, 1901, 107.
89. 'Recollections', NLW, Glyn Richards Collection.
90. ibid.
91. Sparham to Directors, CWM, 16 July 1900.
92. ibid. (John), 10 August 1900.
93. Sparham to Directors, 16 July 1900.
94. Latourette, *Missions China*, op. cit., 472-4, 525; Broomhall, op. cit., Book Seven, 478.
95. CWM, 2 October 1900, and, 'I am sure it is false policy *not* to ask for indemnity', 17 January 1901, 29/11/00. 31 December 1900. Cousins, an LMS director, but speaking personally, agreed with Griffith John, Cousins to John, 17 August 1900, CWM, China East, Outgoing. When the CIM made it known to the authorities that no compensation would be claimed or accepted, 'they were incredulous', Broomhall, op. cit., Book Seven, 479; A. Goold, 'An Argument Against Indemnity', *Chinese Recorder*, December 1890.

96. ibid., 17 July 1900.
97. *Cambridge History of China*, op. cit., vol. 11, Part 2, 126-7.
98. Broomhall, op. cit., Book Seven, 466-70 for CIM.
99. ibid., 464.
100. Stephen Neill, op. cit., 288.
101. CWM, 17 January 1901.
102. ibid., 7 July 1900.
103. 'Recollections', NLW, Glyn Richards Collection.
104. ibid.
105. CWM, 27 August 1900, Wardlaw Thompson, op. cit., 526.

Chapter 7
1. CWM, 31 January 1901. Robert Arthington died at Teignmouth, 9 October 1900; was of the family of Arthington the brewers. Head of the family closed the business because of the moral dangers. Robert himself lived like a hermit in order to support such societies as the BMS and LMS, 'The last penny of the money will be spent next June'. 'The Millionaire who became poor', *Chronicle*, January 1936; CWM, China East, Outgoing, Directors to Griffith John, 14 December 1900.
2. *Voice From China*, op. cit., 237, CWM, 15 May 1901.
3. ibid.
4. Wardlaw Thompson, op. cit., 500-1.
5. *Voice From China*, op. cit., 240; CWM, 26 March 1901; Griffith John, 'Good News from China', *The Examiner*, 11 April 1901.
6. Wardlaw Thompson, op. cit., 502; Griffith John, 'The Opening of Hunan', *Chronicle*, November 1891.
7. 'Reminiscences', NLW, Glyn Richards Collection.
8. CWM, 8 January 1902.
9. ibid.
10. ibid., 19 May 1902, Thompson, op. cit., 503.
11. *Voice From China*, op. cit., 242.
12. ibid.
13. CWM, 23 April, 19 May 1901.
14. *Voice From China*, op. cit., 242, Griffith John, 'Striking at the Heart of Heathendom', *Chronicle*, 1902, where John says that the work was made possible by a gift of £100 from Mr W. Beare, Clapham Park, who had just died.
15. *Voice From China*, op. cit., 243.
16. CWM, 29 May 1903, *Voice From China*, op. cit., gives 26.
17. Griffith John, 'Ten Days with the Deputation in Central China', *Chronicle*, June 1904.
18. *Voice From China*, op. cit., 243-4; CWM, 10 December 1902.
19. CWM, 29 July 1905.
20. ibid., 5 April 1901.
21. ibid., 12 February 1904.
22. *Voice From China*, op. cit., 245.
23. ibid., 245. Jonathan Spence refers to the impact of Griffith John's call for

missionaries to come to Hunan, *The China Helpers*, op. cit., 163.

24. 'A New Chapel at Hankow', *Chronicle*, July 1904.
25. ibid.
26. John to Sparham, 6 March 1902, NLW, Glyn Richards Collection.
27. CWM, Report for 1902.
28. ibid., 23 November 1903.
29. ibid., 18 March 1903.
30. ibid., 23 November 1903.
31. 'A School of the Prophets for Central China', *Chronicle*, August 1904. Griffith John said that he had been 'often tried' during this period, 'But I have found with John Elliot that prayer and pains through faith in Christ can do anything.' 'Mission Field', *British Congregationalist*, 27 September 1906.
32. *Chronicle*, August 1904, op. cit.
33. John to Mary, 7 February 1907, NLW, Glyn Richards Collection.
34. 'A Visitor at the Hankow Hospital', *Chronicle*, March 1904.
35. CWM, 8 January 1902.
36. ibid., 31 July 1902.
37. ibid., 18 March 1903.
38. ibid., 29 May 1903.
39. ibid., 19 July 1903.
40. ibid., 3 April, 5 June 1905.
41. ibid., 30 August 1904.
42. ibid., 4 June 1905.
43. Broomhall, op. cit., Book Seven, 507, 510, 512. A photograph of W. A. P. Martin, Griffith John and Hudson Taylor was taken on two occasions during Hudson Taylor's stay in Hankow, 29 April and 29 May, Broomhall, op. cit., 505, 506, 653 n. 36; Wardlaw Thompson, op. cit., opposite 42. There are a number of photographs of Griffith John in the CIM Collection, SOAS, CIM/Photographs/Albums.
44. CWM, 4, 5 February 1905.
45. ibid., 24 March 1905.
46. ibid., 26 June 1905.
47. Kuling, Saturday (September 1902), NLW, Glyn Richards Collection.
48. ibid., Kuling, 19 September 1904, also 9 December 1904, 3 April, 28 June, 9 September 1905.
49. CWM, 3 October 1905. A friend, Mrs de Selincourt, Balham, London, urged Griffith John to continue with his translation work: 'This I feel is the greatest work you have, and will be your enduring and most beautiful monument.' Griffith John to George Sparham, 10 December 1906, NLW Glyn Richards Collection.
50. CWM, 30 October 1905.
51. ibid., 28 January 1905.
52. John to George, 5 October 1906, 'Apel Oddiwrth Dr Griffith John', *Y Dysgedydd*, Tachwedd 1906.
53. 'Jiwbili Dr Griffith John', *Y Dysgedydd*, Hydref 1906.
54. John to Mary, 22 January 1907, NLW, Glyn Richards Collection.

55. ibid., 6 March 1907, and writing to George, 'I am glad to see in every copy of the Tyst resolutions or letters or both touching the 100,000 sixpences scheme', 5 January 1907.
56. ibid., 7 February 1907.
57. The Wills Brothers. 'They built Highbury Chapel, Bristol, and contributed generously not only towards the building of more than thirty chapels but to a large number of other good causes', R Tudur Jones, *Congregationalism in England, 1662-1962* (London, 1962), 289.
58. Wardlaw Thompson, op. cit., 533f., and Hughes, *Griffith John*, op. cit., xix, give an account of two meetings, but there were three of them.
59. 'Dr Griffith John's Jubilee Celebrations', press cuttings, NLW, Glyn Richards Collection. 'Jiwbili Dr Griffith John', *Y Tyst*, 6 Chwefror 1905.
60. ibid.
61. Wardlaw Thompson, op. cit., 535; 'He Has Loved Us', *Chronicle*, March 1905.
62. ibid., Hughes, *Griffith John*, op. cit., 146-7.
63. CWM, 14 February 1906.
64. ibid., 1 March 1906.
65. ibid., 16 February 1906; 'China is my home, and to talk about going anywhere else as to a *home* sounds strange', ibid., 28 February.
66. ibid., 2 April 1906, 7 April 1906. Although very ill, Griffith John did not retire from the work, as Broomhall states. Broomhall, op. cit., Book Seven, 669.
67. 'Dr John's Farewell', *Chronicle*, May 1906; 'Dr John's Farewell to Hankow', ibid., August, 1906.
68. John to Mary, 23 August, 24 November 1906, NLW, Glyn Richards Collection, CWM, 18 May 1906.
69. John to Mary, 27 December 1906, NLW, Glyn Richards Collection.
70. ibid., 15 December 1906.
71. ibid., 2 January 1906.
72. CWM, 2 October 1906.
73. For Pierson, D. L. Pierson, *Arthur T. Pierson, A Biography* (London, 1921). The reference to the Revival in Wales in NLW, 24 December 1905, Glyn Richards Collection. Pierson referred to Griffith John in *Acts*, 360-1.
74. John to Mary, 21 December, John to George, 24 January 1906, NLW, Glyn Richards Collection.
75. e.g., 27 September, 4 October 1906, 10 January 1907, *British Congregationalist*.
76. John to George, n.d., and 1 March 1907; contacted by Mr Ehnes, who wanted Griffith John's support in the work of distributing literature in the United States and Canada.
77. CWM, 21 May 1907.
78. ibid., 14 June 1907; 4 September 1902, NLW, Glyn Richards Collection.
79. 23 (August or September) 1906, 5 March 1907, NLW, Glyn Richards Collection.
80. 'Mission Field. Dr Griffith John on the Educational Movement in China', *British Congregationalist*, 27 September 1906.

81. ibid.
82. ibid.
83. John to Mary, 21 December 1906, NLW, Glyn Richards Collection.
84. ibid., to George, 5 November, 3, 21 December 1906.
85. ibid., 4 March 1906.
86. ibid., 17 December 1906.
87. ibid., e.g., 24 January, 10, 24 December 1906, 28 January, 14 February, 31 March 1907.
88. Hughes, *Griffith John*, op. cit., 152.
89. CWM, 23 January 1907.
90. John to George, 24 December 1906, NLW, Glyn Richards Collection.
91. ibid., 24 January 1906; for the response of Congregationalists, R. Tudur Jones, op. cit., 351, 352, 354.
92. 15 December 1906, NLW, Glyn Richards Collection.
93. ibid., 24 December 1906.
94. 'I am glad to see what you say about the New Theology. It is reassuring', CWM, 22 April 1907; Horton: 30 May 1907, NLW, Glyn Richards Collection; 'His deep devotion, brilliant intellect and social interest made a combination which appealed to many', R. Tudur Jones, op. cit., 326.
95. 23 January 1907, NLW, Glyn Richards Collection.
96. ibid., 12 October 1907.
97. CWM, 2 January 1908, 5 November 1907.
98. ibid. On his arrival visitors poured in during the whole of the day; a band in the garden played 'Men of Harlech'—'News from the Front', *Chronicle*, March 1908.
99. CWM, 23 December 1907.
100. ibid., 2 January 1907.
101. ibid., 24 January 1908.
102. ibid.
103. ibid.
104. ibid., 27 January 1908.
105. ibid., 14 February 1908.
106. ibid., Foster to Cousins, 24 February 1908.
107. ibid., McFarlane to Directors 30 January, including Minutes of D.C. 16 January 1908.
108. ibid., 5 May 1908. The situation was serious in Hankow. Bonsey was in Kuling because of a nervous collapse, and Upward was suffering from nervous trouble. 'I have endeavoured so as to arrange that things might go on without utter collapse, and I am thankful to say that there are many evidences that good results are being attained. Still it is neither wise nor safe to leave too much work entirely in Chinese hands, at a Central Station.' Sparham to Cousins, 29 April 1908.
109. ibid.
110. ibid., 3 July 1908.
111. ibid., 3 November 1908.
112. ibid., 17 December 1908.
113. ibid., 19 August 1909.

114. ibid., 7, 11 October—'His earnest craving for work is pathetic'; 8 November 1909.

115. ibid., 5 November 1909.

116. ibid., 15 April 1910.

117. ibid., 10 October 1910, 8 February, 11 March 1911.

118. ibid., 23 June, Kuling August 1911; 'Dr Griffith John', *Chronicle*, September 1911.

119. 'The overthrow of the Manchu dynasty was the end of a long decline which began in the nineteenth century and was accelerated by Western intervention in China. Many signs presaged it: failures in the military and diplomatic fields, agrarian revolts and the declining loyalty to the gentry', Chesneaux, op. cit., 376.

120. CWM, 12, 13 October.

121. ibid., 15, 20, 27 October 1911.

122. ibid., 27 October, 1 November.

123. ibid., 27 October.

124. ibid., 8 November.

125. 'Reminiscences', NLW, Glyn Richards Collection.

126. ibid.

127. 'Angladd y Dr Griffith John', *Y Tyst*, 7 Awst 1912; 'A Noble Life. Funeral of the late Dr Griffith John', *South Wales Evening Post*, July 1912; 'Reminiscences', NLW, Glyn Richards Collection. Hymns sung at the funeral: 'Paham yr wylwn am y rhai', 'Beth sydd imi yn y byd', 'Daeth yr awr i'm ddianc adre', 'Our God, our help in ages past', 'Bydd myrdd o ryfeddodau'. 'Gwasanaeth Angladdol Dr Griffith John', Funeral leaflet, Swansea Public Library. It is strange that J. Reason says, 'He died peacefully in his daughter's home in 1912, eighty-one years old', *Griffith John*, op. cit., 24. He did not die in his daughter's home, and he was eighty years old.

128. Broomhall, op. cit., Book Seven, 510.

129. 'Reminiscences', op. cit.; 'Memorial Service', *Chronicle*, October 1912.

130. *Y Tyst*, op. cit., and numerous tributes appeared in newspapers and periodicals, including *Herald of Wales*, 3, 10, 17 August, *South Wales Daily News*, 26 July, *The Daily Chronicle*, 26 July, *The Westminster Gazette*, 26 July, *The Christian World*, 1 August, *Y Dysgedydd*, Mawrth, Medi, Hydref, *Chronicle*, January, September, December, 1912, *Geninen Gwyl Dewi*, 1 Mawrth 1913.

131. 'Canmlwyddiant Cenhadol y Dr Griffith John', *Y Dysgedydd*, Rhagfyr 1931; reports in *Y Tyst*, 24, 31 Rhagfyr 1931; summary by Myfanwy Wood, 'The Griffith John Centenary Meetings', CWM, China Personal.

132. [Garden] 'Marks Memory of missionary born in Swansea', *South Wales Evening Post*, 25 November 1963; Prógramme of the opening, with photograph of the house where Griffith John was brought up, NLW, Glyn Richards Collection; some wrong dates on the programme: e.g., accepted into church membership when he was 8 years old, not 10; entered College in 1850, not in 1852.

Chapter 8
1. *Chronicle*, 1905, op. cit.
2. 'Reminiscences', Glyn Richards Collection.
3. Foster, *Memoir*, op. cit., 7
4. Frederick A. Atkins in the *Chronicle*, January 1908.
5. Journal, op. cit.
6. Discussion in *Cambridge Modern History*, vol. 10, part 1, ch. 11; Wardlaw Thompson, op. cit., 256; Lutz, op. cit., 3.
7. *Chronicle*, March 1905, December 1912.
8. 'Reminiscences', op. cit.
9. Quoted by Wardlaw Thompson, op. cit., 200-1.
10. 'Reminiscences', op. cit.
11. ibid.
12. ibid.
13. CWM, John to Cousins, 6 April 1898.
14. Wardlaw Thompson, op. cit., 378.
15. *Voice From China*, op. cit., 255.
16. ibid., 259.
17. ibid.
18. ibid., 174, 165-6.
19. ibid., 171, 176.
20. ibid., 177.
21. ibid., 178.
22. Griffith John, *The Reason Why* (Hankow, 1903), 7; 'Supreme Motive', *Voice From China*, op. cit.
23. *Voice From China*, op. cit., 117-18.
24. ibid., 96-7.
25. ibid., 111.
26. ibid., 101.
27. ibid., 99.
28. What preaching meant to Griffith John is seen clearly in the articles, 'Y Maes Cenadol', *Y Dysgedydd*, Tach.–Rhag., 1871.
29. Wardlaw Thompson, op. cit., 199.
30. ibid., 183.
31. G. G. Warren in the *Chronicle*, October 1912, op. cit., and in the *China Mission Year Book*, 1912, ed. D. MacGillivray, 185.
32. Wardlaw Thompson, op. cit., 297.
33. Reminiscences', Glyn Richards Collection.
34. Wardlaw Thompson, op. cit., 221.
35. *Voice From China*, 98; 'Where is heaven? In being with Christ, in being like Christ, and in sharing with Christ in His eternal glory. I want nothing more', ibid., 102.
36. ibid., 97. Christ died for all, 'This is Christ's world; He died for the whole of it', 25.
37. A. J. Broomhall, op. cit., Book Seven, 524.
38. Timothy Richard, *Conversion of the Millions in China*, vol. 1 (Shanghai, 1907), 13.

39. ibid., 14.
40. ibid., 81, 87; Latourette, *Missions China*, op. cit., 378-80; Albert J. Garnier, *A Maker of Modern China* (London 1945), 54-5.
41. Sparham, 'Griffith John and his Work', *Chronicle*, April 1905.
42. Griffith John, *China and Her Call*, op. cit., 10.
43. *Missionary Journalist in China*, op. cit., 139.
44. Lionel Caplan, ed., *Studies in Religious Fundamentalism* (MacMillan, 1987), 157, and quoting I. David, *God's Messengers* (1983), 88.
45. A. J. Broomhall, op. cit., Book Six, 461 n. 31.
46. *Voice From China*, 79; 'The Gospel to Paul was not one among many, but the one; it was not a compound of Jewish and Grecian elements, not a product of the faiths of the world, but a new force which had come down from heaven itself, fresh from the hand of God', 116.
47. 'Reminiscences', Glyn Richards Collection.
48. Wardlaw Thompson, op. cit., 458.
49. *Voice From China*, op. cit., 116.
50. *Y Beirniad*, vol. 3, 1862, cf. *Voice From China*, op. cit., 76-8.
51. A. J. Broomhall, op. cit., Book Six, 110; Arnold Foster, *Memoir*, op. cit., 69-71.
52. 'The Divine Christ, The One Saviour of Men', *Sermons by Welshmen in English Pulpits*, ed. Daniel Walters (London, 1898).
53. Bennett, *Missionary Journalist*, op. cit., 192.
54. CWM, Report 1903. Other aspects of his work: published *Hymns of Adoration*, originals and translations from 'Sankey and sacred minstrelsy of the Welsh', notice in *Chinese Recorder*, December 1876; with John Archibald and C. W. Allen edited *Central China Monthly* during 1905. Was restarted by C. W. Kastler in 1909, *The China Mission Year Book*, 1910, 347.
55. Wardlaw Thompson, op. cit., 289-90.
56. William Bolton, *Chronicle*, April 1905.
57. Tribute in the *Chronicle*, October 1912.

Sources

Manuscripts

Aberystwyth: National Library of Wales
Glyn Richards Collection
NLW Deposit 132B
Add MS 384D

Cambridge: University Library
British & Foreign Bible Society Collection

London: Public Record Office (Kew)
FO/17 1127, 1128
School of Oriental & African Studies, Council for World Mission (CWM)
Collection
China Inland Mission (CIM) Collection

Bibliography

a. Books written by Griffith John
Hope for China (London, 1872)
China: Her Claims and Call (London, 1882)
Spiritual Power for Missionary Work (London, 1882)
Sowing and Reaping (London, 1897)
The Reason Why (Hankow, 1903)
A Voice from China (London, 1907)
Then and Now in China (London, 1907)
The Supreme Motive in Foreign Missions (London, 1882), Welsh Translation, JBA
Y Rheswm Paham (London, 1915)

b. Biographies of Griffith John
Berry, W. B.	*Griffith John* (London, 1908)
Bitton, Nelson	*Griffith John* (Sunday School Union, London, 1913)
Cousins, G.	*Hanner Can Mlynedd yn China* (Llundain, y Gymdeithas Genhadol, 1905, cyfieithiad William Davies, Llandeilo?)
Hughes, H. M.	*Griffith John, Arwr China* (OUP, 1914)
Miles, J.	*The Life of Griffith John* (Llundain, y Gymdeithas Genhadol, c.1908)
	Griffith John, Apostol Mawr China (Llundain, c.1931)
Reason, Joyce	*Griffith John of China* (Pocket Pioneer, 1950)

Rees, Hopkyn   *Byr Hanes y Cenadwr Cymreig* (Dolgellau, 1905)
Robson, William   *Griffith John* (London, 1901)
Thompson, Wardlaw   *Griffith John* (London, 1906, 2nd ed. 1908)

c. Other works

Anderson, J. N. D.   *The World's Religions* (Leicester, IVP, 1975)
Barabas, Steven   *So Great Salvation* (Marshall, Morgan & Scott, 1952)
Bird, Isabella   *The Yangtze Valley and Beyond* (Virgo, 1985 ed.)
Brine, Lindsey   *The Taeping Rebellion* (London, 1862)
Broomhall, A. J.   *Hudson Taylor and China's Open Country* (7 vols. from 1981)
Broomhall, Marshall   *The Bible in China* (London, 1934)
Bryson, Mary   *John Kenneth Mackenzie* (New York, n.d.)
Caplan, Lionel ed.   *Studies in Religious Fundamentalism* (MacMillan, 1987)
Canton, William   *History of the British & Foreign Bible Society* (vol. 5, London, 1911)
Carson, D. A.   *The King James Version Debate* (Baker Books, 1979)
Chesneaux, Jean   *China from the Opium Wars to the Revolution of 1911* (Harvester Press, 1977)
Ch'en, Jerome   *China and the West* (London, 1979)
Covell, Ralph   *W. A. P. Martin* (Christian University Press, 1978)
Davies, John   *Y Lloffyn Aeddfed* (Abertawe, 1852)
Davies, E. T.   *Religion in the Industrial Revolution* (Cardiff, 1965)
Dictionary   *Concise Dictionary of the Christian World Mission*, eds. Stephen Neill, Gerald Anderson, John Goodwin (Lutterworth, 1970)
Dictionary   *Dictionary of Welsh Biography* (London, 1959)
Edkins, Jane R.   *Chinese Scenes* (London, 1863)
Edwards, Hywel Teifi   *Cwm Tawe* (Gomer, (Llandysul, 1993)
Evans, E. Lewis   *Cymru a'r Gymdeithas Genhadol* (Llandysul, 1945)
Evans, Leslie Wyn   *Education in Industrial Wales* (Cardiff, 1971)
Fairbank, John King   *Christianity in China* (Cambridge, Mass. and London, 1985)
Fairbank, John K. ed.   *The Cambridge History of China* (CUP, 1978)
Foster, Amy   *Arnold Foster, Memoir* (London Missionary Society, 1921)
Garnier, Albert J.   *A Maker of Modern China* (London, 1945)
Girdlestone, R. B.   *Suggestions for Translators* (London, 1877)
Glover, Archibald E.   *A Thousand Miles of Miracles in China* (London and Glasgow, 1931 ed.)
Griffiths, Ralph ed.   *The City of Swansea, Challenges and Changes* (Alan Sutton, 1990)
Hughes, A. E.   *The Invasion of China by the Western Powers* (London, 2nd ed. 1968)
James, Leighton   *Griffith John—Founder of the Hankow Mission* in Congregational Studies Conference Papers 1990 (EFCC)
James, William   *Canmlwyddiant Eglwys Ebenezer, Abertawe* (Abertawe, 1904)

Jones, David   *Before Rebecca* (Allen Lane, 1973)
Jones, Gwilym H.   *Newydd a Hen yng Nghymraeg y Beibl* (Undeb y
                              Gymraeg, 1988)
Jones, Ieuan Gwynedd   *The Religious Census of 1851* (vol. 1, Cardiff, 1976)
Jones, R. Tudur   *Congregationalism in England, 1662-1962* (London,
                              1962)
Lambert, R. W.   *Drink and Sobriety in Victorian Wales* (Cardiff, 1983)
Latourette, Kenneth Scott   *A History of Christian Missions in China* (London,
                              1929)
Lovett, Richard   *History of the London Missionary Society* (vol. 2,
                              London, 1899)
Lovett, Richard   *James Chalmers* (London, 1902)
MacGillivray, D. ed.   *China Mission Year Book* (1912)
Neill, Stephen   *A History of Christian Missions* (Penguin, 1964)
Owen, Geraint Dyfnallt   *Ysgolion a Cholegau'r Annibynwyr* (Llandysul, 1939)
Records   *Records of the Protestant Missionary Conference, 1877*
                              (Shanghai, 1877)
Rees, Thomas and   *Hanes Eglwysi Annibynol Cymru*
  Thomas, John   (4 vols. Liverpool, 1871-1875)
Rees, Thomas   *History of Protestant Nonconformity in Wales*
                              (London, 1883)
Report   *Report of the Commissioners of Inquiry into the State
                              of Education* (1847)
Register   *Annotated Register of LMS Missionaries* (SOAS)
Richard, Timothy   *Conversion of the Millions in China* (vol. 1, Shanghai,
                              1907)
Richards, Glyn   *Braslun o Hanes Ebenezer, Abertawe* (Llanelli, 1954)
Roberts, J. A. G.   *China Through Western Eyes* (Alan Sutton, 1991)
Stanley, Brian   *The Bible and the Flag* (Leicester, Apollos, 1960)
Spence, Jonathan   *The China Helpers* (London, Sydney, Toronto, 1969)
Stephens, T. ed.   *Album Aberhonddu* (Merthyr, 1898)
Skilton, John ed.   *The New Testament Student and Bible Translation*
                              (Presbyterian & Reformed, 1978)
Taylor, Howard Dr. & Mrs *Hudson Taylor and The China Inland Mission*
                              (London, 1921 ed.)
Taylor, Howard Mrs   *Pastor Hsi* (London, 1954 ed.)
Thomas, John   *Y Diwygiad Dirwestol* (Merthyr, 1885)
Thomas, Norman Lewis   *The Story of Swansea's Districts* (Neath, 1965)
Walters, Daniel ed.   *Sermons by Welshmen in English Pulpits* (London,
                              1898)
Wei, Betty Peh-Ti   *Shanghai, Crucible of Modern China* (OUP, 1990 ed.)
Wehrle, Edmund S.   *Britain, China and The Antimissionary Riots, 1891-
                              1900* (Minneapolis, 1966)
Williams, D. G.   *Y Ddwy Gymanfa Fawr* (Llanelli, 1927)
Williams, Glanmor ed.   *Swansea* (Christopher Davies, 1990)
Williams, Gwyn A.   *The Merthyr Rising* (Croom Helm, 1978)
Williams, John   *Eglwysi Annibynol Abertawe* (Merthyr, 1915)

Williams, John Toriel   *Annibyniaeth ym Mlaendulais* (Aberdar, 1924)
  and Jenkyn Morgan
Yu-Chang, Wu   *The Revolution of 1911* (Peking, 1962)

Periodicals and Newspapers

Cambrian Newspaper
Chinese Recorder
Honourable Society of Cymmrodorion Transactions
Journal National Library of Wales
Journal of the North China Branch of the Royal Asiatic Society, N.S., V, 1868
Missionary Chronicle
Monthly Reporter
North China Herald
South Wales Evening Post
Swansea Leader
The British Congregationalist
The Evangelical Magazine
The Nonconformist and Independent
The Wesleyan Methodist Magazine
Y Cronicl Cenadol
Y Diwygiwr
Y Dysgedydd
Y Ganwyll
Y Geninen
Y Tyst
Yr Amserau

Glossary

Chung Wang   outstanding Taiping military leader
Foo   prefecture, sub-division of a province
Gentry   holders of degrees/literati
Grand Canal   waterway linking the Yangtze and North China
Kan Wang   Shield King; Taiping leader Hung Jen-kan
Mandarin   an official; a language
Pagoda   oriental temple
Sedan   covered chair on two poles
Tael   a measure—ounce of silver;
              3 taels = £1 sterling, or = US $1.63
Taoism   Chinese philosophy and religion, founded by Lao-tzu
Viceroy   Governor General of one or more provinces
Yamen   official residence of a Mandarin

Index

A

Allen, J. Young, 109, 159, 176
Allen, Richard, 49
Alliance Mission, *see under*
    Missionary societies
Alliott, Richard, 29
Alltwen Independent Chapel, 23
American Bible Society, *see under*
    Bible societies
American Episcopal Church, *see*
    under Missionary societies
American Presbyterian Mission, *see*
    under Missionary societies
Archibald, John, 102, 103, 107, 117,
    131, 181

B

Baptisms, 97, 101, 105, 146, 147-8,
    153, 156, 168
    baptising lepers, 170
    preparation for, 50-2, 148
Bedford College, 29
Bevan, Ll. D., 112
Bevan, Thomas (Madagascar), 17, 30
Bible societies
    American Bible Society, 124
    British and Foreign Bible Society,
        29, 81, 107, 132, 133, 134, 138
    National Bible Society of
        Scotland, 102, 107, 110, 132,
        133, 134, 138, 155
Bible translation, *see under* John,
    Griffith: literary work
Blodget, Dr, 133, 134
Boardman, W. E., 94
Bolton, William, 170, 173
Bonsey, Arthur, 117, 141, 147, 161,
    183, 187
Bowring, Sir John, 62
Boxer rebellion, 162-4
Brecon Congregational College,
    26-7, 30

British and Foreign Bible Society, *see*
    under Bible societies
Bryant, Evan, 76, 79, 101, 107, 110,
    125, 136
Bryson, Thomas, 79, 107, 111, 205
Buddhism, 77
Burdon, Dr, 133, 134
Burdon and Blodget Version, *see*
    under Chinese Bible versions

C

Cambridge Seven, The, 128
Campbell, R. J., 181-2
Canton, 35, 42
Carey, William, 32, 67, 182, 195
Central China Religious Tract
    Society, 131, 180
Chalmers, James, 86
Chalmers, John, 134-5
Chang Kai-shek, 150
Changsha, 103, 150, 152, 155, 167,
    168, 169, 171, 174, 180
Chefoo, 60
Chengtu, 82, 85, 144-5
China, Her Claim and Call, see under
    John, Griffith: literary work
China Inland Mission (CIM), *see*
    under Missionary societies
Chinese Bible versions
    Burdon and Blodget Version, 134
    Delegates' Version, 132
    Mandarin Version of NT
        (Medhurst), 128
    Peking Version of NT (northern
        Mandarin), 128
    Schereschewsky version of OT,
        128
    Union Version for China (whole
        Bible), 135
    Wen-li New Testament (John),
        133, 138
Chinese inns, 124-5, 126

Chinese language, 37
Chinese national workers, *see also*
   John, Griffith: national workers
   Chu Shao An, 71
   Liu, 97-8
   Lo Hiang-Yung, 73, 77
   Pau Ting Chang, 74
   Peng Lau-Seng, 151, 152, 155,
     156, 157, 169
   Peng Pang Ts'ien, 161, 163
   Sian, 98, 101, 104, 106
   Shen Tsi-sing, 71-2, 92
   Tung, 103-4, 105-6, 111
   Wang-king-fu, 124
   Wang-Lien-King, 153, 156
   Wei, 98, 100-01
   Yang Pan-king, 146-7
   Yii Ki-Fang, 73-4
Cholera, 15, 24-5
Christian's Pathway to Power, The, 94
Christian's Secret of a Happy Life, The
   (Hanna Smith), 94
Chungking, 84, 123, 124, 145
Church buildings, 77, 79, 90, 107,
   111-12, 118-19, 123, 157, 169, 171
Clarke, Sidney, 175
Confucius, 47, 77, 204
   Analects of, 127
   Confucianism, 109, 204
Congregational Union of England
   and Wales
   chairmanship declined, 126, 144,
     177
   Jubilee collection for G.J., 175-6
   Jubilee meetings (1881), 112
Cousins, George, 170, 173
Cox, Josiah, 71, 77
Cumberland Mission, The, *see under*
   Missionary societies
Cwm-nant, 149

D

Dale, R. W., 112
Davies, David (Ebenezer), 16, 17
Davies, E. T., 25
Davies, Edward (Brecon College),
   26, 27, 30

Davies, Peter, 17
Davies, Thomas (Ebenezer), 18, 21
Delegates' Version, *see under*
   Chinese Bible versions
Divinity School, *see under* Hankow
Douglas, Carstairs, 109
Duff, Alexander, 49
Duthie, James, 29
Dyer, Samuel, 133

E

Ebenezer Independent Chapel, 16-
   21 *passim*, 26, 30, 175-6, 187-8
Edinburgh, 86
Edkins, Joseph, 37, 38, 39, 55, 57, 91,
   127, 134
Education, *see under* John, Griffith
English Presbyterian Mission, *see*
   under Missionary societies
Evangelism (forms of)
   books and tract preparation and
     distribution, 39-40, 81, 82, 85,
     130-31, *see also* Scriptures,
     books and tract distribution
   Bible translation, *see under* John,
     Griffith: literary work
   establishing schools, 69-70, 79,
     180, *see also* John, Griffith:
     education
   medical missionary work, 70, 91,
     115-16, 173-4, *see also under*
     John, Griffith
   personal witness, 40, 74, 101
   preaching, *see under* John, Griffith
Evans, Silyn, 187

F

Father Kavanagh, 25
Finney, Charles, 25, 96
Foster, Arnold, 92, 111, 130, 142, 143,
   161, 164, 176, 177, 184
Fowler, Dr, 143-4, 170
Frazer, Sir Everard, 163

G

Gardner, Christopher, 150-1
Gate of Virtue and Wisdom, The

(tract), 131
Gillison, Dr, 117, 141, 142, 143
Good Words to exhort the age, 54
Grieg, 155, 157, 167-8, 169, 171
Griffith John College, 184
Griffiths, David (Madagascar), 17, 27-31 *passim*
Griffiths, Evan, 20, 21, 22, 25, 30
Griffiths, Henry (Brecon College), 26, 27, 28
Gutzlaff, 54
Gwynfe, 86

H
Hangchow, 45, 55
Hankow (Hupeh province), 41, 60, 65; description of, 65-6, 67; first convert, 68; opening of first chapel (Kia Kiai), 68-9; opening of schools, 69; first hospital, 70-1; Wesleyan mission, 71; hospitals built, 111, 141; strategic impor-tance of, 118; Hankow Tract Society, 108; enlarged hospital, 173-4; new chapel built, 119-20; Divinity School, 161, 172-3, 205; refugee missionaries, 146; refugees during Boxer troubles, 162; 50 years ministry celebra-tions, 176-7; reopening of enlarged chapel, 172; integrated worship, 172; last return of Griffith John, 182-3
Hanyang, 65, 66, 80, 123, 172
Harries, Joseph (Gomer), 19
Hengchow, 152-5 *passim*, 163-4, 167, 168, 169, 171
Hiaukuan, 98, 101, 103-4, 106-7, 111
Higher Christian Life, The (Boardman), 94
Hill, David, 46, 71, 79, 107, 108, 119, 134, 149
Holy Spirit, 93-8 *passim*, 108-9, 198
Hopkins, Evan, 94
Hsi, Pastor, 75
Hughes, A. E., 62
Hunan province, 103, 117-18;

description of, 151; anti-foreign feeling, 150-1; first convert, 153; appeal for missionaries, 153-5; growth in the church, 156, 157, 171; Boxer persecution in, 163-4, 167
Hung Xin-quan, 53-4, 63

I
Ichang, 82, 85. 123
Infant baptism, *see under* John, Griffith
Irving, Edward, 201

J
Jacob, Elijah (Ebenezer), 21, 22, 24, 26, 30, 31
Japan, 123, 131, 144

JOHN, GRIFFITH
early influences, 15-22; boy preacher and theological student, 22-8; call to mission field, 27-8; doctrinal position, 28-9, 33; ordination and marriage, 30; voyage to China, 31-3; mission-ary journeys from Shanghai, 38-45, 55-63; periods in Taiping rebel territory, 55-60, 61-2; arrival at Hankow, 65; long journey of 1868, 81-6
——
Biography of, 14, 178-9
comparison with Timothy Richard, 88, 200-02
contribution, summary of, 205-7
character. 191-5
China, future of, 165
Chinese religions, 202-05
doctrinal position, 28-9, 33, 199-200
application to missionary thinking, 200-02
application to other religions, 202-05
education
general education, views on, 180

schools, 69-70, 79, 160-61, 172,
    180
theological training, 161, 172-3
infant baptism, 52-3
literary work
  Bible translation/revision,
    131-9, 175, 205; *basic texts*, 137;
    completion of Wen-li NT, 133;
    method, 132-3, 137-9; *new
    Mandarin version*, 134; *princ-
    iples of translation*, 137;
    revised Wen-li NT, 134
  A Voice from China, 34, 64, 88,
    114
  China, Her Claim and Call, 140
  Reason Why, The, 34,
  tracts, 53, 107, 130-1, 205
medical missionary work, 70-1,
  79, 91, 115-16
  Leper hospital, 143-4, 170, 173-4
  support, 141-2
missionary work, views on, 33,
  41, 48-51, 169, 197-8
modernist teaching, 181-2
national workers
  financial support, 69, 70, 79, 80,
    90, 92, 157
  importance of, 49, 69, 71-4, 79,
    80, 156
  training, 143
opium, views on, 35, 51, 121-2
personal spirituality, 74-6, 92-3,
  96-7
physical features, 36, 191
pioneer work, 65, 80, 81-6, 91,
  117-18, 151-7, *see also*
  Missionary journeys
preaching, 23, 41, 45--9 (content
  of, 46-7; method, 47-9), 67, 84,
  97, 101, 106, 112, 118, 130, 190,
  198-9, 202, 205
  itinerant, 108, 148, 199
Taiping rising, sympathy for, 62-3
        ---
last meeting with Hudson Taylor,
  174; ill-health, 86, 149, 174, 177,
  178, 184-6; Jubilee celebrations

(1905), 175-7; leaving for
    America, 177-8; stay in
    America, 178-82; newspapers
    and periodicals, 179; return to
    Hankow, 182; last farewell to
    China, 186-7; last days and
    funeral, 187-8; centenary cele-
    bration (1931), 188

John, Jeannette (formerly Jenkins),
    92-3, 111, 112, 116, 120-1
John, Margaret Jones, *nee* Griffiths,
    30-1, 49, 86, 87, 89, 89-90, 141
Jones, David (Madagascar), 17, 30
Jones, Morgan, 17
Journey of 1868, 81-6
Jukes, Edward, 29

                    K
Kan Wang, 54, 57, 59, 60, 61
Keswick teaching, 94, 95-6
Kiangsi province, 102
Kianguin, 43
Kingshan, 147-8
Korea, 117, 131, 144
Kucheng killings, 145, 146
Kuling, 149-50, 155, 184, 185, 186

                    L
Latourette, 110
Law of Liberty in the Spiritual Life, The,
    94
Legge, James, 54
Lewis, Dr George, 26
Leper hospital, *see under* John,
    Griffith: medical missionary work
Liang Ch'i-ch'ao, 159
Life of Christ, The (Edward White), 29
Life of Faith, The, 95
Literature distribution, *see*
    Scriptures, books and tract distri-
    bution
Liu village, 101-2, 124, 125
Liu Wang, 58, 60
Liverpool, 188
Lockart, Dr, 36-7, 111
London Missionary Society (LMS),

see under Missionary societies
Madagascar, 17, 27, 28, 30-1, 89
Machynlleth, 86
Mackenzie, Dr Kenneth 71, 79, 92, 98, 99, 100, 110
Malagasy Bible, 29
Manchu dynasty, fall of, 186
Mandarin Version of NT (Medhurst), *see under* Chinese Bible versions
Marshman, William, 131
Martin, W. A. P., 109, 158
Mawbey, Dr, 111, 115-16
Medhurst, Walter, 36, 37, 54, 57, 128
Medical missionary work, *see under* John, Griffith
Meller, T., 29
Meyer, F. B., 185
Milne, William, 54
Mission Hymn Book, The, 126, 127
Mission premises, *see* Church buildings
Missionaries
appeal for (Hunan), 153-5
expulsion from Szechwan, 145-6
financial support, 107, 128-30
missionary type, 64, 91-2, 109, 128, 140, 195-7
training, 126-8
Missionary co-operation, 107-10
Missionary journeys, 81-6, 102-3, 104-6, 117-18, 124-6, 152-3, 155-7, *see also* John, Griffith: pioneer work
Missionary societies
Alliance Mission, 157
American Episcopal Church, 107, 108, 144
American Presbyterian Mission, 157
China Inland Mission (CIM), 46, 91, 95, 108, 109, 123, 129-30, 144-5, 151, 199
Cumberland Mission, 157
English Presbyterian Mission, 115
London Missionary Society (LMS), 16-17, 28, 53, 79-80, 86, 95, 128, 130, 142, 157, 171
Moddfey [Myddfai], 30
Moody, D. L., 94, 112
Morgan, Campbell, 181, 182
Morrison, Robert, 54, 131
Moule, Bishop, 133, 136, 137, 138
Muirhead, William, 37, 38, 40, 42, 44, 108, 120, 132, 134

N

Nanchang, 102
Nanking, 58-61 *passim*, 63, 71, 72
Nanking, Treaty of, 35
National Bible Society of Scotland, *see under* Bible societies
National Holiness Movement, 94
National workers, *see under* John, Griffith
Nevius, John, 201
Ningpo, 35
Non-Christian religions, 202-5

O

Onllwyn (Seven Sisters), 22
Opium, 35, 51, 121-2
Owen, George S., 136, 137-8
Owen, William, 92, 107, 111, 116, 149, 188

P

Paley, William, 204
Palmer, Walter and Phoebe, 94
Peking, 42, 146, 158, 163
Peking Version of NT, *see under* Chinese Bible versions
Phillips, Thomas (Neuadd-lwyd), 17
Pierson, A. T., 179
Pilgrim's Progress, The, 53, 127 (W. C. Burns translation)
Pinghu, 40, 41, 49-50
Pioneer work, *see under* John, Griffith
Plough Chapel, Brecon, 27
Polygamy, 51
Prayer, 93, 97, 112-13, 140, 196-7
Preaching, *see under* John, Griffith
Preaching and singing festival, 156
Progressive Lessons (Edkins), 127

R

Reason Why, The, see under John,
   Griffith: literary work
Rees, Hopkyn, 187, 199, 205
Rees, Thomas, 33, 187
Rees, William, 18, 19, 22
Reform after Sino-Japanese War,
   157-61
Reid, Dr, 70, 71, 141
Religious Tract Society, 108, 131
Revival, 25-6, 93-4, 95, 96, 97, 174
Richard, Timothy, 49, 159, 200-02
Roberts, Evan (revivalist), 174
Roberts, Issacher, 54, 58, 59, 60
Roman Catholics, 46, 84, 104-5

S

Salvation Army, 94
Schereschewsky, 132
Schereschewsky Version of OT, *see
   under* Chinese Bible versions
Schools, *see under* John, Griffith:
   education
Scriptures, books and tract distribu-
   tion, 39-40, 45, 66, 77, 81, 82, 84,
   85, 86, 102, 107-8, 126, 130-1
Shanghai, 35-6, 44-5, 53, 57-8, 108
Shanghai conferences: (1877) 88,
   108-10, 203; (1890) 135
Shansi province, 162
Shantung province, 60
Shaw, Bernard, 182
Simmons, E. B., 134
Sino-Japanese War, 144, 157-8
Smith, Pearsall, 94
Smith, Stanley, 128
Soochow (Suchow), 39, 41, 42, 43,
   54-5, 57, 58
Sparham, George, 117, 124, 141, 142,
   143, 152, 161, 167, 184, 185, 205
Sparham, Mary, *nee* John, 117, 141,
   163
Studd, C. T., 128
Sun Yat-sen, 159, 186
Sungkiang, 38-9, 40, 41
Swansea, 15, 17, 20, 24-5, 30, 86, 187,
   188

Szechwan province, 81, 83, 123-4,
   144-6

T

Taiping rebellion, 53-5
   belief of, 56-7, 61-2
   missionary relations with, 55-60
Talmage, 112
Taoism, 77
Taylor, Hudson, 36, 46, 91, 95, 107-10
   passim, 129-30, 155, 159, 164, 174,
   200, 201, 203
Thomas, John (Liverpool), 120
Thompson, Wardlaw, 14, 80, 142,
   178-9, 187
Tientsin, Treaty of, 41-2
Total abstinence, 21-2
Triads, The, 35-6
Trials and dangers, 44-5, 78, 84-5, 99-
   100, 103, 117-18
   anti-foreign riots in Szechwan,
   144-6; in Hunan, 152-3
   Boxer rising in Hunan, 163-4, 167
Tsingkiangpu, 43-4

U

Union Version for China (whole
   Bible), *see under* Chinese Bible
   versions

V

Voice from China, A, see under John,
   Griffith: literary work

W

Wei village, 98-100, 111-12
Wen-li New Testament, *see under*
   Chinese Bible versions
Wesley, John, 96
Wesleyan Mission, *see under*
   Hankow
Williams, John (Onllwyn), 22, 24
Williamson, A., 31, 36, 38, 40, 107
Wilson, John, 107, 123, 124
Wilson, Robert, 61, 65, 66, 75, 77, 184
Women, 80-1, 90, 91, 109

Wookey, A. J., 113
Wooshan, 83
Wu Yu-Chang, 158
Wuchang, 65, 66, 77-80, 108, 111, 186
Wylie, Alexander, 36, 37-8, 51, 55, 79, 81, 82-3, 84-5, 107, 108, 199

Y
Yingshan, 125-6
Yochow, 103, 117, 154, 155, 157, 169
Young People's Missionary Movement, 179

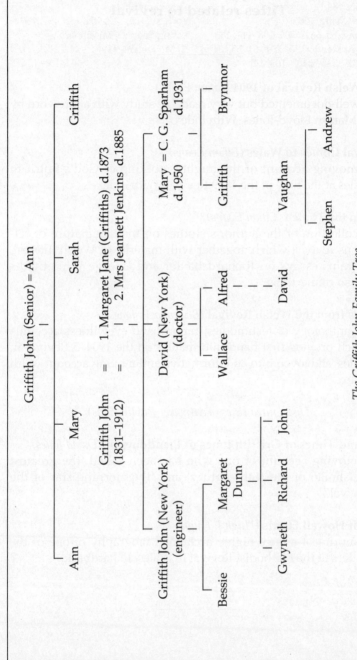

The Griffith John Family Tree

NLW, Glyn Richards Collection

Bryntirion Press
Titles related to revival

The Welsh Revival of 1904 *(Eifion Evans)*
A well-documented but very readable study with a foreword by
D. Martyn Lloyd-Jones. With index.

Revival Comes to Wales *(Eifion Evans)*
A moving account of the mighty working of God's Spirit in
Wales at the time of the 1859 Revival. With index.

Fire in the Thatch *(Eifion Evans)*
A collection of the author's studies on the true nature of religious revival, which, together with material of Welsh interest,
contains essays on Richard Baxter and George Whitefield's
Welsh connections.

Voices from the Welsh Revival *(Brynmor P. Jones)*
An anthology of testimonies, reports and eyewitness accounts
which provide first-hand information on the 1904–5 Revival in
Wales, all woven into an informative and moving account. With
index.

Distributed titles (Tentmaker Publications)

Life and Times of Griffith Jones of Llanddowror *(David Jones)*
A moving account of one who has been called 'the greatest
Welshman of the 18th century' and 'the morning star of the
Revival'.

Life of Howell Harris *(Hugh J. Hughes)*
A reprint of a once highly acclaimed biography of one of the
leaders of the Methodist Revival in Wales. In hardback.

Titles from the
Bryntirion Press

3 companion volumes

Christian Missionaries *(Owen Milton)*
31 chapters on great missionaries of the last four centuries (including Griffith John). Illustrations, maps and index.

Christian Preachers *(Nigel Clifford)*
The lives and achievements of 31 of some of the outstanding men of the Christian Church. 26 illustrations and an index.

Christian Hymn-writers *(Elsie Houghton)*
A collection of brief biographies of some of the great hymn-writers. 50 illustrations and index.

Covenanting with God *(Gwyn Davies)*
A study of the spirituality of the past, focusing attention on covenants between individuals and God and on church covenants. As well as examples from Wales, it deals with the role of covenanting in the lives of such men as Matthew Henry, Jonathan Edwards and C. H. Spurgeon.

Taught to Serve *(Noel Gibbard)*
An account of a continuing work of God from the beginnings of the South Wales Bible College, Barry, up to the present Evangelical Theological College of Wales, Bryntirion, Bridgend. With index.

Pursued by God (a translation by *Eifion Evans*)
A selective translation with notes of the Welsh religious classic *Theomemphus* by William Williams of Pantycelyn. The volume also includes an introduction and a survey of Williams' life and work.

The Great Reformation *(R. Tudur Jones)*
A readable and wide-ranging analysis and survey of the beginnings of Protestantism, which ranges from Iceland to Poland, from Wales to Spain, by one of our foremost church historians.

Recent titles from
Bryntirion Press

Welsh Calvinistic Methodism *(William Williams)*
A third edition of a book first published in 1872, being a historical sketch of the Presbyterian Church of Wales, capturing the essence of a profound spiritual awakening. Introduction and notes by Gwyn Davies with an appendix by D. Martyn Lloyd-Jones. In hardback and paperback.

Christmas Sermons *(D. Martyn Lloyd-Jones)*
An exposition of the Magnificat in four sermons preached in 1959 at Westminster Chapel, London.

Daniel—Servant of God under Four Kings *(Geoff Thomas)*
A lively exposition with many telling illustrations and challenging applications for today, originally given in the form of addresses at the EMW Conference at Aberystwyth, Wales in 1998.

Gypsy from the Forest *(David Lazell)*
A new account of the remarkable life and service of the international evangelist Gipsy Smith (1860–1947).

True Happiness *(D. Martyn Lloyd-Jones)*
An exposition of Psalm One originally preached as four New Year sermons in 1963 by one of the foremost preachers of our time.

God Spoke to Them *(Peter Williams)*
Character studies of 26 Old Testament figures, based on a series of sermons preached at Bournemouth.

Living Water *(John Benton)*
With its sub-title—*finding real life in Jesus*—this is a vivid evangelistic exposition of John, chapter 7, verse 37.

Cast Out but not Forsaken *(Janice Wiseman)*
A moving and challenging autobiography of a convert to the Christian faith from an Orthodox Jewish home.

Talking it Over *(Tom Holland)*
An unusual book which uses a series of conversations between a pastor and members of his congregation to help us think through various important aspects of prayer.

Into All the World *(Norman Shields)*
A survey of what the Bible teaches about mission and the need to declare the gospel to people of every culture.

48f convert China starting with the common people.
49 the less educated as missionaries.
53ff Taiping rebels.